Biblical Themes in World Literature

ALSO BY SOL LIPTZIN

History of Yiddish Literature
The Maturing of Yiddish Literature
The Flowering of Yiddish Literature
The Jew in American Literature
Generation of Decision
Germany's Stepchildren
Arthur Schnitzler
Shelley in Germany
Richard Beer-Hofmann
The Weavers in German Literature
Lyric Pioneers of Modern Germany
The English Legend of Heinrich Heine
Historical Survey of German Literature
From Novalis to Nietzsche
Eliakum Zunser
Peretz
Heine

Biblical Themes in World Literature

by
SOL LIPTZIN

KTAV PUBLISHING HOUSE, INC.
HOBOKEN, NEW JERSEY
1985

COPYRIGHT © 1985
SOLOMON LIPTZIN

Library of Congress Cataloging in Publication Data

Liptzin, Solomon, 1901-
  Biblical themes in world literature.

  Bibliography: p.
  Includes index.
  1. Bible in literature. 2. Bible. O.T.—Legends.
I. Title.
PN56.B5L5   1985   809'.93382   84-19457
ISBN 0-88125-063-5

MANUFACTURED IN THE UNITED STATES OF AMERICA

Table of Contents

Preface	vii
1. Rehabilitation of Lilith	1
2. Defiant Cain	13
3. The Tower of Babel	25
4. Princess Hagar	39
5. Rebekah's Beguilement of Isaac	54
6. Lady Asenath	62
7. Schiller's Moses	74
8. The Death of Moses	81
9. Rahab of Jericho	93
10. Jephthah's Literary Vogue	102
11. Samson in the Twentieth Century	113
12. Ruth and Medea	121
13. Saul's Tragedy	128
14. The Love of David and Michal	144
15. Nabal and Abigail	155
16. Noble Jonathan	164
17. Abishag the Shunammite	170
18. The Judgment of Solomon	180
19. Solomon and the Queen of Sheba	187
20. Sulamith Unallegorized	204
21. Solomon's Humiliation	215
22. Elijah in Yiddish Literature	228
23. The Literary Impact of Jonah	236
24. Job and Faust	250
25. In the Days of Job	254
26. The Cult of Moloch	259
27. Belshazzar's Folly	273
28. The Biblical Tradition of Democracy	282
Afterword by Elie Wiesel	293
Bibliography	295
Index	309

To my daughters
Yelva Lynfield and Karen Sitton

Preface

The present study calls attention to biblical characters, ideas, and events that have stimulated the creative imagination of writers in diverse lands and centuries, primarily occidental lands and recent centuries. It may add to our understanding of the Hebraic mind, because the Book of Books has shaped the Hebraic people since this people's birth, accompanied it throughout its long history in its homeland and in the Diaspora, and still exerts an enormous influence upon its contemporary rebirth in Israel.

Poets, novelists, dramatists have been stimulated to reinterpret ever anew biblical happenings and biblical personalities. They have done so in accordance with the spirit of their own era and their own country in many works of ephemeral interest but also in literary masterpieces of enduring value. Since the subject is inexhaustible, only a selection of biblical themes and of their literary transformations has been made. Themes thoroughly investigated by scholars in easily available studies have been excluded.

1

Rehabilitation of Lilith

The literature and the folklore of Jews, Christians, and Moslems has much to tell about Lilith, not a drop of whose blood is human but who was made like a soft, sweet woman. Some of these tales go back to Babylonian-Assyrian sources of close to four thousand years ago, perhaps even to a still older period when the Sumerians were the most civilized people inhabiting the region between the Tigris and the Euphrates, a region from which the patriarch Abraham stemmed.

The original stories of the mysterious, tormented goddess, demon, or woman are lost in the night of time. However, there is the legend of Lilith as the first wife of Adam, the most fascinating of all the legends about her. It is rather late, appearing in the Talmud, expanded by the kabbalists, flourishing among Yiddish-speaking Jews of Eastern Europe, and favored as a romantic theme by poets, novelists, and dramatists of Europe and America until our own day.

Most versions vilify her, since they were written by the descendants of her successor, Eve, Adam's second wife. Nevertheless, all the calumnies and imprecations hurled at her have not obscured her loveliness nor tarnished her radiant, golden hair. Her soft-shed kisses still enticed Dante Gabriel Rossetti's young men into her net, and her melodious voice and flashing eyes still lured Yitzkhak Leibush Peretz's Monish away from his absorption in the folios of the Gemara and led this pious youth to abandon God and the Torah in her arms.

It was not, however, until the dawn of our century, the century that has fought so vehemently for the liberation of woman from the dominance of man, that attempts were begun to rehabilitate Lilith as Adam's proud mate, who refused to bow to his claim of male superiority, a claim which her successor, Eve, accepted as God-ordained. It was Eve, and not Lilith, who was responsible for the Fall of Man and the expulsion from Paradise. And it is the children of Eve, not those of Lilith, who have made a sorry mess of our planet, despoiling it of its ecological harmony.

Only once does the Bible mention Lilith. She is listed in Isaiah 34:14 among the creatures that will settle in the desolated land of Edom and find a resting place there. It is not clear, however, what sort of creature the prophet had in mind, and this lack of clarity has plagued translators and commentators down the ages. The Septuagint translates *lilith* as "tailless ape." The Vulgate Latin rendering designates her as Lamia, in Roman folklore, a female demon, half-woman and half-serpent, a vampire who lured men in order to suck their blood. Luther, in his German translation, conceived of Lilith as a *Kobold*, a gnome or goblin who dwells in mines and subterranean caves and contaminates silver with a worthless ingredient which the chemists now call cobalt. The King James English version translates *lilith* as "screech-owl." The American Revised Version of 1901 calls *lilith* a night-monster, and the Revised Standard Version of 1952 a night-hag, thus completely negating the aspect of beauty which oral tradition always assigned to her.

It was once assumed that the name *lilith* had been derived from *laila*, the Hebrew word for "night," since she was generally thought of as a creature of the night. However, this etymology is no longer accepted, since the name already occurs in ancient, pre-Hebraic inscriptions as *lilit*, *lilu*, and *lilitu*.

There is no evidence that Isaiah referred to the Lilith who was the first consort of Adam. This notion arose later, in talmudic times, as a result of a difficult problem posed by the two stories of creation in the earliest chapters of Genesis. The sages of the

Talmud, who never doubted the literal accuracy of the biblical text, were perplexed by the fact that these chapters gave two apparently contradictory versions of the creation of woman. The first chapter narrates that, on the sixth day of creation, God fashioned the human species in His own image—"male and female He created them"—both simultaneously and in the same manner. The second chapter of Genesis, however, relates that Adam still had no mate suitable for him when all other living creatures were already paired. In order to provide him too with a mate, the Lord caused a deep sleep to fall upon him. During this sleep a rib was taken from him and fashioned into a woman with whom he could be happy, since she was bone of his bone and flesh of his flesh.

The contradiction between the two chapters was resolved by the conjecture that Adam had two wives. One was created at the same time as he. Although she could not claim priority, she felt justified to claim equality with him, a claim which he refused to recognize and which led to constant quarreling and ultimate separation. Adam's second wife, made from his rib, was content to subordinate herself to him. The first was Lilith, the second was Eve.

Lilith, in legendary lore, was conceived as a winged creature, hence one who, though stemming like Adam, her consort in Paradise, from *adama*, "earth," nevertheless aspired to rise upward beyond the all-too-earthly. She anticipated the modern revolt of woman against the double standard of morality. When Adam insisted on subjugating her to his will, she balked and fled from the Garden of Eden, which was a paradise for him who lorded over all species, but not for her who was too proud to bend under his yoke. She sought refuge with Lucifer, the lucent archangel, and was precipitated with him to the abyss.

Because of her relationship with this chief rebel against God's authority, the rabbis of the Talmud saw her as the mother of evil (*Baba Bathra* 73a), as the enemy of Adam's offspring by Eve. She was reputed to be roaming about at night, appearing to men in their dreams and fastening herself upon any man asleep alone in a room (*Shabbat* 151b). Angry at her successor, Eve, she sought to steal in the night infants newly born to Eve's descendants and to carry them off to the desert, her usual dwelling place.

In classical mythology, Lilith was identified with Lamia, the beloved of Jupiter. Her face was that of a woman, and her body that of a serpent. She was the vampire who gave birth to the monstrous Scylla. St. Jerome noted that Lamia was called by the Hebrews Lilith—"et lamiam quae Hebraiae dicitur Lilith."

The *Alphabet of Ben Sira*, a manuscript of the ninth or tenth century, gave a detailed version of the medieval conception of Lilith. It was the principal source for the *Zohar*'s assertion that she was Adam's first wife (*Zohar* I, 19b, 39b; III, 19a). It may also have been, together with the Talmud, the chief source for Johann Andreas Eisenmenger's description of Lilith in his venomously anti-Semitic volume *Entdecktes Judentum*, whose many German editions since 1700 stimulated German poets and whose English translation of 1732 made her known to English readers.

In the Walpurgis Night scene of Goethe's *Faust*, Mephistopheles points Lilith out to his companion Faust and warns him to beware of her, now that he has been rejuvenated, since she never again lets go of any young man whom she lures with her beautiful hair (*Faust* I, ll. 4119-4123).

Eastern European Jewish folklore wove many legends about her. The most widespread of these related that she stood at the foot of the beds of lying-in women and tried to snatch newborn babes from the arms of their mothers. Superstitious women feared her. To ward her off, it was customary to hang an amulet around the neck of a newly born infant, an amulet inscribed with the names of the three angels—Snwy, Snanwy, and Smnglf—who had terrorized her after her flight from Eden. Equally effective in warding off her pernicious power were the "childbirth tablets" which were inscribed with magic formulas and which were nailed to the walls of the lying-in room. While the greatest danger faced infants during their first night, boys were in peril of being snatched away until their circumcision on the eighth day. Girls had to be protected against Lilith's wiles until their twentieth day. She was especially dangerous to infants who had been begotten sinfully.

Western European writers, primarily romantic writers who were fascinated by the exotic and the occult, found in Lilith a most attractive subject. Among French writers, Alfred de Vigny in 1857 depicted her as the personification of sensuality; Victor Hugo in 1886 identified her with the Egyptian goddess Isis and saw her as the mother of innumerable evil spirits; Remy de Gourmont, in his play *Lilith* of 1892, presented her as an imperfect creation of God, who discarded her by tossing her to Satan, the Prince of Evil, and then corrected His error by creating Eve as a more suitable mate for Adam. Among English poets, Robert Browning humanized her in his lyric of 1883, "Adam, Lilith and Eve;" but it was Dante Gabriel Rossetti, the Pre-Raphaelite painter and poet, who was most charmed by her. He painted her in 1864, and for this portrait of his imagination he wrote the following exquisite sonnet:

> Of Adam's first wife, Lilith, it is told
> (The witch he loved before the gift of Eve,)
> That, ere the snake's, her sweet tongue could deceive,
> And her enchanted hair was the first gold.
>
> And still she sits, young while the world is old,
> And, subtly of herself contemplative,
> Draws men to watch the bright net she can weave,
> Till heart and body and life are in its hold.
>
> The rose and poppy are her flowers; for where
> Is he not found, O Lilith, whom shed scent
> And soft-shed kisses and soft sleep shall snare?
> Lo! as that youth's eyes burned at thine, so went
> Thy spell through him, and left his straight neck bent,
> And round his heart one strangling golden hair.

More elaborate was Rossetti's depiction of Lilith in his ballad "Eden Bower," which he completed in 1869, five years after his painting and his sonnet. While in his painting he portrayed her as a radiant, beautiful woman in a rose-filled boudoir combing her rich golden hair, and while in his sonnet he depicted her as an ever-alluring Lorelei who is still the bane of enticed young men, his ballad reverted to the primeval, legendary era of Adam and Eve in the Garden of Eden. The ballad is in the form of a plea by Lilith to the serpent, who had been her lover before she had been turned over by God to Adam, who was created long after her. She implores her King-Snake to lend her his serpentine shape for an hour, so that she can avenge herself on Adam, who has become faithless to her, and on Eve, her successor. Then the hearts of the human pair will ache as her own heart aches.

The rehabilitation of Lilith is a twentieth-century development of the legend. But already in 1889, Anatole France attempted, in his short story "La Fille de Lilith," to win sympathy for her offspring. Leila, the daughter of Lilith, is beautiful and immortal like her mother. To a young Parisian, who loves her passionately and whom she leaves in order to return to her oriental home, she bequeaths an amulet which contains a prayer. When the prayer is deciphered by a learned priest, it proves to be a plea for release from her immortality. "My God, grant me Death, so that I may enjoy Life. My God, grant me Remorse, so that I may experience Joy. My God, make me the equal of the daughters of Eve."

The priest then gives the young man an insight into the world of Lilith and her daughter. Their permanent home was among the pre-Adamites, who were wiser and fairer than the post-Adamite mortals. When Lilith was replaced in Adam's affections by Eve in the Garden of Eden, he was still in a state of innocence. Not participating in Adam's first transgression against God, Lilith was not tainted by original sin and therefore escaped the curse pronounced upon Eve and Eve's offspring. She knows neither pain nor death. She need not atone, and her soul need not be redeemed. Her daughters are immortal like her and live beyond good and evil.

This story parallels the German legend of Tannhäuser and his beautiful paramour, immortal Lady Venus, a legend which formed the source for Heinrich Heine's verse narrative and for Richard Wagner's opera.

The Scottish novelist George Macdonald also attempted a rehabilitation of Lilith in his dream-romance of 1895, which was only adequately appreciated generations later and whose translation into German by Uwe Hermes in 1977 aroused considerable interest. The English poet and critic W. H. Auden evaluated it as equal if not superior to the best of Edgar Allen Poe. Rainer Hoffmann, who called attention to it in the *Neue Züricher Zeitung* of May 6, 1978, hailed it as a masterpiece of myth-fiction, which revealed for us a landscape of fairyland that is worth traveling on.

Vane, the hero of Macdonald's fantastic novel, returns to his ancestral home, a rambling, abandoned, old house, and finds in the garret an aerial portal which opens upon dreamland. When he steps out of the portal, he finds himself in a seventh-dimensional world that encompasses much more than the three-dimensional, spatial world in which our conscious life, though not our dream-life, is spent. In that all-embracing world beyond life and death, most of the physical and many of the mental laws are different than those we normally apprehend with our few senses. There two objects can exist in the same place at the same time. There Lilith and the Shadow to whom she is subject represent the forces of evil, while Adam and Eve in various transformations represent the forces of good.

Traveling among the constellations, Vane arrives at the city of Bulika, which is ruled by Lilith, a princess older than the land under her sway, an evil person with a terrible past, a vampire who sucks the blood of Eve's children and seeks to destroy them. For Lilith, Vane too is a tame animal to feed upon, a human fountain for a thirsty demoniac. And yet, this queen of hell is not beyond redemption. Her own daughter, who survived Lilith's destructive urge and was divinely fostered, with angels as her playmates, has become the guardian of the Little Ones who escaped from Bulika. Through her love, her mother Lilith, after much suffering, is freed from dependence upon the Shadow and is prepared to submit to the Universal Will, even as do Eve, Adam, and all who have seen through the illusions of the cycle of life and death.

Joseph Victor Widmann, the Swiss dramatist, went beyond Anatole France and George Macdonald in rehabilitating Lilith. In his poetic play *Der Heilige und die Tiere* (1905), he showed her as the vassal of Asasel, forced to do his bidding and to tempt with her loveliness the saintly hero of the drama, and yet revolting against her fate. When the hero resists her wiles, she is filled with awe at his purity, understanding, sympathy, and holiness. She cannot proceed with luring him and retreats before the radiance that streams from his compassionate eyes. When he addresses her pityingly as a poor, wayward spirit, she is overcome with shame and revulsion because of her role as the eternal temptress.

In 1908, three years after Widmann's biblical drama, Isolde Kurz sought to rehabilitate Lilith in her long verse narrative *Die Kinder der Lilith*. As the daughter of the Swabian poet Hermann Kurz, she had revolted against the ideal of woman which was dominant in respectable German circles when she grew up and which degraded woman to the humiliating level of a "demütige Magd oder Weibchen—Leib ohne Seele." She had heard the clarion call of Ibsen against the bourgeois concept of marriage. She recalled that the girls of her generation and her upper middle class were groomed primarily for marriage and were brainwashed to be proud of their vassalage to husbands. Such women accepted their own intellectual impoverishment as an asset that heightened their attractiveness as dolls or darlings. In order to please suitors, many girls pretended to be less knowledgeable and weaker than they really were. They were not expected to bring intellectual gifts into their marriage but to be a *tabula rasa*, a blank page on which the man was to write his text.

Isolde Kurz was familiar with the legend of Lilith as a haughty, winged demon who did not get along well with Adam, who flew away from him after a quarrel by invoking the Ineffable Name, and who thereafter dwelt in grottos as a dangerous vampire.

The poetess regarded this legend as an absurdity. Why should the omniscient God have selected so evil a mate for Adam? And why were wings bestowed upon Lilith and not upon Adam? Having wings, she undoubtedly shared with the angels the ability to fly from place to place and to gain deep insight into what transpired on the terrestrial planet. But she also shared with mortals the need for food and the reproductive instinct. Did God have some higher purpose when He combined these traits in Lilith? And was the denigration of Lilith in the lore of the Jews a later development of the original legend, the result of ensuing centuries of lesser esteem for women?

Isolde Kurz undertook to restore to Lilith her pristine eminence, cleansing her of the later legendary excrescences, even as Euripides had rehabilitated the alluring, demonic Helen and had exonerated her of faithlessness by presenting her, in his drama *Helen*, as the model of a loyal wife who had escaped from her captor Paris and had hidden for many years in Egypt until she could be reunited with her husband, Menelaus. A fate similar to Lilith's had also overtaken the radiant Aphrodite, goddess of love, who had been degraded during the Middle Ages and lived on in popular imagination as a demon, not unlike Hekate or Cybele, as a temptress who sat at crossroads and lured young men to passion and death, a demon whom John Keats had immortalized in his ballad "La Belle Dame Sans Merci," whom Richard Wagner had depicted as Lady Venus in his opera *Tannhäuser* and as Kundry in his opera *Parsifal*, and whom Algernon Charles Swinburne had rehabilitated in his poetic monologue "Laus Veneris," preferring her even to the Virgin Mary.

The Lilith legend, as reinterpreted by Isolde Kurz, clarified and justified apparent contradictions in God's plan when He fashioned this strange creature, half-angel and half-human. According to Kurz, God had, in the course of aeons, tired of the eternal sameness, of absolute perfection, of seraphic choirs forever intoning hymns of praise. He longed for change, growth, decay, disorder straining toward order, imperfection evolving and ameliorating. He therefore created life and its many species of fauna and flora that covered land and sea. However, these did not sufficiently satisfy Him. He wanted a species that could encompass The All in thought and imagination and that would be worthy of accompanying Him, so that He would not be lonely in His uniqueness. He therefore formed Adam out of a clod of earth, out of *adama*, and gave him as a mate the most resplendent of the winged spirits, the bright, airy Lilith. With her many charms and whims, she was to inspire and goad earthbound Adam to creative activities and to unceasing progress toward perfection.

From their daily dissensions and reconciliations, clashes of will and harmonious reunions, there were born stimulating thoughts and there arose the beginnings of art. It looked as if man were advancing toward the blessed goal which God designed for him. But Lucifer, the lustrous archangel closest to the Divine Presence, feared that before long man would displace him and become his successful rival. Hence, he put an obstacle in the way of man's upward climb. When Adam was asleep, he created out of one of his ribs Eve, a creature unwanted by God, a woman who was merely body, unleavened by spirit, and who enticed her mate into sensualism and indolence.

Eve destroyed Adam's love for Lilith, his bright, splendid, graceful first mate, who was no less spirit than sense. Becoming aware of Adam's degeneracy under the influence of Eve, Lilith fled in despair. Eden, the abode of their bliss, went up in flames. Banned from Paradise, Adam begot with Eve sensual, wolfish offspring who were enmeshed in guilt and were suffering. But God's plans cannot be forever thwarted. The angel Gabriel revealed to Adam before his death that Lilith too had born a son to him who was being raised by seraphim and would descend to earth in ever new transformations, as prophet, as poet, as leader of his purely human brothers or half-brothers. Though his radiant influence would be vitiated to a large extent by the children of Eve, who would rally together under the slogan "He is one and we are many," there is progressive improvement, and ultimately all the children of Adam will slough the legacy of Eve and evolve upward toward spiritual perfection, the final goal God wants them to attain.

In the poetic epic *Ashmedai* (1904) by the Yiddish folklorist S. Anski, who is best remembered as the author of the often-staged mystical drama *The Dybbuk*, Lilith is introduced as the consort of Ashmedai and his chief ally in luring righteous souls to lust and perdition. She experiences moral regeneration when she wrestles with an immaculate Zaddik and is defeated by him. Anski portrays her as more beautiful than Delilah, Tamar, Sulamith, the Queen of Sheba, Queen Vashti, and Queen Esther. Adoring Ashmedai as a god, she always does his bidding. But the saintly rabbi in a Jewish townlet, by his goodness, changes her personality from a creature of evil to a penitent, yearning for salvation from evil. The Zaddik sees in her not the spirit of temptation but a being in need of purification. His boundless compassion cleanses her of her immoral attributes. She obeys him and follows his instruction. She devotes herself to feeding and healing orphaned children, who then call her "mother." The Zaddik, who earns his livelihood by the sweat of his brow and the toil of his hands, becomes a model for her. She too spends her days in good deeds and her evenings in prayer and religious meditation. Hailed by Ashmedai before a court of demons, she is condemned to be punished by continuing her new way of life. Then she will suffer as the loneliest of creatures, since the pious will always keep in mind her past as the alluring Lilith, and the secular and impious will mock her ostentatious modesty. She will be at home neither in heaven nor in hell and will roam the earth as a stranger, misunderstood and accursed.

The most magnificent rehabilitation of Lilith was undertaken in English literature by George Bernard Shaw. In his play of 1921, *Back to Methuselah*, he portrayed her as the personification of the force of Creative Evolution, as the mother of Adam and Eve, and hence of the entire human race.

The play begins with the first human pair in the Garden of Eden. It continues on to the year 31,920, as far as thought can reach. It concludes with the sage insight of Lilith, who wonders whether her labor in creating man and woman was enough of an achievement or whether she should labor again so as to bring forth something that would sweep mankind away. After weighing all possibilities, she feels that she can be reasonably content with her offspring and that she should not supersede them. She has been patient with the human race for many aeons, even though this race has tried her sorely. Her patience has been rewarded. Mankind, ever dissatisfied, has worked its way up from cruelty and hypocrisy and has redeemed itself from vileness. "The impulse I gave them in that day when I sundered myself in twain and launched Man and Woman on the earth still urges them: after passing a million goals they press on to the goal of redemption from the flesh, to the vortex freed from matter, to the whirlpool in pure intelligence that, when the world began, was a whirlpool in pure force."

According to Shaw, it was Lilith who gave her daughter Eve the greatest of gifts: curiosity. This prevented stagnation and is opening up to the human race ever new vistas. "I am Lilith: I brought life into the whirlpool of force, and compelled my enemy, Matter, to obey a living soul." When the final goal will be attained toward which mankind reaches out, when the whirlpool will be all life and no matter, then Lilith herself will also be superseded and become only a legend and a lay that has lost its meaning. "Of Life only there is no end; and though of its million starry mansions many are empty and many still unbuilt, and though its vast domain is as yet unbearably desert, my seed shall one day fill it and master its matter to its uttermost confines. And for what may be beyond, the eyesight of Lilith is too short. It is enough that there is a beyond."

With this optimistic faith in the creative evolution of life, the aged British sage ends his dramatic masterpiece, his rehabilitation of Lilith after the calumnies of many generations, his idealization of her as the primal creator of the human species, as the cause of all suffering, progress, and evolution from matter to spirit.

In 1976, the periodical *Lilith* was founded by leading members of the Jewish Feminist Organization of America in order to further the struggle for woman's liberation from still-persisting disabilities. The editors held that the demonic image of Lilith had reflected and shaped men's thoughts and feelings about women for many preceding generations but that at last the time had arrived for a reassessment of the Lilith myth. Lilith was not a wild-haired, vengeful witch but a rebel against tyranny.

In many ways, she could be a model for Jewish women and the patron saint of the contemporary movements that sought to liberate women from age-old disabilities and assure them equal rights in every field of endeavor.

The twentieth century, in its revaluation of values, is rehabilitating much-abused and long-vilified Lilith and is restoring her to her pristine splendor.

2

Defiant Cain

According to the Bible, God created the world and established the world order. No living thing, from the lowliest plant to the most magnificent animal, can question His establishment. All must react with the mute language of impulse or instinct to the environment in which they have been placed. The tiger must rend and the lamb must accept its destiny to be rent. Man alone God made in His image, and upon him alone He bestowed the gift of free will. However, when Adam and Eve used this gift for the first time, when they willed against God's prohibition and ate of the fruit of a forbidden tree, they were so severely punished that they never again willed against God's established order. Nevertheless, the faculty which enabled them to distinguish between good and evil and which they acquired by their single act of disobedience was handed down by them to their descendants.

When Cain, their firstborn son, made use of this faculty and exercised his freedom of will in order to question God's fairness and to reject God's decision exalting Abel, his younger brother, above him, he was condemned as a criminal and as a rebel against the Supreme Authority by the biblical narrator and by all the later theologians and literary interpreters who bowed their necks under the yoke of religious authorities. In Christian lore, Abel was idealized as the innocent sufferer and as the first martyr. His fate was regarded as a prefiguration of the Christian savior. Cain, on the other hand, was depicted as the incarnation of evil. This tradition was followed throughout the Middle Ages and in the religious spectacles of the Renaissance and the Age of Baroque.

From the Age of Enlightenment, however, Cain has been viewed with greater tolerance, and since the Age of Romanticism he has even been idolized by creative spirits who themselves rebelled against the establishment and who themselves became outcasts because they dared to will against the social, political, and religious environment of their day. As the anti-establishment hero, Cain reached the summit of defiance against the universal order and God's authority in Lord Byron's dramatic mystery of 1822 and in the European versions under Byronic influence.

The most influential treatment of the Cain theme in the generations before Byron was that of the Swiss writer Salomon Gessner in 1758. His idyllic *Der Tod Abels*, composed in five cantos of lyrical prose, centers about the hard-working firstborn son of Adam rather than about his gentler brother. Gessner displays great sympathy for the serious, manly tiller of the soil, beside whom the more light-hearted shepherd pales. Cain is the eagle, and Abel the dove. Toiling on the raw earth from dawn to dusk in order to eke out a living for his family, Cain has neither the leisure nor the inclination to sing hymns to God as does Abel, who sits idling away the daylight hours while the sheep graze. Cain is good and noble, a fine husband and a loving father. However, he is not satisfied with God's world and hence cannot dissolve in sweet smiles and sentimental tears of happiness. He compares himself to the raging storm and the torrential stream. He has no hatred in his heart toward Abel and would not intentionally hurt him. He becomes an innocent fratricide when he is aroused to anger by a horrible dream in which he sees his own descendants clubbed and enslaved by Abel's descendants, a nightmare induced by Anamelech, an infernal spirit of Lucifer's retinue. On awakening, Cain impetuously strikes a blow with his club at his brother, but is immediately seized by remorse when he realizes that he has unwittingly brought death into the world. His murderous deed was a momentary aberration of his real nature, and he is ready to atone for the pain he inflicted upon Adam's family. Though Adam is ready to forgive him, his own conscience drives him forth into the unknown. In his remorseful, bleak existence, however, he will be comforted by his faithful wife, who shared his joy and is willing to share his misery. Accompanied by her and by his children, he goes out into the desolate wastes where no human foot has yet trodden.

Gessner's idyllic epic enjoyed a worldwide vogue surpassing that of any other literary work in the German language until his day. *Der Tod Abels* was translated into English, French, Italian, Dutch, Portuguese, Spanish, Swedish, Czech, Hungarian, and other tongues. The sentimental Swiss author was hailed as the new Theocritus. In England, his work was as popular as Bunyan's *Pilgrim's Progress* and Defoe's *Robinson Crusoe*, the two bestsellers of the eighteenth century. Byron read it when he was eight years old, and Wordsworth, in *The Prelude*, compared it with the works of Shakespeare and Dante. (See Bertha Reed's study *The Influence of Gessner upon English Literature*, 1905.)

Coleridge intended his own prose-poem *The Wanderings of Cain* to be a continuation of Gessner's idyl. In a prefatory note, he mentioned that he wrote it in 1798, the year of his intensive collaboration with Wordsworth, although it was not published until thirty years later. He planned this work to be written on the scale of *The Ancient Mariner*. It was to consist of three cantos in lyrical prose. Wordsworth was to write the first canto, and he the second, before either or both poets embarked upon the third canto. However, the only part completed was the second canto, since Wordsworth could not adapt himself to the spirit of Gessner. Coleridge's wanderer Cain does indeed have the same traits as the German model of which it is a continuation. Cain is still the questioning, discontented son of Adam. Accompanied by his own innocent little son Enos, he roams through the forest in the moonlight, pursued by his conscience and yearning for death or at least for blackness to cover him. His countenance bears the marks of agonies that were, are, and will continue to be.

On emerging from the forest, he beholds a strange Shape whose limbs and face are like those of Abel and whose voice is full of lamentations. When Cain asks the Shape why one who found favor in the sight of God during life is now lamenting so bitterly, the Shape replies that there is one God for the living and another for the dead. Abel, who was beloved by the God of the living, was snatched away from His power and dominion by the death-dealing blow. Cain, on the other hand, who brought sacrifices to the God of the dead, may be accursed and wretched all the days of mortal life but can look forward to relief from toil and pain after death. When the afflicted Cain wants to know who and where is the God of the dead, Abel undertakes to lead him over the white sands to where an answer can be found.

The second canto ends as Cain, Abel, and Enos set out on this journey. Though the third canto was never written, Coleridge's imagination, stirred by the Cain theme of remorse and atonement, carried this theme with him into his most famous poem *The Ancient Mariner*, composed soon after *The Wanderings of Cain*. The face of the strange mariner is like the face of Cain, and just as a mark was branded upon Cain after the murder, so the albatross was hung about the mariner's neck after the latter's crime. The expiation that Coleridge may have planned for Cain in the unwritten canto he bestowed upon the wandering mariner with the glittering eye and hoary face.

Friedrich Schiller, in his philosophic-historic study *On the First Human Society According to the Mosaic Source* (1790), freed Cain from the sentimentalism that in the eighteenth century hovered over the first murderer. The German poet and dramatist depicted man's evolution from the animal stage, when man always reacted to experience as instinctively as did all of nature's creatures, to a truly human stage, when he reacted on the basis of free choice and an increasing use of reason. Man's release from the tyrannical but unerring guidance of instinct, and his groping with his gradually developing reasoning faculties, after he had partaken of the fruit of the tree of knowledge, may indeed be characterized as a fall from a paradisiacal existence. It was, however, a fall from which he was to emerge in the course of millennia to an ever higher level of existence, with ever greater freedom and enlightenment.

In the early part of man's long upward climb, when the first human pair, after expulsion from the Garden of Eden, give birth to Cain, the agriculturist, and Abel, the herdsman, the seeds for future conflicts between members of the human species are sown. While the herdsman's flock can graze everywhere, the herdsman can idle away all hours and roam from place to place. The agriculturist, on the other hand, is bound to a fixed abode. He is enslaved to the bit of soil which he has to till, water, and harvest with his bare hands and the sweat of his brow, and has to defend his produce against wild animals and the ravages of nature in periods of flood and drought. He has to regard his brother, the herdsman, as the favorite of heaven. He comes to envy, hate, and despise him, his good fortune, and his idleness. Both come into collision when the herdsman's flock, having grazed bare the untilled earth, intrudes upon the cultivated fields. Then the bitterness lodged in the heart of the hard-working agriculturist finds explosive expression and leads him to use against his own brother the same club with which he has driven off wild animals. Thus began the strife of man with man. As an aftermath of this horrible fratricide, however, law had to be introduced into human society in order to regulate the behavior of later offspring toward each other.

Cain's murderous act was spontaneous and not premeditated. It came about because he no longer lived in a state of innocence, as did his parents before their expulsion from Eden, and because his newly functioning reason had not yet evolved social laws to tame individual instinctive behavior.

In contrast to the sentimental and humanitarian versions of the eighteenth century that pleaded for greater tolerance toward the erring, accursed Cain, the most influential nineteenth-century version, that of Lord Byron, presented Cain not as the accused, crushed person who merited understanding and compassion but as the accuser against God and as a rebel against the world establishment.

Byron's defiant Cain resembles the Greek titan Prometheus, who loved mankind and revolted against the injustice and tyranny of Zeus, since the Lord of Olympus withheld from man the gift of fire, the basis for progress and civilization. The oldest son of Adam and Eve makes use of his reason, the precious but fatal gift acquired by the sin of his parents, and becomes an uncompromising seeker of absolute truth. His reason tells him that this is not the best of all possible worlds. Indeed, it is not even a good world. He, therefore, refuses to pay homage to the omnipotent Creator who demands of all creatures, including man, unquestioning obedience and blind submission to the establishment.

Just as Goethe, under whose influence Byron stood while composing his biblical mystery, begins his masterpiece *Faust* with a Prologue in Heaven, in which the archangels sing the praise of God, with Mephistopheles alone failing to join in, so too Byron begins his poetic drama with hymns to the Lord by Adam, Eve, Abel, and his sisters Adah, the wife of Cain, and Zillah, the wife of Abel. Only Cain is silent. He has nothing to ask of God and can think of nothing for which to thank Him. When Adam points out that just to be alive is reason enough to be thankful, Cain replies that life is but transitory and death the inevitable end and the more enduring state. To his parents' expression of remorse for having brought death into the world by their eating the fruit of a forbidden tree, Cain counters that they should have gone a step further and also have plucked the fruit of the other forbidden tree, the tree of life that was in the midst of Eden. Then they would have been in a position to defy God successfully. Cain tells his parents and his wife:

> I sought not to be born; nor love the state
> To which that birth has brought me. Why did he
> Yield to the serpent and the woman? or
> Yielding, why suffer? What was there in this?
> The tree was planted, and why not for him?
> If not, why place him near it, where it grew,
> The fairest in the center? They have but
> One answer to all questions, "Twas His will,
> And He is good!" How know I that? Because
> He is all-powerful, must all-good, too, follow?
> I judge but by the fruits—and they are bitter—
> Which I must feed on for a fault not mine.

Defiant Cain

For Adam's ears these are blasphemous words, but Cain insists that to taste the fruit of knowledge and of life was good and not evil. He cannot, however, convince his parents. They are resigned to their expulsion from Eden and to their suffering on earth as a deserved punishment for their sin of disobedience, and they warn their son not to let himself be ensnared to rebel against the established order. But Cain remains incorrigible. Adam may have been tamed down; Eve may have forgotten the mind which made her thirst for knowledge even at the risk of an eternal curse; Abel may be humbly offering up the firstlings of his flock to the despotic Creator; but Cain will not bow to the heavenly Tyrant. He accepts the offer of Lucifer, a kindred defiant spirit, to conduct him through the abyss of space and to show him worlds upon worlds made and unmade by the Lord enthroned in eternal solitude beyond space and time.

Flying through the star-studded constellations in the company of Lucifer, Cain becomes aware of how tiny and inferior is the terrestrial planet in the vastness of the universe. Emerging beyond the brink of space and the realm of life, both arrive in Hades, the silent, gloomy abode of swimming shadows and enormous shapes, the realm of the monstrous dinosaurs and pre-Adamites who once inhabited the earth and other orbs, and who are now lodged in the habitation of Death. The principal lesson Lucifer imparts to Cain, his human ally, is to make use of the gift of reason and not to believe what is contrary to the experiences of the senses. He tells Cain:

> One good gift has the fatal apple given—
> Your reason:—let it not be overswayed
> By tyrannous threats to force you into faith
> 'Gainst all external sense and inward feeling.
> Think and endure, and form an inner world
> In your own bosom—where the outward fails;
> So shall you nearer be the spiritual
> Nature, and war triumphant with your own.

Cain returns to earth a sadder and wiser man. Though surrounded by the love of his wife Adah and the smiles of his son

Enoch, he cannot desist from brooding on his recent experience in space when he perceived the earth as no more bright or significant than a little shining firefly. He cannot grasp why the search for knowledge was and is branded as a sin that requires atonement or why the Creator must be bribed with burnt-offerings such as the worshipping Abel sacrificed daily. Nevertheless, Abel ultimately succeeds in persuading his skeptical brother to forgo gloomy speculations and to offer fruit of the tilled soil to the Lord. However, while Abel's prayer during the sacrifice is a hymn extolling God's justice, goodness, and mercy, Cain's prayer is permeated with skepticism and lacking in humility. He cannot bring himself to whine for forgiveness of sins when he does not feel himself guilty. He rather wants to know which sacrifice is more pleasing to the Omnipotent, Abel's blood-drenched offering of a slaughtered sheep, whose limbs reek to the sky with sanguinary incense, or his own sweet and blossoming produce of agricultural toil spread on the unstained turf.

The answer comes when the fire upon the altar of Abel kindles into a column of the brightest flame, while a whirlwind throws down the altar of Cain and scatters the fruit far and wide. Apparently, God prefers flesh-offerings and the fumes of smoking blood. The so-called Lord of justice, goodness, and mercy seemingly pays little heed to the pain of a bleating mother who still yearns for her missing, slaughtered offspring or the pangs of the victim under the pious knife. In an outburst of rage at such a God, Cain attempts to destroy the smoking altar. When Abel tries to stop him in this impious deed, Cain snatches a brand from the altar and strikes him. But immediately remorse assails Cain. He who loved life so fervently and abhorred the thought of death so deeply has himself become guilty of ending a human life. The mark branded on his brow burns him less than the thoughts within his brow. He would gladly give up his own life to redeem his brother from the dust. But what has been done cannot be undone. He will betake himself to the most desolate region east of Eden. Abel is at peace, but he, the wanderer and eternal seeker of absolute truth, will never know the blessing of peace.

Byron, who called himself the wandering outlaw of his own

dark mind, mirrored himself in Cain. The poet's transformation of the first murderer into an heroic fighter against falsehood, servility, and injustice influenced not only his own romantic generation but also later ones, and not only his own country's versions but also those of other literatures. Jacob Rothschild's excellent study, *Kain und Abel in der deutschen Literatur* (1933), and Auguste Brieger's *Kain und Abel in der deutschen Dichtung* (1934), deal in great detail with the German dramas, epics, and lyrics that felt the impact of Byron's *Cain*.

In France, Baudelaire's "Abel et Cain," included in his finest poetic collection *Les fleurs du mal* (1857), contrasts the seed of Abel, who form the establishment, with the seed of Cain, who resist the establishment. The poem reaches a climax in the final stanza, which predicts the destruction of God's established order and foresees Cain's offspring scaling heaven's walls and hurling God to the ground.

While Victor Hugo's Cain poem, "La conscience," included in the cycle *La legende des siècles* (1859), is free of Byronic influence, Leconte de Lisle's poem "Qain," which ushers in the *Poèmes barbares* (1869), is permeated with such influence. It reflects the bitterness and atheism of this pessimistic Parnassian poet and is an extremely powerful expression of divine culpability for the miserable human lot. As in Byron's *Cain*, God is shown to be a sad and jealous deity, deserving of hatred. Though Qain seeks a world of kindness and happiness, he is precipitated into crime against his will. While Byron ends Cain's revolt against God on a note of despair, Leconte de Lisle ends his poem with a vision of the overthrow of Jehovah and Qain's reconquest of Eden. (For a detailed analysis of "Qain," see Alison Fairlie's study *Leconte de Lisle's Poems on the Barbarian Races*, 1947, pp. 244-279.)

The defiant Cain also appears in Gérard de Nerval's *Tale of the Queen of the Morning and Solomon, the Prince of the Genii* (1844). In this tale, Adoniram, the last of Cain's descendants, a rival of Solomon for the affections of the Queen of Sheba, is escorted by Tubal-Cain to the sanctuary of fire in a subterranean kingdom. There he meets Cain. This ancestor is depicted as of a superhuman beauty, despite the sadness of his eyes and the pallor of his lips. Cain explains that he is the child of Eve and of Eblis, the angel of light. Adam, who was kneaded out of mud, was only his foster-father. Cain's life was a life of sacrifice. He experienced ingratitude, injustice, bitterness. Adam did not love him. Eve preferred Abel and pampered him. While Cain's sweat irrigated the land and compelled the soil to produce, Abel idled throughout the day and slept beneath the sycamore, leaving the flocks to stray and graze by themselves. When Cain complained and appealed to God for a decision and when both brothers offered up sacrifices, Cain's complaints, appeals, and sacrifices were scornfully rejected because the jealous God preferred mediocre minds to genuine geniuses. Though Cain, thereafter, brought murder into the world by slaying his brother and was forced to atone, was not God far more guilty when He drowned multitudes in the waters of the Deluge?

The wrathful defiance of Cain, the anti-establishment hero, continues until the twentieth-century versions. In the drama of the Viennese expressionist Anton Wildgans, *Kain* (1920), and in George Bernard Shaw's *Back to Methuselah* (1921), the oldest son of Adam still retains the Byronic aggressive attitude toward God and the universe. Shaw's Cain tells Adam and Eve that it was Abel and not he himself who invented killing. Cain lived by the tilling of the hard soil and ate the fruits of the earth. But Abel was the discoverer of blood. Abel kept himself alive by eating meat. "His meal cost him a day's glorious health-giving sport and an hour's amusing play with the fire." Cain, who continued to drudge and dig, envied his brother's freedom and happiness. Then the great idea came to him: why not kill Abel just as Abel killed the beasts? Why not also live by the chase, by the killing, and by the fire? He did so, and thereafter he felt stronger, happier, freer. He felt that he had risen beyond mere man to become a hero and a superman.

Cain, the first murderer, and not Abel, the victim, is the central figure in most versions of the century from Byron to Shaw. Jewish writers, on the other hand, continue to center their attention upon Abel, in whom they see their own fate prefigured. Thus, Elsa Lasker-Schüler's lyric "Abel," included in her

Hebräische Balladen (1913), asks the Jewish question of Cain: why did you kill your brother? Abel was living a peaceful life that was pleasing to God. His face was a golden garden, and his eyes were nightingales. The strings of his soul were vibrating with God's bright melody. But Cain could not endure his brother, the prototype of the Jew, and murdered him. Since then, the blood of the innocent victim cries out from the earth and colors even heaven.

Several of the sonnets in the cycle *Biblische Sonette*, which Uriel Birnbaum, the much-tried Viennese Jewish lyricist, completed in exile before his death in 1956, are devoted to Cain. In one sonnet, Adam and Eve fall back in horror at the sight of their gloomy, bloodstained son, upon whose brow God's sign had been branded, but his sister clings to him, pitying the distraught criminal. She will never disown their relationship. In another sonnet, Cain is shown revisiting Abel's grave after centuries of wandering far from Eden. He finds that the lot of the brother who died so young was much happier than his own, having been spared life's travails. Leaving Abel's grave, old Cain catches sight of the tree of life in the Garden of Eden, but he does not raise his hand to pluck its fruit. The tired wanderer rejects eternal life. He has had enough of unwanted years. He turns his back also upon Eden's splendor and its angels. When Cain finally dies, he is not mourned. All who are present at his burial feel a sense of relief. They do not want to be reminded of their ancestor and his crime.

In the post-Holocaust period, German versions of the Cain theme stress the murderer's remorse after his terrible deed, while the deed itself is muted. In the collective volume edited by Joachim Illies and entitled *Brudermord—Zum Mythos von Kain und Abel* (1975), Friedrich Kienecker analyzes several of the more than twenty recent literary treatments of the Cain theme. Typical of these are Christa Reinig's lyrical dialogue "Gott Ruft Kain" (1967) and Walter Helmut Fritz's poem "Kain" (1971). The former takes issue with the contemporary Cains who want to obliterate the memory of their atrocious behavior. God seeks out Cain and finds him reading a newspaper. In their dialogue, God asks him: what happened to Abel? Cain answers that he does not know, that he did not read anything about Abel in the daily press, and that he has forgotten happenings of long ago. When God insists: "So you know nothing and heard no outcry?" Cain replies that he did hear but he passed by, indifferent to the outcry. After all, what concern is it to him now, decades after the tragic events of the Holocaust?

The poem of Walter Helmut Fritz also condemns the German tendency to forget the unpleasant past. Cain of the 1970s no longer wanders over the fields with a club. He can now kill at a vast distance without looking his victim in the eye. He need not feel any personal responsibility. He neither hears nor knows the identity of the slain. He no longer even has to reply that he is not his brother's keeper. His face is marked with absolute indifference. He is living in a world devoid of moral values and hence feels no guilt and no need to atone.

A generation after Auschwitz and Maidanek, Hiroshima and Nagasaki, the blood of Abel still cries out from the ground. How does the contemporary Cain face up to the innocent blood he shed? Does he, a member of the only species that can distinguish between good and evil, bear personal responsibility for his murderous deed, or can he disclaim responsibility by putting the blame on the established world order, against which he may at best rage, but whose bidding he feels he must patriotically obey? These questions continue to reverberate in the literature of our day even as they stirred the conscience of sensitive creative spirits in earlier generations.

3

The Tower of Babel

The episode of the Tower of Babel, as narrated in Genesis 11:1-9, testifies to man's aspiring to reach heaven by his own united efforts, even against the will of God. It has its parallel in the Greek story of the Titans who piled Pelion on Ossa and tried to ascend to the realm of the Olympian divinities. But, unlike the Greeks, who saw this effort as part of a struggle between immortals for supremacy, the biblical tale is of mere mortals, descendants of Adam and Noah, who were undaunted by the punishments meted out to their forefathers for disobedience to God, such as expulsion from Paradise and the catastrophe of the Deluge. These human beings of a postdiluvian generation dared to challenge the Creator of the Universe. Endowed with the attribute of reason and under the leadership of Nimrod, a heroic rebel against God's establishment, they were animated by a common purpose and spoke a common tongue. They attracted God's attention as their tower rose ever higher and higher. He descended from the heaven to which they aspired and was filled with astonishment at their monumental achievement. They were reaching out beyond the earthly limitations He had set for these creatures of earth. To frustrate their arrogant striving, He confused their tongues. Without a common language, they could no longer counsel together and hence could not engage in this or any other venture of such magnitude. He also weakened them further by scattering them over the face of the entire earth. Since then, human beings have been moving in different directions and have never again known unity. Even their efforts during the present century to establish a viable League of Nations and an effective United Nations have not been crowned with great success.

Though Genesis does not specifically mention that Nimrod was the initiator of the building of the tower, most commentators since Josephus Flavius have made this assumption, because he was recorded to be the strongest personality of the generations between Noah and Abraham. He was the first ruler who wanted to encompass all mankind under his dominion. This grandson of Ham succeeeded in uniting the Mesopotamian cities on the plain of Shinar into the great power later named Babylonia. The symbol of his mighty domain was to be a lofty ziggurat in the heart of its capital, the metropolis of Babylon, even as the Eiffel Tower is today the symbol of France's capital.

Biblical scholars have tried to discover the historical basis of the tower narrative. Archaeologists have explored ruins throughout the Middle East and conjectured which of these might have been known to the biblical people. The original tower that gave rise to the story was probably rebuilt after its destruction and was destroyed again and again in the course of many warring centuries.

An inscription of Nabopolasser, the father of Nebuchadnezzar, records that he rebuilt the Tower of Babylon in honor of the god Marduk, with its foundation deep in the earth and its pinnacle striving heavenward. Nebuchadnezzar continued with the building of this grandiose structure whose pinnacle was to compete with the sky. This was probably the tower which the Jews who were exiled to Babylon saw in the sixth century B.C.E. and which the Greek historian Herodotus saw when he visited the city in the middle of the following century. He described it as consisting of eight towers, each erected upon the other, with a great temple crowning the topmost tower. In this temple there was reputed to be a golden table and a large couch on which a lady chosen by God among the women of Babylon spent her nights. The priests claimed that God himself came down to the temple and slept with her on this couch. Herodotus, however, does not vouch for the authenticity of these nightly divine encounters in the temple. He merely reports them as hearsay.

References to Babylon's tower recur in the works of the Greek geographer Strabo and the historian Diodorus, both of whom lived during the reign of Emperor Augustus, and in the prophecies of the Jewish sybil a century and a half earlier. A sybil was a seeress who in ecstatic moments foresaw and foretold events to come—above all, dire events. In order to make her oracular utterances more credible, she spoke of past events as if she had also foreseen them. The so-called Jewish sybil, a few of whose oracular verses have been preserved, stemmed supposedly from Hellenistic circles in Alexandria, a center of the Jewish Diaspora in the middle of the second century B.C.E. Her incantations survey the early history of the world and report on the Tower of Babel erected after the Deluge by the descendants of Noah, who still spoke a common language and who were living in Assyria after their descent from Mount Ararat, the resting place of Noah's ark. Their plan to reach the starry heaven was, however, frustrated by God, who sent a storm to topple the tower before it could be completed. Thereafter, dissension broke out among them and they scattered in three directions, peopling the three realms over which ruled Cronus, Titan, and Japetos (Japhet), realms which engaged in constant warfare with each other.

Josephus Flavius, who quoted the sybil, was thoroughly familiar with Greek historical sources as well as with biblical ones. Unlike Philo, who, in the treatise *On the Confusion of Languages*, attempted a complicated allegorical interpretation of the tower episode, Josephus assumed the factual reality of the tower's existence. In his *Jewish Antiquities*, he mentioned that God suggested to the descendants of Noah, who had come down from the mountains to the plains of Senaar, and who had multiplied rapidly, that they send out colonies to cultivate other parts of the earth and to enjoy an abundance of the earth's fruits. But Nimrod urged them to stay where they were and to trust in their mightiness. He promised them that he would avenge the destruction of the civilization of their antediluvian ancestors. He would build a tower higher than the waters could reach, so that, if God were inclined to inundate the earth again, its inhabitants would have a safe shelter. The people went to work and built the towering structure at a tremendous speed because of the multitude of available laborers. Seeing their mad enterprise, God put an end to it by confusing their speech and sowing discord among them.

Since Hellenistic and Roman days, the Tower episode has engaged the popular imagination and has been embellished in arts and letters by Jews, Christians, and Moslems. In a six-volume study, entitled *Der Turmbau von Babel* (1957-1965), Arno Borst analyzed most of this material.

For the Middle Ages, the tower was the symbol of human arrogance and human defiance of God's order. The boldness of the sinning multitudes stemmed from the fact that, despite the population explosion after the Flood, mankind remained a united community and spoke a common tongue, the Hebrew in which God conversed with Adam, and Adam with his descendants. The unity of the human race came to an end when God scrambled spoken Hebrew to such an extent that seventy, or seventy-two, languages arose from its fragments, and these were spoken by the seventy, or seventy-two, peoples dispersed over all continents. At the end of days, however, fragmented humanity will be reunited, and mankind will then sing the Lord's praises in the unscrambled, original Hebrew. As it is said in Zephaniah 3:9, "For then I will convert the peoples to a purer language, that they may all call upon the name of the Lord, to serve him with one consent."

Stories about the *dor haflaga*, the generation of the Tower of Babel, were embellished and expanded by rabbinical sages century after century. They were recorded in compilations such as *Bereshith Rabba, Pirke de Rabbi Eliezer*, and *The Chronicles of Jerahmeel*. The former two commentaries were the principal sources for the detailed narrative in the *Tseno Ureno*, which has been a bestseller down the centuries since its first printing in 1616. This Yiddish commentary on the Bible was especially designed for women readers. Like its sources, it attributed the plan of the tower to Nimrod, a wicked tyrant whose power over his fellow men emanated from the God-tailored coat which he inherited from his grandfather, Ham. God had made this coat for Adam as replacement for the fig-leaves, and Noah had taken it into the ark. When Nimrod, the slave of a slave, put on this coat, all beasts and birds prostrated themselves before him, and all men obeyed him. Upon his command, the tower was built, and, though never completed, it reached a height of twenty-seven miles. Rabbi Eliezer's narrative mentioned seven miles, but the *Tseno Ureno* added another twenty, thus giving the tower a more impressive height. The staircases were in the east and in the west. The laborers carrying bricks ascended from the east and descended in the west, so as not to get in each other's way. However, if a person fell down from the dizzying height and was killed, no great ado was made, since he was easily replaceable, but if a brick fell down, there was weeping at its loss, because a great effort would be needed to replace it.

English poets, well versed in biblical lore, often referred to the Tower of Babel. Thus, Edmund Spenser, in a sonnet published posthumously in 1599 and prefixed to the English translation of Cardinal Contarini's *The Commonwealth and Government of Venice*, reminds us that ancient Babel, Empress of the East, upreared its building to threaten the sky, and tyrannical Rome, the Babel of the West, also upraised its airy towers to great heights. Yet both are fallen and lie buried in ruins. But fair Venice, flower of the world's delight, persists in its beautiful structure, because Venice is more righteous than Babylon or Rome.

John Donne, comparing the joys of this world with those of the next, holds that, just as the builders of Babel's tower could not have found enough material in the entire earth to serve as a base for their structure, so too the world is too poor a foundation upon which to erect true joy such as is to be found only in the afterworld.

John Milton, in his epic *Paradise Lost*, has the Archangel Michael give Adam a panoramic view of future events. Book XII previews events after the Deluge. At first, the survivors and their offspring would be content to till the soil, reap goodly crops, and live in peace. But then an ambitious person would arise who was not content with fair equality. He would be a mighty hunter, not of beasts but of men. He would arrogate unto himself dominion over his fellows and would dispute God's sovereignty. He would set out with a crew to build a city and a tower whose top was to reach to heaven. But God, who often descends unseen to visit our planet, would notice what these men were doing, and He would not like it. He would deride them and garble their native language so that they would not understand each other and would have to stop building.

> ... Great laughter was in Heaven
> And looking down to see the hubbub strange,
> And hear the din. Thus was the building left
> Ridiculous, and the work *Confusion* named. (XII, ll. 59-62)

The etymology of Babel as meaning "confusion" was accepted by Milton, unaware that the Babylonians derived the name from *babilu*, which in their tongue meant "Gate of God."

The antimonarchical Milton has Adam angrily condemn the execrable descendant who assumed authority to rule over his brethren, whereas God gave man dominion only over beast, fish, and fowl but not over his own species. Besides, what a wretched fool was this first tyrant not to realize that, even if he completed the tower, he could not breathe in the thin air above the clouds!

A generation after Milton, and two years after a bloodless revolution toppled James II from the throne of England, the philosopher John Locke sought to exonerate Nimrod from blame in the Tower episode. In the first of the *Two Treatises of Civil Government* (1690), Locke refuted the doctrine that absolute monarchy was grounded in the divine right of kings, as claimed by the Stuarts. He rather maintained that the right of rulers to rule was based on the consent of the people to be governed. It was not Nimrod who was responsible for the decision to erect the Tower of Babel. It was rather the people who reached this decision and authorized the building. The people said: "Come, let *us* build *us* a city and a tower, with the top in heaven, and let *us* make *us* a name, lest *we* be scattered abroad upon the face of the whole earth" (Genesis 11:4). The people built as free men for themselves and not as slaves for a lord and master, because they wanted a permanent settlement so as not to be dispersed.

Daniel Defoe, a younger contemporary of Locke, attributed the entire project of the tower to the machinations of Satan. In *The Political History of the Devil* (1726), he theorized that after the Flood Satan did not find it as easy to bring about man's degeneracy as in antediluvian days. His first major opportunity came when he persuaded mankind to start the Tower of Babel. The building was designed chiefly as a storehouse for provisions in case of a second Deluge. But God thwarted Satan and put an end to the diabolic enterprise, not in anger but in pity for the dreaming human creatures. The collapse of the project was Satan's first great disappointment. He had always triumphed earlier, as in the case of Eve, Cain, and when he got the sons of God to engage in promiscuous, voluptuous living with the daughters of hell. After man's dispersion from Babel, Satan had to learn many tongues if he wanted to set human beings upon each other as one sets dogs upon each other. He was responsible for the growth of oppression, invasions, bloodshed. Warring human beings lost their former beautiful, angelic features and were distorted into furious monsters, into veritable devils. War was Satan's masterpiece. King Nimrod was but the first of many tyrants. He was baited by Satan with dreams of empire, the same bait which ensnared all Majesties down to Louis XIV of France. King Nimrod the First was later idolized as a god under the name of Belus, then Baal.

Among the more original eighteenth-century interpretations of the Tower story was that of the German philosopher and poet Johann Gottfried Herder. He regarded the entire narrative as a *Spottsage*, a satire on the first usurper, Nimrod. In Herder's eulogistic work on biblical literature, *Vom Geist der ebräischen Poesie* (1782), he presented Nimrod as a mighty ruler of Babylon who wanted to build himself a royal residence with a tall tower as the monument of his greatness and his people's subjugation. He persuaded his subjects that such a tower would guarantee them security and lasting unity. The higher it rose, the more did it impinge upon God's domain above the earth. Fearing that the builders would never desist from encroaching upon His territory, God put His finger to their lips, confusing their speech and putting an end to their united effort. Babel became the symbol of man's humbled pride, the symbol of insolence punished. Nimrod, the mighty hunter who wanted to rise on the shoulders of a betrayed and enslaved human herd, suffered disgrace when he challenged the Lord. The gigantic project became the laughing-stock of later generations.

Goethe, who early came under Herder's influence, defended the Promethean striving of the builders of the tower. He did not look upon their dispersion as a curse and as God's punishment for their arrogance. The swarming of the human race over the entire earth, even as the ants, was a blessing, though a mixed blessing. It enabled man to populate all lands, but it also brought about the ensuing disunity. The builders were only a few generations removed from the catastrophe that wiped out the previous race of mortals, save for Noah and his family. The postdiluvians were nourishing themselves by raising herds of cattle. However, to find sufficient pasture, they had to roam ever further from their center. Their desire to build a tower visible from great distances arose from their wish not to cut themselves off entirely from their roots. They wanted to be able to find their way back again to their ancestral ground. If God ruined their project, it was because He did not want them to be happy and wise, numerous and united, too near to heaven.

The English romantic poet William Wordsworth, in the long poem *The Excursion* (1814), harked back to Herodotus in the verses on the Tower of Babel. Generalizing that in earlier stages of society apathy was unknown because religion prevented apathy, he offered as evidence illustrations from Jewish, Persian, Babylonian, Chaldean, and Greek modes of belief. The Babylonian god was Belus. For this divinity, the people of Babel, with immense toil, upreared tower planted upon tower, so that, when Belus descended nightly to rest on his splendid couch in the eighth tower, the highest one, he could overlook the winding Euphrates and the vast city of his devoted and contented worshipers (*The Excursion*, bk. IV, ll. 682-693).

The romantic drama *Der Turm zu Babel* by the postromantic German poet Julius Rodenberg formed the libretto for the opera by the Russian composer Anton Rubinstein. Its first performances in 1870 in Königsberg, Berlin, and Vienna attracted wide attention. It has, however, rarely been staged since then. Nimrod is the opera's main character. Proud of his achievement, as his workers build the tower ever higher, he boasts of his soon being able to challenge God in heaven and not merely on earth. Abram warns him that God can be approached only in humility and not in defiance. He implores Nimrod to desist from sinning against God by building the impious edifice. The enraged Nimrod orders this insolent herdsman to be flung into the glowing kiln in which the bricks are being made. When Abram emerges unscathed by the fire, the people attribute the miracle of his salvation to God. But which God? Was it Baal, or was it Abram's God, or was it a third divinity? Nimrod silences the quarreling factions, adherents of different gods, and sends them back to work on the tower. As for the rebellious Abram, he is to be hurled from the tower and to find his grave at its bottom. But again a miracle intervenes. Amidst thunder and lightning, the tower topples and the people scatter in fear. As Nimrod contemplates the ruins, he is converted to the worship of the one true God, the God of Abram. At the end, Abram sees the three groups descended from Noah—the Semites, Hamites, and Japhetites—wander off in different directions, but he also foresees their finding unification again in the course of time, since they are all God's children. They will then know universal peace and will again speak a common tongue. The world will be a golden Paradise, irradiated by love.

A fiercer spirit pervades Heinrich Hart's blood-drenched *Nimrod* (1888), the second poetic narrative of a projected gigantic epic in twenty-four parts, entitled *Das Lied der Menschheit*. Before his death in 1906, this German poet and critic, who championed realism, even when dealing with remote ages and far-off lands, succeeded in completing three of the twenty-four narratives and only fragments of others. He wanted to present on a grand scale mankind's progress from primitive savagery to the present complex civilization, and even beyond the present on to distant millennia. *Nimrod* deals with the transition from the nomadic way of life to a more settled condition, the forging on the banks of the Euphrates of wandering bedouins into a united people under the leadership of a titanic personality. Nimrod battles his way to supremacy. He becomes the first king. He then builds the first city and a tower from which he can survey the entire area over which he rules. However, in his immeasurable conceit as the sovereign of Babel, he conceives of himself as the god of the earth, and he challenges Bel, the god of the starry sky. He hurls his flashing lance at the firmament above him. The reaction of Bel comes in flashes of lightning and peals of thunder, which topple the tower. It seems as if man's defiance is answered with mocking laughter by a power greater than man.

The German novelist Josef Ponten began his novel *Der Turm zu Babel* before the First World War but did not complete it until the war's end, since he had to spend much of the time after 1914 fighting on various European battlefields. When this novel finally appeared in 1918, the German Empire, which had arisen in the 1870s under the strong, guiding hand of Bismarck, was crumbling into ruins. Ponten mirrored its rise and fall in his narrative of a master-builder whose grandiose vision of erecting a tower that would scrape the sky ended only as a dream because, as in the biblical Tower of Babel, construction could not proceed when confusion in communication set in among the members of the family.

After reading the biblical tale of the tower project, Ponten's master-builder wishes he could have lived in the generation that conceived such a project. He even makes sketches of how a similar tower could still be built nowadays. He entitles his envisaged structure "The Babylonian Tower: An Attempt At Its Reconstruction." This structure is not to be an iron needle like the Eiffel Tower but is to have a broad base and to be made of massive old stones. If his vision is never realized and the tower is never built, it is because, as in ancient days, misunderstandings arise, communication stalls, each member of the master-builder's family pulls in a different direction. At the end, the aged master surveys the wreck of his hopes, the finale of the dream dreamed in his youth in the 1870s, when even the impossible seemed possible.

Stefan Zweig's *Der Turm zu Babel* was written in the midst of the First World War but after the initial patriotic enthusiasm for the conflict had begun to wane in the Austrian capital, which was his home. This literary gem was an expression of Zweig's faith in the reconstruction of European unity after its collapse. He had witnessed the shattering of the bonds of friendship which he had forged across national boundaries before 1914. Unable to join the chorus of European writers who preached hatred, he had at first lapsed into silence. But, by 1916, he resumed broken contacts with the French novelist Romain Rolland, the Belgian poet Émile Verhaeren, and other Europeans in hostile lands who had earlier influenced his thinking. He began work on his pacifistic drama *Jeremias*, in which, under the guise of biblical events of a distant past, he bewailed the insane behavior that gripped his own generation and his own continent, which was in essence a spiritual and cultural unity. However, before *Jeremias* was completed and staged in neutral Switzerland in 1917, he made known his own views on the Europe that he wished to see rebuilt after the war.

In his biblical allegory of the Tower of Babel, he pointed out that the tower vision arose when human beings after the Deluge found themselves on a dangerous, pathless, desolated earth. As they looked up to the pure, radiant sky above them, there was born in their souls a longing to aspire toward heaven, and they united to build a tower that would reach up to it. When God looked down upon these tiny creatures, He at first smiled at their apparently naive, harmless amusement. But, as He saw the foundation pillars of the tower growing ever stronger, He feared that these united Lilliputians, endowed with the spirit He had implanted in their species, would continue in their task until they could challenge Him. In their unity lay the key to their strength. And so He destroyed this unity by confusing their tongues. Not understanding each other, they quarreled and abandoned the grandiose common enterprise. They scattered and built individual homesteads, each family for itself. The tower became a ruin and ultimately a legend.

For thousands of years human beings continued their selfish existences as strangers separated by borders that were breached only for plunder. But the vision of their lost unity never died within them. Gradually they began to interchange ideas and to revive communication across boundaries. Life became richer as they discovered that a unity of arts, science, and commerce was possible amidst diversity. On Europe's soil a new Tower of Babel arose, not as a monument of brick and cement but as one of fraternal solidarity. The tower's foundations were sublime spiritual substances gathered from the wisdom of the Orient and the Occident. Each nation added its contribution, and the tower grew until its spire reached an unprecedented height. In the intoxication of unity, the European builders were nearing heaven. They felt themselves to be creative even as was God. However, the God who had destroyed the first Tower of Babel sensed the danger to His superiority that a united humanity posed, and so He again sowed confusion. Again people raged against each other. They threw away the tools of peace and took up arms. Destruction replaced creativity. The new Tower of Babel, symbol of European solidarity, was crumbling as the war went on. It may take a long time before the interrupted common work can be resumed, but the tower must rise again from its ruins. After the war, the nations must again find their lost unity.

As a literary champion of the reconstruction of Europe's spiritual and cultural unity, Zweig was untiringly active in liberal causes until the Nazis overran his native Austria and forced him to flee from country to country. When the Second World War broke out, the Good European, as he was wont to call himself, saw the third Tower of Babel collapsing, and he could no longer sustain any faith that on Europe's ruins a fourth tower could be built. As a refugee in Brazil, he ended his life in 1942.

The pessimistic mood that drove Zweig to his death dominated German literature after the Nazi regime left Germany in shambles. This mood was reflected in the cynical plays of the dramatist Friedrich Dürrenmatt. The Tower of Babel occupied this Swiss writer's imagination since his youth. In a sketch that he drew of it, he showed its tottering pinnacle rising to a height comparable to the earth's radius. Human beings are too small to be seen, and even mountains appear to be tiny. Long, transparent ribbons, apparently emanating from God's glory, seem to be tugging at the tower and will soon topple it to the ground.

In the play of 1957, *Ein Engel Kommt Nach Babylon*, Dürrenmatt explains how this grandiose tower enterprise came to be undertaken in ancient days, as senseless an enterprise as similar ones today. An angel, disguised as a beggar, comes to Babylon, whose ruler, Nebuchadnezzar, has just overthrown his opponent, Nimrod, after being Nimrod's footstool for nine hundred years. The angel brings with him Kurrubbi, a newly born cherub, who is to be handed over to the lowliest man. The play ends with the tyrant Nebuchadnezzar, in despair at Kurrubbi's disappearance, giving the order to herd mankind into one great enclosure. In its midst, he intends to raise a tower which will pierce the clouds and reach his enemy, God. "I will oppose to the creation out of the void the creation of the spirit of man, and we shall see which is the better: my justice, or the injustice of God." From this city the lowliest beggar, a lover of freedom, flees to the wide open spaces with Kurrubbi, the spirit of love. They leave behind them the mighty but unstable structure of steel and stone as they face the colorful and wild unknown, the beautiful earth of beggars, and a new dawn of dangers and promises.

Among the most recent reinterpretations of the Tower of Babel is the long poem published under this title in 1979 in Israel by the Yiddish poet Hirsh Osherowitch. He wrote it, however, in Vilna during 1964 and 1965, the years when the Great Thaw that followed Stalin's death had not yet come to an end and when biblical themes were no longer frowned upon as subversive.

The poem is an affirmation of man's faith in himself and in his ability to give reality to magnificent dreams, such as the dream of the Tower of Babel. Our species may have been created out of the dust of the earth, but spirit has been breathed into it. We love the firm earth upon which we have been planted, but we also aspire to rise beyond our earthly condition and to touch the realm of the radiant sun, even though it scorch us. Not only in ancient Babylon but also in the present century did we take bricks and stones, sand and loam, and built a tower, so that, like the angels, we could be with God. For, are not angels merely human beings with wings? Though we have no wings, we can emulate the heavenly host by ascending to God by means of the tower which already extends beyond the clouds that cover the cellar called Earth. The winged eagle can no longer reach us as we toil upward, but, alas, the cynical serpent manages to creep upward with us and to sow dissension among us. Truth is mated with falsehood and becomes a stone with which a comrade cracks another comrade's skull. Once stones begin to be hurled, there is no stopping them until the entire structure totters and collapses.

The poet, in heavily veiled, interspersed hints, tries to get the idea across that the structure built by the Soviet Nimrod may be collapsing but that man's dreams remain indestructible, and it is the dreams that make humanity godlike.

In the many literary versions of the Tower of Babel legend, from its biblical beginning until its present configuration, man's irrepressible, boundless, upward striving finds expression. Though this striving is often condemned as arrogance and defiance of the established order, it also mirrors the greatness of the human species, a species that is not content to stay within the bounds set for it by God or fate or the genetic code but rather that wills to build towers with spires reaching up to dizzy heights, even to heaven itself. Such towers may topple and fall, as did the first Tower of Babel, but upon the ruins new towers will be built again and again as sublime monuments of man's indomitable spirit.

4

Princess Hagar

The story of Hagar is told in Genesis 16 and 21. It is a strange story and does not cast a favorable light upon the first patriarchal couple, Abraham and Sarah. While religious commentators have sought in various ingenious ways to justify the mistreatment of Hagar, modern poets and novelists have been almost unanimous in their sympathy for her and in their condemnation of her master and mistress.

Genesis 16 tells us that Sarah was childless for a long time. She had a handmaid, Hagar, who was of Egyptian origin. She offered this handmaid to her husband as his concubine in the hope that Hagar might conceive and she could then adopt Hagar's child as her own. But, when Hagar, on becoming pregnant, behaved disrespectfully toward her mistress, Sarah complained, and Abraham, her docile husband, told her that she could do with her maid whatever she pleased. Thereupon Sarah dealt harshly with her, and Hagar ran away. She got as far as Shur in trying to make her way to her native Egypt, but ultimately she turned back or was forced to turn back. The child she bore to Abraham was Ishmael.

A different portrait of Hagar is presented in Genesis 21. There Hagar is no longer the proud young woman who brooks no ill-treatment after Abraham has raised her to a position of greater prestige as his concubine. She is a broken, submissive, mature woman, a mother worried about the future of her son Ishmael, now that Sarah has at last also given birth to a son, Isaac, who is growing up and would soon contest Ishmael's birthright. When Sarah demands that Abraham cast out the bondwoman Hagar and his firstborn son, since he now has another heir, her own son, the docile husband, though unhappy at this request, nevertheless again complies. He rises up early in the morning, provides Hagar and her son with bread and a jug of water, and sends them away to the Negev desert south of Beersheba. Mother and child would have perished if they had not found a well of water at the last possible moment and were thus able to survive in the harsh wilderness of Paran.

Among the earliest surviving interpretations of the Hagar story were those of the Hellenistic philosopher Philo of Alexandria, the apostle Paul, and the Roman Jewish historian Josephus Flavius, all three of whom wrote in Greek.

Philo and Paul attempted allegorical interpretations of the confrontation between Hagar and Sarah, while Josephus preferred to deal with the confrontation as a factual event.

Writing under the influence of Neoplatonic and Stoic philosophers, Philo evaluated the liberal arts as the handmaid of philosophy, and thus as inferior to philosophy, the mistress. Hagar, the handmaid of Sarah, symbolized for him such liberal arts as grammar, astronomy, rhetoric, music, while Sarah herself symbolized Wisdom and Virtue. Abraham, the symbol of Mind, desires to have children by Virtue, but, unable to do so at once, he is persuaded to espouse Virtue's handmaid, the lower instruction, the liberal arts. Sarah, or Wisdom, refrains from reproaching him with his backwardness or complete impotence in generation. She would also offer similar advice to us in such a situation. "Instead of upbraiding us for our misfortune, Wisdom tells us: 'Go in, then, to my handmaid, the lower instruction given by the lower branches of school lore, that first you may have children by her.' For afterwards you will be able to avail yourself of the mistress's company to beget children of higher birth" (Philo, Loeb Classics ed., IV, 465).

Philo takes up the question as to why Sarah does not give

Hagar to Abraham immediately after their arrival with this Egyptian maid in the land of the Canaanites, but rather after they stayed there for ten years. His answer, in typical allegorical fashion, is that, after emerging from childhood, symbolized by Egypt, a person has to go through a period of adolescence in Canaan, and only then, when he has attained sufficient maturity as a reasoning being, can he wed Hagar: "It is quite natural, then, that the mating with Hagar should take place when ten years have elapsed from the arrival in the land of the Canaanites; for we cannot desire the training of schools the moment we become reasoning beings, as understanding is still soft and flaccid. That only comes when we have hardened our intelligence and quickness of mind and possess about all things a judgment which is no longer light and superficial, but firm and steady" (ibid., IV, 519).

Philo wants us not to condemn Sarah's ill-treatment of Hagar as a typical example of women's jealousy. "It is not women that is spoken of here; it is minds—on the one hand, the mind which exercises itself in the preliminary learning; on the other hand, the mind which strives to win the palm of virtue and ceases not till it is won." (ibid., IV, 551).

Like Philo, the apostle Paul also attempts an allegorical interpretation of the Hagar story, but unlike Philo's Neoplatonic approach, his is a Christian approach. In his Epistle to the Galatians (4:21-31), he is interested in proving the temporariness of the old religion to which the Jews were still clinging, the Sinai covenant which has been superseded by the new covenant of Christianity. Hagar, the bondwoman, and Ishmael, her son, symbolize the slavery of the old covenant, while Sarah, the free woman, and Isaac, her son, symbolize the freedom of the new covenant. Ishmael was born after the flesh, but Isaac was born by promise. As Hagar was a bondwoman and Ishmael a child of bondage, so too is the old Jerusalem a city linked in bondage to the Sinai covenant. The new Jerusalem, however, stands for freedom from bondage. It is linked to the new covenant. The Christians are the children not of the bondwoman but of the free woman. Let the Galatian Christians, therefore, refuse to be forced under the Sinai covenant, lest they be cast out and fall under the doom of Hagar and Ishmael. Let them accept the freedom offered them by the second, later covenant entered into by God and man.

Unlike the Alexandrian philosopher Philo and the Christian apostle Paul, who attempted allegorical interpretations, the historian Josephus preferred factual interpretations of biblical and Jewish events. He was writing in the closing decade of the first century for an audience consisting of educated Greeks and Romans rather than of Hellenistic Jews or new converts to Christianity. He, therefore, eschews esoteric discourses. In his *Jewish Antiquities*, he tries to present biblical Jewish characters in a favorable light as human beings with human motivations. In his narrative, Abraham is a good husband who is distressed at his wife's sterility. Sarah is a good wife. To please him, she brings him one of her handmaidens, the Egyptian Hagar, that he might have children by her. This servant, on becoming pregnant, has the insolence to abuse her mistress and to assume queenly airs, as though the succession were definitely to pass from Abraham to her still unborn son. When Abraham permits Sarah to chastise her, Hagar, unwilling to endure humiliation, attempts flight but is persuaded to return. She is forgiven and behaves better thereafter. Sarah, at first, cherishes Ishmael as if he were her own son, seeing that he has to be trained as heir to the chieftaincy. However, when she herself gives birth, she fears that Ishmael, as the older child, might hurt Isaac after the death of Abraham. She, therefore, urges her husband to send Hagar and Ishmael to settle elsewhere. As a good human being, Abraham refuses, thinking that it is brutal to send off an infant child with a woman destitute of the necessities of life. But afterwards, as a good husband, he yields to his wife's entreaties. Fortunately, Hagar survives her ordeal of thirst in the desert. She later meets some shepherds and, through their care, escapes her miseries. She raises her son to be the ancestor of powerful tribes.

Jewish biblical commentators throughout the Middle Ages refused to tolerate any flaws in the character of the revered first patriarch and his wife. They generally tried to find excuses for their behavior toward Hagar. Only Nachmanides (1195-1270), in commenting on Genesis 16:6, concludes that Sarah sinned and so did Abraham. That is why God heard Hagar's lament when she ran away from mistreatment and gave her a son whose descendants would plague the descendants of Abraham and Sarah.

Hagar's independence of mind and action, so untypical of slaves and bondwomen, was due to the fact that she had been a princess in Egypt, the daughter of Pharaoh, before she was made to serve Sarah. The claim that she was of royal origin was already voiced in the second century by Rabbi Simeon bar Yohai, a disciple of Rabbi Akiva. It is attributed to this sage in *Genesis Rabbah*, an aggadic Midrash based on very early oral and written sources. It is repeated by Rashi (1040-1105), and by many other expounders of the Bible thereafter.

According to *Genesis Rabbah*, when Sarah was in Egypt with her husband, who introduced her as his sister, Pharaoh wished to add her to his harem because of her great beauty, but was prevented by divine intervention in her behalf. He then discovered that she was Abraham's wife and returned her to him along with rich gifts. He bestowed his daughter Hagar upon Sarah, saying that it was better for Hagar to be a handmaid in Sarah's blessed household than to be a mistress in another house. It was Sarah who persuaded the reluctant maid to be united with Abraham. She urged Hagar on with the words: "Happy art thou to be united to so holy a man." After Hagar conceived, Sarah was especially nice to her. When ladies came to visit Sarah, she would ask them also to visit Hagar. However, Hagar soon began to feel superior to her mistress. She would gossip to the visitors and tell them: "My mistress Sarah is not inwardly what she is outwardly. She appears to be a righteous woman, but she is not. For, had she been a righteous woman, she would not be barren. See how many years have passed without her conceiving, whereas I conceived in one night." When this gossip was reported to Sarah, she complained to her husband. He was in a quandary and decided not to interfere, saying to Sarah: "After we made Hagar a mistress, shall we make her a bondwoman again? I am constrained to do her neither good nor harm." It was Sarah, and not Abraham, who dealt harshly with Hagar and caused this proud Egyptian princess, who was her property and not her husband's, to run away.

Pirke de Rabbi Eliezer, an aggadic collection whose final text of the ninth century also goes back to earlier sources, repeats the legend of Hagar as the daughter of Pharaoh and thus explains the maid's defiance of her mistress, to whom she does not feel in the least inferior even when forced into servitude.

The same aggadic work also tries to excuse Abraham's later yielding to Sarah's demand that Hagar and Ishmael be cast out by explaining that young Ishmael, who grew up with the bow and became an archer, once saw Isaac sitting by himself and shot an arrow at him to slay him. Sarah saw this and insisted that Ishmael and Hagar be sent far away to prevent a future calamity if a more accurate arrow should be aimed at Isaac. Although Abraham felt this demand to be exceedingly cruel, he could not gainsay his wife or put Isaac's life in constant jeopardy.

With the rise of Islam, legends of Hagar and Ishmael, the revered forebears of powerful Arab tribes, proliferated among Arab writers. Max Grünbaum in his *Neue Beiträge zur semitischen Sagenkunde* (1893) summarized many of these legends. Abraham and Ishmael were regarded as the founders of the Kaaba, the sacred shrine at Mecca, toward which Moslems turn when praying, even as Jews turn toward Jerusalem. In Islamic lore, Sarah and Isaac are in the background. Hagar is idealized, and Sarah's behavior is deprecated. Hagar and her son are sent into the desert leading to Mecca. There Allah lets the well of Zemzem arise. When Arab tribesmen see birds flying in its direction, they realize that only where there is water will birds congregate. They follow in the same direction and find Hagar at the well. They let her share their milk, and she lets them share in the water.

According to another Moslem legend, Abraham himself brought Hagar and Ishmael to Mecca, when Sarah wanted them far away, and years later, after his son married, he visited him twice. These visits too became the source of fascinating legends.

Many of the legends that circulated in oral and written form among Jews since the beginning of the common era became far more widely known when they were incorporated in the commentaries of Rashi and of Nachmanides (Ramban), commentaries reprinted throughout later generations and still studied today in schools and synagogues. Women read these legends in the *Tseno*

Ureno, their Yiddish biblical commentary, which interlaced biblical passages with parables, allegories, short stories, anecdotes, and admonitions. The *Tseno Ureno* has been reprinted in numerous editions since 1616. For centuries, Jewish mothers used to read its chapters to their children on Saturday afternoons, and the moral text helped to mold the character and values of their young sons and daughters. Every act of the revered patriarchs and matriarchs was either condoned or, if this was impossible, was shown to have brought down suffering as retribution for aberrations. In the Hagar story, the maid's misbehavior toward her mistress was blamed for her misfortunes. Sarah, who was barren for ten years in the land of Canaan and more years before entering Canaan, thought that by giving her maid to Abraham, she too would merit having children. Abraham was not really interested in having a child with Hagar, but he listened to his wife because he did not want to offend her. Sarah was so upset because Abraham did not reprove Hagar for gossiping that she even cast an evil eye on Hagar, who then miscarried. The retribution meted out to Sarah for this sinful behavior was the shortening of her life. She was to have lived as long as Abraham, but she died prematurely by forty-eight years. Abraham's weakness in permitting her to mistreat Hagar was also sinful and resulted in his offspring with Sarah later falling under the dominance of Hagar's offspring, a conclusion earlier voiced by Nachmanides.

As to the question why Abraham did not give Hagar enough water to last mother and child for the entire journey through the desert, the answer was offered that the water would have been sufficient normally, but that Ishmael was feverish and drank an inordinate amount of the precious liquid, so that the jug was soon emptied.

Another question asked was: why did not the all-knowing God let Ishmael perish of thirst before he could grow up and cause trouble, through his descendants, to the Jews, God's chosen people? The answer, which was taken over from Rashi, was that Ishmael was still an innocent child when he was expelled into the wilderness, and God does not punish evil which has not yet been committed.

Abraham later compensated Hagar for his earlier behavior toward her by marrying her after the death of Sarah, and Hagar bore him seven more children. It is true that, according to the Bible, the wife he married in his old age was Ketura. However, Ketura is identified as Hagar, upon the authority of Rashi. *Ketura* is the Hebrew word for "incense," and Hagar bore this name after she repented of her idolatry and her deeds were then as beautifully fragrant as incense. The *Tseno Ureno* also repeats a second etymology that Rashi gives for Ketura, namely, that the word is derived from *keter*, Chaldean for "knotted, tied up," because Hagar, after her expulsion and until her reunion with the aged Abraham, lived closed up and lonely; otherwise Abraham probably would not have been allowed to take her back, since a woman may not return to her first husband after she has lived with a second husband.

Jewish, Christian, and Moslem legends formed the basis for the best-known Dutch version of the Hagar theme, the long narrative poem *Hagar* by Isaac da Costa (1798-1860). The poet was the scion of a patrician Marrano family to which belonged also the excommunicated Jewish dissenter Uriel da Costa. The family had escaped from Portugal to Amsterdam at the beginning of the seventeenth century and reverted to Judaism. Isaac da Costa, however, came under the influence of the Christian religious writer Willem Bilderdijk (1756-1831) and was baptized in his twenty-fourth year. He ultimately ended as the curator of the Theological Seminary of the Free Scottish Church in Amsterdam, and his maturer biblical verses were given a Christian slant. His *Hagar* (1847) is generally regarded as his finest poem and was for a time popular as a school text in Holland. It begins with Hagar's first flight into the wilderness and her return. It continues with her being cast out into the wilderness after the birth of Isaac. Her son Ishmael later becomes the ancestor of the Arabs, who proceed to make great conquests, especially after the appearance of Mohammed. God's promise to Ishmael is fulfilled when the Mohammedan realm attains to enormous splendor. However, the resurgence of Christendom since the era of the Crusades results in the decline of Islam. Ultimately, Ishmael's descendants will have to submit to the Christian savior, the descendant of Isaac, even as Hagar, after her original flight, had to submit to Sarah.

The English poets who have dealt with the Hagar theme during the past two centuries find no justification for the patriarch who exposed his child and its mother to the inhospitable desert. They are more interested in the human drama than in theological explanations. In the poem "Hagar in the Desert" by Mary Tighe (1773-1810), we see the injured, hopeless, weary mother wandering on, indignant and forlorn, with her scorned child. We participate in her anguish as she watches her Ishmael dying of thirst, and we exult when divine relief finally comes to the two lonely figures. In the sonnet "Hagar" by the Victorian poet Hartley Coleridge (1796-1849), the son of the more famous poet Samuel Taylor Coleridge, we sympathize with the angry, wronged, outcast mother as she sits with her famished child in the desert. God too feels with her in her undeserved disgrace, and He sends an angel to cheer her and to revive her child.

The narrative poem "Hagar in the Wilderness" by Edwin Arnold (1832-1904), whose long epics of exotic Asian lands once delighted Victorian readers, depicts Hagar in the scorching desert-noon reconciling herself to her nighing death after the last drop of her shriveled flagon has been drained. She bewails her little son, who must share her fate. She cannot imagine that Abraham, who gave him life, would knowingly rob him of life. She still defends the patriarch as wise and gentle, and blames the bitter-hearted Sarah for their distress. For a moment, a cry of joy bursts from Ishmael's bosom as he discerns glistening water in the distance. But his mother recognizes it as a desert mirage and sinks into despair. "Man had no mercy—God will show us none." But God is merciful and unseals their sight so that they behold a real, sparkling spring in the desert sand. They quaff the liquid life and learn the lesson all of us must learn: to hope ever anew and not to despair.

The poem "Hagar in the Wilderness" by Nathanial Parker Willis (1806-1867) concentrates on Abraham's agony in having to yield to Sarah's demand. He speaks no word to Hagar nor looks upon her face. He merely lays his hand in silent blessing on the fair-haired boy as he sends both mother and son into the wilderness.

In the poem "Hagar Departed" by the American religious poet Edward Everett Hale (1822-1909), it is again Sarah who bears the chief blame rather than her husband. It is Sarah, a mother, who drives another mother from home. She alone is dry-eyed, while the patriarch, Hagar, and the child Ishmael weep. If salvation comes at the critical moment, it is because God, and not man, hears the outcast mother's agony and the orphan's cry of anguish in the wide desert.

The five stanzas of the lyric "Hagar" by the young Scottish poet Francis Lauderdale Adams (1862-1893) describe a hungry mother wandering through the night with her baby in her arms and finally lying down to die. The famished child wails and wails. The mother creeps away, yet still hears the wailing. She finally takes a jagged stone and beats the child on the head. It gives only a single moan and is silent forever. No miracle comes to the modern Hagar, such as came to the biblical one, though the sun rises in the eastern sky—and the day is Christmas Day.

Equally bitter is the tone of the German lyricist Irene Forbes-Mosse (1864-1945), whose poem in thirteen stanzas "Hagars Klage" voices woman's resentment that she is treated like a puppy with whom a man plays and then casts off, or like an unbefriended little dog whom man feeds and then points to the door: "Go, it is enough!" This is what happened to Hagar. It is not merely the dryness of the desert that makes her thirst for water. It is also injustice that makes her thirst for justice, and loneliness that makes her thirst for comradeship.

Condemnation of the man who disports with woman and then casts her off permeates the three lyrics about Hagar by Itzik Manger (1901-1969), the Rumanian Yiddish troubadour, who resurrected biblical characters as if they lived and breathed in an East European townlet of the early twentieth century. The first lyric portrays Hagar's last night with Abraham. She sits in the kitchen beside a smoky lamp and weeps when he tells her that she must go. Sarah has threatened him with divorce unless he gets rid of Hagar. The maid takes out the gifts that the patriarch once gave her when he took her out for a walk near the railroad. She laments that the love of a man floats away and disintegrates like the smoke of the lamp or of the locomotive. Where is she to go now with her little baby? And yet, she still bears some love for her seducer, and she will not leave the floor unswept or the pots and plates unwashed before departing. The second lyric takes place at dawn, as Hagar prepares to leave Abraham's house by coach in order to catch the morning train. While he haggles with the coachman, she calms her little Ishmael: "Don't weep, my darling. That's our fate. That's how patriarchs with long, pious beards behave." But she herself cannot restrain her tears as she thinks of her uncertain future. She wonders whether the pious Abraham senses what goes on in her heart, now that the coach stands ready to drive her far, far away from him. In the third lyric, the weeping Hagar sits at the crossroads, not knowing whether to turn eastward or westward. Fortunately, the Turkish sultan passes by with a caravan and recognizes her as Abraham's maid, from whom he and other Moslems stem, according to the prophet Mohammed. He kneels before her and thanks Allah for having found her. Hagar sits confused at this sudden change of fortune, while a silver half-moon glistens in her hair.

While Manger's ironic lyrics about Hagar were penned during his light-hearted pre-Nazi years, before exile and illness saddened him, the Yiddish lyricist Rikudah Potash, who began her poetic career in pre-Holocaust Poland, wrote her "Hagar" after she found refuge in 1934 on the soil of her new homeland. In Jerusalem, she came under the influence of the German expressionist poet Else Lasker-Schüler, who had also escaped the Nazi deluge. Nevertheless, the tender, elegiac biblical poems of Rikudah Potash remained free of expressionistic explosive hysteria. In her "Hagar," she depicts the exiled mother and child in the wilderness, where all the elements are hostile. The hot dust of the desert falls upon Hagar's hair, the caked earth upon which she treads is unproductive, the fiery, blood-colored sky hangs heavy above her. Amidst this desolation, where is she to find refuge with her little boy? Weeping she wanders on and on. Nowhere can she cool her tears.

The poem was composed when the Nazis were dominant. The

apparently hopeless fate of the exiled Hagar mirrored the situation of many Jewish mothers in Eastern and Central Europe.

The South African poet Lewis Sowden (1905-1974), who also found refuge in Israel after struggling against apartheid, saw in Hagar the precursor of all who are held in bondage. In his *Poems on Themes Drawn from the Bible* (1960), he includes, under the title "Ishmael," three monologues by Hagar, Sarah, and Abraham. Hagar calls on the God of bondmen and bondmaids to loosen their shackles. She feels that in the desert God is nearer to the enslaved. He will exercise mercy and will not let her son die. Sarah justifies her own behavior in wanting the alien menial banished before the son of this slave can claim a share in Abraham's bounty. Abraham realizes that if, in dividing his heritage, he were to give more to one son, he would arouse envy in the other son and destroy their brotherhood. He can teach the unity of God but is helpless to teach the unity of man. Hagar and Ishmael are exiled to the desert in order to expiate their master's sins, but they will return, after learning wilder ways, to claim their own.

As a fighter for the liberation of the blacks of South Africa from dominance by the whites, Sowden foresaw a coming conflict between both, after the blacks will have learned the wilder ways of terrorism. In the end, perhaps brotherhood will come into being.

While poets could concentrate on a single episode of the Hagar story, generally the casting out of Hagar and her child, novelists had to paint an entire panorama of the world in which this biblical event took place, the world between the Nile and the Euphrates. Twentieth-century archaeological discoveries from the patriarchal era have enriched our understanding of arising, dominant, and decaying civilizations in this region that was teeming with peoples of different levels of culture. Among these peoples were the nomadic and seminomadic Habiru, of whom we learned from tablets uncovered at Tel-el-Amarna in Egypt, at Mari on the Upper Euphrates, and at Nuzi, about 150 miles north of Baghdad. The similarity of the names Habiru and Hebrew led novelists, who could afford to be less critical than biblical scholars, not only to identify both as one and the same grouping but also to catapult Abraham into the leadership of the Habiru nomads. Two novels that sought to reconstruct imaginatively the Abrahamitic generation at the close of the third millennium before the common era, and laid great stress on the Hagar episode, were *Father Abraham* (1935) by the Canadian scholar and novelist William George Hardy and *Hagar* (1958) by Cothburn O'Neal.

Hardy was a professor of classics at the University of Alberta and the author of several biblical novels. He was familiar with the excavations then being concluded by the British archaeologist C. L. Woolley, who had uncovered Ur of the Chaldees and its civilization, dating from the time of Abraham. He therefore began his novel in Ur with the young lad Abraham, the son of Terach, an Aramean immigrant and maker of images, and he traced Abraham's growth in a lifelong search for the supreme God. The novelist conceived of Sarah as the princess of the wandering Habiru. She it was who saved Abraham from crumbling Ur when the city came under the rule of the conquering Hammurabi, king of Babylon. As Sarah's husband, Abraham attained to great power, becoming the undisputed chieftain of the Habiru, whom he indoctrinated into the worship of the one God, invisible and all-powerful. When famine swept over Canaan, Abraham led his tribe down to Egypt. There the beautiful Sarah attracted the notice of Pharaoh, who wanted her as his favorite concubine. He gave her Hagar as her servant. Hagar was the daughter of the concubine whom Sarah had displaced and who, in accordance with the prevailing custom, had committed suicide. On discovering that Sarah, who had been introduced to him as Abraham's sister, was also Abraham's wife, Pharaoh feared divine vengeance and sent the couple back to Canaan, together with Princess Hagar. It was in Canaan that the drama was then played out between Sarah, queen of the Habiru, and Hagar, the daughter of Pharaoh, who had become her bondwoman. It was a human drama, with human passions swirling about the main characters. It ended when Ishmael, who had witnessed human sacrifices being offered up to Baal by the Canaanites, bound Isaac hand and foot and put him on an altar of wood to slay him. Then did

Abraham free himself from his fascination for Hagar and sent her back to Egypt with her son.

Cothburn O'Neal's novel also attempted a reconstruction of the life of the Habiru nomads under the leadership of Abraham. When they wander on to Egypt and Pharaoh discovers that Sarah is a married woman, he fears that plagues will descend upon his land because of his wanting her as his concubine. To appease her God, he gives her his daughter Hagar. This highly cultured Egyptian princess then lives on as Sarah's property in the tents of the uncultured Habiru. Upon the behest of her mistress, she has to bear a child to Abraham. But, after Isaac too is born, Sarah can tolerate no rival claimant as Abraham's successor and casts out Hagar and Ishmael. After severe hardships in the desert, both are rescued by Phicol, an exiled Egyptian aristocrat and warrior, who commands the army of King Abimelech of Gerar. Phicol is proud to marry a daughter of Pharaoh. Her son is thus assured of attaining to great power in the Wilderness of Paran.

The novelist emphasizes that Sarah acted not out of malice toward her Egyptian maid and toward Abraham's firstborn son but rather in order to effect a separation between the Habiru, over whom Isaac was to rule, and the Canaanites, among whom Ishmael was to carve out a kingdom for himself.

Abraham's sacrifice of Hagar and Ishmael in order to mollify his wife and to secure the inheritance for his younger son had little appeal to dramatists. Franz Lindheimer, in his verse drama of 1896, *Hagar's Love* (*Hagars Liebe*), attempted to do justice to this theme and failed. Karl Wolfskehl, in his sad, exilic, New Zealand years, wrestled with this theme in his projected poetic drama *Abram*, but apparently never completed this work. Only a single monologue by Hagar, when she was cast out and faced death, appeared posthumously in 1960.

Abraham's inner conflict, whether or not to appease his wife and reluctantly sacrifice his firstborn son, could not arouse universal sympathy, as could his religious conflict, whether or not to yield to the will of God, who demanded absolute submission in the sacrifice of Isaac. In the Hagar story, our sympathy is not with Abraham but rather with the princess who became a bondwoman, the concubine who was misused by her master and mistress and then abandoned. She is at the center of our interest, and not the patriarch, as in the Akedah theme. All the subtle and ingenious excuses offered by well-meaning theologians, poets, and novelists cannot absolve Abraham and Sarah of guilt. Their behavior toward Hagar is deplorably human and, therefore, suffers from moral imperfection. The Bible does not gloss over human weaknesses but rather shows man, be he patriarch, king, or commoner, striving to rise above his erring, imperfect condition in his ascent to a more moral level of existence.

5

Rebekah's Beguilement of Isaac

The Bible presents two contrasting images of Rebekah, the wife of Isaac. One is of the young maiden at the well of Aram-Naharaim, virginal, good-natured, obedient, gracious, and very beautiful. When Eliezer, who was sent by his master, Abraham, to find a suitable mate for Isaac, catches sight of her and asks her for a little water of the pitcher she has just filled, she not only gives him to drink but also volunteers to draw water from the well for his camels until they have had their fill. The other image is of the mature Rebekah, wise and wily, unhappy with her son Esau and his Hittite wives, inciting her second son, Jacob, to deceive her old, blind husband.

The chief character trait common to Rebekah in her young years and in her old age is courage. She displays this courage when she, who has never ventured far from her birthplace, is ready to depart from it immediately with the strangers from beyond the desert, even without the suggested delay, the ten days of leave-taking advised by her brother Laban. She also displays this courage late in life when planning and executing the beguilement of Isaac and getting him to bless Jacob, the son preferred by her, rather than Esau, the son preferred by him.

Young Rebekah's encounter with Eliezer at the well has been a favorite subject for pictorial artists in their illustrations of the many precious biblical manuscripts ever since the Vienna *Genesis* of the fifth century. The scene is also depicted in mosaics and frescoes of medieval cathedrals, including those at Palermo, Monreale, Amiens, and Pisa. In the Renaissance and Baroque periods, the Italian Guido Reni, the Frenchman Nicolas Poussin, the Spaniard Bartolomé Murillo, and the Austrian Josef Anton Zoller created notable paintings of this scene. Albert Bertel Thorvaldsen, the most famous of Danish sculptors in the nineteenth century, and Marc Chagall among contemporary artists reverted to this popular subject. Though the older Rebekah had less fascination for sculptors and painters, she is favored more often by twentieth-century writers. These emphasize her role in the deception of Isaac. They include the Austrian dramatist Richard Beer-Hofmann, the English dramatist Laurence Housman, the German novelist Thomas Mann, the French novelist Jean Cabries, the American novelist Irving Fineman, as well as many lyrics in diverse tongues.

Beer-Hofmann, in his poetic drama *Jaakobs Traum,* begun in 1909 and published only as the First World War was nearing its end in 1918, opens with a conflict between the aging but still resolute Rebekah and the alien wives of Esau. To these Hittite women, who upbraid her for her beguilement of her blind husband, she explains that the broken old man whose life is ebbing so sadly was always but a pale twig who grew up in the shadow of the resplendent Abraham. It was the son of the renowned Abraham she married, the mighty Abraham who defeated four kings at Laish, the magnificent lord who offered hospitality to God and His angels at Mamre. The weakling Isaac was attracted to the robust hunter Esau. The unseeing Isaac hesitated to bestow his blessing, when Jacob stood before him, and it was not his father's blessing that Jacob received but the ancestral blessing of Abraham that erupted from the lips of the aged Isaac.

Though Isaac himself does not appear in the play at all, an image of him emerges from the words of Rebekah and Jacob. It was the tragic fate of young Isaac to have been sacrificed on Mount Moriah, not physically but emotionally. The child that was placed there on the altar, and that gazed, wide-eyed with fear, upon the knife hovering over him in his father's hand, bore the scars of that horrible moment ever thereafter. He who had trusted his beloved and adored father, and who had seen this father ready to murder in an onset of religious frenzy, could never in later years trust anyone or feel sure of himself.

When Edom, the name under which Esau appears in Beer-Hofmann's play, is called back from the hunt and informed of the betrayal perpetrated during his absence from home by his mother and his brother, he is raging mad and refuses to listen to the admonition of Rebekah not to disturb the sleep of his father, whose days may be coming to an end. Edom forces his way into his father's tent but soon emerges sobbing. He demands that his mother explain why she dislikes him so much and harmed him so grievously. She defends her behavior toward him. A son who spends his days hunting and his nights carousing with alien wives has become a stranger to her and should be able to dispense with her affection.

When Edom threatens to avenge the wrong done him and to slay his brother, Rebekah adjures him to desist. She promises that Jacob will stay far away from the family home in Beersheba. Isaac and she herself are nearing their end. Soon he, Edom, will be lord of all their possessions. But Edom reminds her that it is Jacob who has the ancestral blessing and, if alive, will retain it. Only with Jacob's death can the nefarious deed be undone. Rebekah pleads with her son to be content with the earthly heritage and to desist from pursuing Jacob. To Edom's persistent questioning why Jacob and not he, her firstborn son, was chosen for God's blessing, Rebekah replies: "Because Jacob walks about full of mysterious questions, hearing within himself the doubts, dreams, longings, and imperative voices of his ancestors, while you rejoice in your sure knowledge and satiety; because he does not entomb his God in distant heavens as you do but wrestles with him day by day and breast to breast; because he does not hunt and sacrifice and murder as you do but, rather, pales in the presence of all suffering creatures and speaks to all of them as they to him. That is why the blessing is his—and the burden of the blessing."

These words enrage Edom even more, and he rushes forth,

with murder in his heart. Rebekah, helpless to stop him, turns in prayer to God not to permit an encounter between the two brothers that may result in fratricide but rather to let Jacob arrive safely in Haran, where she spent her happy youth until her marriage.

Beer-Hofmann's portrayal of Rebekah as a matron of strong will and decisive action is followed by Thomas Mann in his novel *Die Geschichten Jaakobs* (1933), the first volume of his Joseph tetralogy. It is she, according to Mann, who initiates the deception of Isaac, while Jacob merely obeys her instructions, trembling and hesitant. She it is who dresses him in his brother's festive garments and anoints him with his brother's oil. She it is who prepares the meal and sends him into the tent to steal the blessing. She anticipates that Jacob will have to flee before Esau, who is out hunting, when he returns with the venison. She has a premonition that she will never see her favorite son again and is prepared for the sacrifice, though her heart aches. Jacob, aware that he wronged his brother, fears that Isaac, on discovering the deception, will curse the two deceivers.

When Eliphas, the son of Esau, catches up with the fleeing Jacob, the latter pleads for forgiveness and explains that he did not plan the betrayal or even wish it. He considers himself to be a victim of his mother's machinations. He was helpless against a woman's cunning. He was enticed to cooperate in the nefarious deed, even as his first ancestor, Adam, was led astray by Eve.

Thomas Mann is not certain that Jacob was sincere in his protestations of innocence and in his explanation to Eliphas, but these did have the effect of saving his endangered life. According to Mann, Jacob did not want to leave home as a thief in the night, burdened with the knowledge of his father's lasting ill-will. Upon his insistence, the strong-willed Rebekah successfully undertook to persuade her docile, pious husband to forgive the deception and to reconcile himself with Jacob, who was about to undertake the long flight, since this son would be finding refuge at Laban's estate and would there most likely choose a wife from among kin and not from among the worshipers of foreign gods.

Laurence Housman, who dramatized the story of Jacob in the

second of his *Palestine Plays* (1942), devotes the first scenes to the betrayal of Isaac by Rebekah and Jacob. Housman interprets the Bible as the record of a long process of trial and error by which the Israelites finally arrived at the pure concept of God, the concept taught by the prophets. While Beer-Hofmann was reverent in his approach to the Bible, and Thomas Mann was ironic, Housman is anti-biblical, even vicious, in debunking the patriarchs and the supernatural miracles. His Jacob is not a good person, and the behavior attributed to him is atrocious. Obeying Rebekah, he cheated his brother and deceived his father. Isaac, old, tired, feeble, is entirely dependent upon his wife and his son Esau. Before dying, he wants to transmit to his firstborn the blessing derived from Abraham. But who is the firstborn? Esau recalls that for a mess of potage he has just sold to the scheming Jacob the right of the firstborn. When Rebekah overhears Isaac suggesting to Esau that a venison feast be prepared for the morrow at which God's blessing to Abraham will be handed down, she prepares for the deception. The frightened Jacob is reluctant to join in her plan but also fears to disobey his resolute mother.

Though Isaac and Esau are angry at Jacob after the deception, they do not curse him. They feel that he has already been punished insofar as fear will always shadow him. Rebekah too is punished for her participation in the fraudulant act in that she will never again see her favorite son. A later scene does indeed show Jacob overcome with terror during his flight. Fear is about him throughout all the years until his reconciliation with Esau two decades later. Only then does he feel secure.

According to the dramatist, Esau is lordly, brave, magnanimous, but not too intelligent, while Jacob is humble, cowardly, greedy, deceitful, but very clever. Jacob will be fear-ridden until he and his brother compose their differences face to face. Then the dream he dreamed at Bethel, the most famous dream in all history, will be realized, and he and his descendants, the race of Jacob, renamed Israel, will know peace and release from fear.

During the Second World War, when Housman's drama was published, the American novelist Irving Fineman also dealt with Rebekah's beguilement of Isaac in the narrative *Jacob* (1941), a fictional autobiography related by the patriarch to his favorite son, Joseph. In telling of his early life, Jacob explains why he cooperated in deceiving his father, though he himself did not initiate the deception. Scorned by his brother and loved by his mother, he early became aware of the unending struggle between the men of force and action and the men of thought and sensitivity. Since Esau could hunt and fight, he was looked up to by the gentle and poetically inclined Isaac, who had lost to the Philistines much of the lands and possessions inherited from Abraham. This loss occurred because he refused to resist by force the Philistine incursions. Jacob, who inherited his father's gentle nature, did not really want to deceive the blind old man and felt that he could get along well even without the blessing. But the forceful Rebekah urged him on, overcame all his scruples, and then sent him off to Laban. Not only would he be safer there than in Beersheba, but there, she hoped, he would choose his own wife. She recalled that the privilege of choosing a wife had been denied to Isaac, whose too illustrious and too domineering father had done the choosing for him. Like so many sons of daring and successful fathers, Isaac was timid, conservative, and obedient. As for herself, she had gone with Eliezer, Abraham's messenger, in order to see the fulfillment of her romantic vision of an unknown prince in faraway Canaan. But, when she met Isaac for the first time, she was disappointed to find him so ordinary and not at all dashing like the famed Abraham, thoughtful but not very talkative. She had been a good wife to him, but she wanted her son to be more independent and not to be forced into a marriage arranged by others.

In the French novel *Saint Jacob* by Jean Cabries, which appeared in 1954, Rebekah is again the principal instigator in the beguilement of Isaac. The first glimpse of her is as an old, much-tried woman, who wanders about in the outdoors after midnight of the eventful day when both her sons left home. She will have to spend the rest of her years alone with Isaac, for better or for worse. Having hatched the plot and hurriedly made all preparations for carrying it through, she had pushed the hesitating Jacob into her husband's tent. Without her encouragement and resolute actions, he would not have deceived his blind father. But, even after the blessing had been obtained, Jacob still lacked the courage and the strength to set out on the long journey to Mesopotamia. Rebekah had to give him of her courage and her strength. She went even further and dared to confront Isaac after the blessing intended for Esau and to plead with him to bless Jacob a second time, so that this son would not leave home with the stigma of a stolen blessing. Thnough she succeeded in mollifying her husband, she knew that the peace which had prevailed down the years in their relationship as husband and wife could no longer be fully restored and that a lasting alienation between her and her firstborn son had set in. Esau told her on parting from her: "I am no longer your son, mother. Jacob alone has been your son from the beginning. I have never had a mother." Rebekah has much to brood on. In a single day she has lost both of her sons. Jacob is fleeing eastward to his uncle Laban, and Esau is heading westward to his uncle Ishmael. Each will experience a different destiny, while their old mother will remain with her ailing husband, lonely and grief-stricken, yet confident that she has done God's will and that she was justified in her apparently unseemly action.

Unlike the novelists and dramatists but like most pictorial artists, lyric poets, confined within the limits of a few verses or stanzas, generally avoided the theme of Rebekah's beguilement of Isaac, since it was far more complex than the simple vision of Rebekah at the well.

The American poet Mark Van Doren and the Yiddish poet Itzik Manger were among the rare exceptions, even as were Rembrandt and Chagall among painters. Van Doren was fascinated by Rebekah, although he did not condone her deception. In his poem "Rebekah," she is as clear-headed and resolute in her old age as in her youth, when she followed Eliezer to be the wife of Abraham's son. Isaac was helpless against her trickery. She was no longer a girl perfect in simplicity. She knew that she was inflicting hurt upon Isaac and Esau, but she felt that she was God's instrument in transferring the blessing to Jacob.

The sonnet "Rebekah" by Itzik Manger presents Rebekah as

weeping at the thought that the two children to whom she gave birth in a single hour are about to leave her within a single hour. She is, however, comforted by the foresight that the two hostile brothers, who in her lifetime are going their separate ways, will be reunited after her death and will then again extend their hands to each other in fraternal reconciliation.

Of the four biblical matriarchs, Sarah and Rachel attract most attention in world literature. Leah is neglected or given a very subordinate role, and Rebekah is generally depicted primarily in her beguilement of her husband. This deception, which cannot be justified by normal human moral standards, was justified by claiming it to be God's will, a higher criterion than man's. In this respect, Rebekah's justification for her conduct is reminiscent of that of the Greek heroine Antigone, daughter of Oedipus.

Antigone rose to fame in literature and has maintained it to this day by acting against a human decree which she regarded as impious, a decree of the state of Thebes proclaimed by its ruler, Creon. She appealed to a higher law than that promulgated by mere man as justification for her action, and she was prepared to pay the penalty of death, if necessary, for her willful defiance of constituted human authority. Similarly, in the beguilement of Isaac, Rebekah acts on the basis of what she believes is a higher law than that of mere man. Isaac may prefer to hand down the ancestral blessing to his firstborn son, the mighty Esau. But she diverts the blessing to her younger son and is prepared to pay the high price for her disobedience: her husband's anger and condemnation, inevitable alienation from her older son, and a lifelong separation from her younger and more beloved son.

6

Lady Asenath

Asenath is mentioned only three times in the Bible. Yet many are the legends that posterity wove about her.

Genesis 41:45 records that when Pharaoh elevated Joseph to be viceroy over all the land of Egypt, he changed Joseph's name to Zaphenath-Paneah and gave him as wife Asenath, daughter of Poti-phera, who was priest of On.

The name Asenath has been interpreted as meaning one who belonged to Neith, an Egyptian goddess. Poti-phera, who was a priest, is not to be confused with Potiphar, Pharaoh's chamberlain, at whose home Joseph served before his imprisonment and whose wife sought to seduce him. However, because of the similarity of names, legends and literary versions later found ingenious ways of combining Potiphar and Poti-phera into a single character. On was later known as Heliopolis, the city of Sun-worship.

A second reference to Asenath, Genesis 41:50, records that unto Joseph were born two sons before the years of famine came, whom Asenath, the daughter of Poti-phera, Priest of On, bore unto him.

The third and final reference appears in Genesis 46:20. In listing the descendants of Jacob, we are again told that unto Joseph in the land of Egypt were born Manasseh and Ephraim, whom Asenath, the daughter of Poti-phera, priest of On, bore unto him.

Although the life of Joseph is narrated in far greater detail than that of any other character in the Book of Genesis, these three meager references are the only ones that refer to his wife and the mother of his children. Of the two Egyptian women who had the greatest influence upon the Hebrew slave who ended up as viceroy of Egypt, much space is given only to the temptress, the wife of his master, whose charms he so strenuously resisted. Though nameless in the Bible, she surfaces in literature and folklore under many appellations. Of these, the most popular were Zuleika and Sephira.

The apocryphal *Testament of Joseph*, the historian Josephus, talmudic sages, early church fathers, Arabian and Persian poets, medieval chroniclers, Renaissance painters and playwrights, baroque novelists, modern lyricists, and contemporary writers and musical composers have vied in glamorizing the fierce passion of the alluring woman so tragically involved with the noble, implacably chaste Joseph. In comparison with her vivid, strong-willed, resourceful personality, Asenath in the biblical narrative is but a shadowy figure, apparently without a will of her own, a mere chattel handed over by the ruler of Egypt to his Hebraic favorite as an additional reward for correctly interpreting the two dreams of the fat and lean cows and the plump and lean ears of corn. Popular imagination, however, refused to reconcile itself to such an unromantic, self-effacing role for the mother of the two powerful tribes of Manasseh and Ephraim. Hence, when Asenath emerges from obscurity at the beginning of the common era, she too is invested with a vivid personality, as tall as Sarah, as charming as Rebecca, as beautiful as Rachel, and even more strong-willed than her earlier rival for Joseph's affection.

It was in Jewish-Hellenistic circles that legends of Asenath were most widespread and were taken over by the earliest Christian writers. It is true that the *Testament of Joseph*, which probably dates back to Maccabean times, and which is the most fascinating of the twelve testaments of the sons of Jacob, goes into great detail in narrating the many unsuccessful efforts of Potiphar's wife to break down the resolute resistance of the chaste Joseph, and that Asenath is there mentioned only as the woman he married and whose body he enjoins his sons to bury near the grave of Rachel, their grandmother. However, by the beginning of the common era, Asenath stories must have circulated among the Jews, especially in the large Egyptian diaspora. There are records of eighty-four medieval manuscripts on the marriage of Joseph and Asenath. Not all of them have survived, but those that did survive in Greek, Latin, Syriac, Armenian, Old Slavonic, and other languages apparently all go back to a common source, a *Joseph and Asenath* romance of the early centuries of our era.

Christoph Burchard, in his *Untersuchungen zu Joseph und Asenath* (1965), analyzed these manuscripts and proved that the European vogue of this romance before the invention of printing and during the centuries soon thereafter was in largest measure due to the Latin version of Vincent of Beauvais (1190-ca. 1264), which is included in his *Speculum Historiale* (ca. 1260), a history of the world from creation until the mid-thirteenth century. This history was the principal source for translations and adaptations of Asenath stories in French, English, German, Dutch, Norse, Danish, Czech, and Polish manuscripts and the earliest printed versions in fifteenth-century France and sixteenth-century Germany.

The original romance, stripped of its later Christian accretions, may be summarized as follows:

In the ancient city of Heliopolis there lived a priest named Pentephres, who was the chief of Pharaoh's satraps and who presided over the worship of the sun-god. He was exceedingly rich and wise and gentle, and he had a daughter, Asenath, who was more beautiful than any maiden on earth. On attaining to the age of eighteen, she was wooed by many lords and princes, including the firstborn son of Pharaoh. She, however, scorned all men and disdained even to look upon them. She dwelt in a tower overlooking the priestly dwelling. This tower contained ten chambers, of which seven housed seven virgins, playmates of her own age, and the other three her precious belongings and her idols. Her innermost chamber had three windows that looked out toward the east, the south, and the north.

Now it came to pass in the first of the seven years of plenty that

Pharaoh sent Joseph to go round all the land of Egypt in order to gather the corn for the royal granary. And when Joseph came to Heliopolis, Pentephres prepared a great feast for him and suggested to his daughter that this wise and influential favorite of Pharaoh would be a fine bridegroom for her. When she heard this, she was greatly angered that an alien, the son of a shepherd, a former slave who lay with his mistress and was cast into the prison of darkness, should now, after his turn of fortune, be considered as a fitting mate for her. She fled to her chamber in the tower when Joseph's chariot neared the gate of her father's house, and she alone failed to welcome him. However, when she looked out of her tower-window and beheld his great beauty, she regretted her hasty, evil words about him. Surely, she thought, he must be a son of God, for who among men could ever beget such beauty, and what womb of woman could give birth to such radiance? When Joseph espied her peeping out of her lofty window, he at first thought of her as another siren out to lure him. But Pentephres assured him that the maiden was his daughter, a virgin who hated every man. In that case, said Joseph, let her descend and I will look upon her as my sister. Asenath was fetched by her mother, who told her to kiss him as a brother. But Joseph said that it was improper for him to kiss or be kissed by a strange woman who was an idol-worshiper. When the eyes of the maiden were filled with tears at these words, Joseph pitied her and blessed her in the name of the Lord, the God of his father Israel.

On the following day Joseph left Heliopolis but promised to return on the eighth day, after completing his collection of corn for Pharaoh. Asenath retreated to her chamber, put off her magnificent robes, girded her loins with sackcloth, sprinkled ashes over her head, broke into fragments all her gods of gold and silver, and fasted for seven days. On the eighth day of her abasing herself, she prayed to the God of the Hebrews, the Lord of mighty Joseph. And when the Lord God heard her confession and saw her penitent humility, he sent to her his archangel Michael, who resembled Joseph save that his face was as lightning. Michael made known to her that God was giving her to

Joseph for a bride. From the tower, the archangel vanished and appeared to Joseph with the same message.

Before the eighth day came to an end, Joseph was back in Heliopolis. And now he kissed Asenath for the first time and gave her the spirit of life, then a second time and gave her the spirit of wisdom, and a third time tenderly and gave her the spirit of truth. Then he left to ask the consent of Pharaoh, who was like a father to him. And Pharaoh made a wedding for Joseph and Asenath and a feast that lasted seven days.

When the seven years of plenty passed and the second year of famine came, Jacob and his kindred settled in Goshen, and the aging patriarch blessed his daughter-in-law. But when Pharaoh's firstborn son saw Asenath, his love flared up, and he plotted to kill Joseph and take her to wife. Unable to induce Simeon and Levi to ally themselves to him, he conspired with Dan and Gad, who envied the good fortune of their younger brother. Besides, Pharaoh's son convinced them that Joseph intended to slay them after Jacob's death. He gave them two thousand men to ambush Asenath. These fell upon the six hundred men who were with Asenath and cut them down, but Asenath, with Benjamin at her side, succeeded in fleeing in her chariot. When Pharaoh's son sought to attack the chariot, Benjamin wounded him with a round stone and killed fifty men who were with him. The alerted sons of Leah slew the rest. Dan and Gad were spared when Asenath interceded for them, but Pharaoh's son died of his wound. Soon thereafter Pharaoh also died after bequeathing the throne to Joseph, who reigned as regent until Pharaoh's suckling son came of age.

Lovely as was this tale of Jacob's favorite son and the glamorous Asenath, it did not satisfy Jewish religious circles, who could not grasp why the hero God chose to be the savior of Jacob and Jacob's descendants had to marry the daughter of a heathen priest, an idol-worshiping Egyptian maiden unrelated to the clan of Nachor, Terach, Abraham, and Isaac. It is true that, like Ruth of Moab, she was converted to the God of Israel. Besides, her uprightness and sincere piety might compensate for her alien origin. And yet, how much more worthy of Joseph would she be if, like the matriarchs Sarah, Rebecca, Rachel, and Leah, she were somehow related from birth to the extended family! And so the legend arose that Asenath was indeed closely related, that she was the daughter of Dinah, the offspring of Shechem's deed of violence. This interpretation was taken over by *Targum Jonathan*, an Aramaic translation and commentary on Genesis completed no later than the seventh or eighth century, and with greater elaboration by *Pirkei de Rabbi Eliezer*, an aggadic work of the eighth century.

If Asenath was the daughter of Dinah, the question then arose as to how she got to Egypt and to the house of Poti-phera or Pentephres, priest of On. The answer arrived at was that her brothers wanted to kill Dinah for blemishing the family's honor, but that the compassionate Jacob sent her away when her pregnancy was discovered or after she gave birth to a daughter. However, just as the son of Hagar was saved by the intercession of an angel, so too was the daughter of Dinah. According to one version, it was the archangel Michael who carried the infant to Egypt and placed her where Potiphera would find her. The childless priest then brought her up as his daughter. Jacob had suspended an amulet around the infant's neck by which she was afterwards recognized. According to another version, Jacob did not send Dinah away into the wilderness, but she herself fled in fear of her life when she found herself pregnant. After giving birth to a girl, she exposed the infant and an eagle carried it off to Egypt, where Potiphera found it and adopted it as his own child. When Dinah, who had been restored to her family, later descended to Egypt with her father and her brothers, she recognized the swaddling clothes in which Asenath wrapped her child as those of her own exposed daughter.

In the versions in which Potiphera, priest of On, and Potiphar, chamberlain of Pharaoh's court, were combined into one person, the Hebrew ancestry of Asenath could not be maintained. Another reason had to be found for God's designating her as a suitable mate for Joseph. The reason arrived at was that she was the person who saved Joseph from death again and again. As a relative of Potiphar, as a princess raised in his home, she became aware of the efforts of Potiphar's wife to entice Joseph. When Potiphar, in the first flush of wrath after hearing his wife's accusation, wanted to have Joseph killed, Asenath related to him a conversation she had overheard which aroused doubt as to the Hebrew servant's guilt. She succeeded in delaying Joseph's trial, and she alleviated his lot during his imprisonment. Potiphar's wife continued to pursue Joseph with her advances, offering him release from prison. On being rejected by him, she tried to poison him, but Asenath again saved him and was, therefore, ultimately rewarded by becoming his wife.

The chaste Joseph was a favorite character in the emerging European drama of the Middle Ages, especially in the sixteenth century. In these plays, the temptation scenes received the main attention, and Asenath is only rarely mentioned.

The first long narrative about Joseph in Egypt, Grimmelshausen's *Keuscher Joseph*, was not published until 1667, and the first novel with Joseph's wife Asenath rather than Potiphar's wife Sefira as the principal womanly figure was the far longer narrative *Assenat* by the more elegant and more sentimental Philip von Zesen, which appeared three years later.

Hans Jakob Christoffel von Grimmelshausen (1610-1676) is today remembered primarily as the author of *Simplicissimus* (1668), the finest German novel of his century. His tales of the adventures during the Thirty Years' War of the amoral canteen-woman Courasche were dramatized by Berthold Brecht and were a box-office success in the post-World War II era, especially in Eastern Europe. Far less known is Grimmelshausen's novel of the chaste Joseph, which appeared under the pseudonym of Samuel Greifnson, and which experienced a second edition in 1671, a third edition in 1675, and the most recent edition in 1968. In 1670, there also appeared the supplementary narrative *Musai*, which dealt with the adventures of Joseph's faithful servant, an Elamite with a perfect knowledge of Hebrew, who acted as the viceroy's Hebrew translator during the various audiences with Jacob's sons before Joseph revealed himself as their long-lost brother. Asenath's questioning of this aged servant, who had been present at the sale of Joseph to the Ishmaelites, about his own past and about the customs and history of the various Asiatic peoples he encountered, as well as her revelations about the heathen gods she worshiped before her marriage to Joseph, were meant both to entertain and to edify readers.

Grimmelshausen's main sources for his Joseph narrative included the Bible, aggadic commentaries on Genesis, Josephus, the Koran, and *Sepher Hayashar*. Asenath is introduced as the daughter of Potiphar, high priest of Heliopolis, and a cousin of Selicha, wife of Potiphar, the third most influential person in the royal capital of Thebes, and the master of the slave Joseph. Asenath overhears Selicha luring Joseph and his dignified but resolute rejection of the temptress. When Selicha catches Asenath eavesdropping and cannot convince her that no woman can resist Joseph's beauty, she invites her to a party to which other gossipping women are also invited. In an elaboration and variation of a scene recorded in the twelfth sura of the Koran, Selicha places a sharp knife near each plate, and at the end of the meal, she has a lemon served to each of her guests, promising a beautiful ring to the one who is the first to complete peeling the fruit. While the women are busy with the peeling, she has Joseph enter, dressed in a silk summer robe that half-reveals and half-conceals his lovely figure, and holding in his hands a water-pitcher and a basin. The women cannot take their eyes off the fair slave. They cut their fingers with the peeling-knives, and Asenath most of all. She is wounded not only in her hand but also in her heart of hearts. Selicha thus proves that Joseph's beauty was indeed irresistible.

When Joseph is afterwards imprisoned, Asenath is the only one convinced of his innocence. She saves him from death, watches over him during his imprisonment until the death of the frustrated Selicha, and then marries him after his liberation and elevation. And the chaste Joseph satisfies himself with her as his only wife, although other great men of his time have an entire assortment of wives and concubines.

Philip von Zesen did not scruple to take over from Grimmelshausen many innovative interpretations and additions to the Joseph theme. To prove the greater accuracy of his own version, however, he gave a detailed account of his own sources and added 186 pages of explanatory notes. His sources ranged far wider than those of Grimmelshausen. He elaborated on *The Testament of the Twelve Patriarchs* and reproduced the greater part of the medieval adaptation of the pseudepigraphic romance of *Joseph and Asenath*. As an aristocrat, Zesen was writing for a more elegant audience than the commoner Grimmelshausen. He characterized his novel as a tale of love, heroism, and statesmanship. He aimed to educate and enlighten his readers and hence included historical, mythological, political, and religious material.

While Grimmelshausen stressed the unsuccessful efforts of the demonic Selicha to drag Joseph down into the swamp of sensuality, Zesen stressed the elevation of Asenath to the spiritual level of her noble Hebraic husband. Zesen stated, in his introduction, that he did not want to write merely another worldly love romance. Of such romances, there were more than enough, including the many translated from Greek, Spanish, Italian, French, and English. His book was rather designed as a moral tale based on Holy Writ, the story of an Egyptian idolatress who became a Hebrew matriarch, the biography of a maiden of noble birth, priestly upbringing, and chaste character. He lavished upon Asenath all the ideal attributes that harked back to the Age of Chivalry. At Asenath's birth, kings and priests bless her. After the infant is brought to the sanctuary of Heliopolis, the archbishop of the sun-god suggests that she be kept apart from the ordinary ways of the world: raised by her nurse and attendants in an isolated castle, and given only girl playmates of her own age but no male companions.

The years pass. Joseph is brought as a slave to Egypt, is sold to Potiphar, and is tempted by Potiphar's wife Sefira, whom he resists. He is imprisoned and then restored to grace after the death of Sefira and the correct interpretation of Pharaoh's dreams. Meanwhile, the archbishop of Heliopolis passes away, and Potiphar is chosen to replace him, thus bringing him from Memphis, the royal capital, to the Heliopolis shrine adjoining Asenath's tower. When the Viceroy Joseph comes on a mission to Heliopolis, Archbishop Potiphar receives him as befits Pharaoh's favorite, and the story continues, as in the medieval romance of *Joseph and Asenath*, until the death of Pharaoh and the assumption of the regency by Joseph. The concluding Book VII spins the story further. It recounts Asenath's charitable role during the years of famine, her great love for the oppressed and the needy, her nursing the sick, her interceding with her husband in behalf of the poor. Her fame spreads throughout all Egypt. Everyone praises her wisdom, and after her death, she is worshiped as Isse or Isis, the goddess of wisdom.

Joseph lives on until the news reaches him in his one hundred and tenth year about the misfortunes that have overtaken his relative, the mighty, prosperous, and upright Job of Uz. This affects him to such an extent that he falls ill and fails to recover. After his death, the Egyptians add him to their pantheon. Reversing the letters of his name, they worship him as the deity Apis. The fame of Joseph and Asenath survived long after the destruction of the Egyptian and the Hebrew states. They are still renowned, and they will be remembered until everything meets its ultimate end.

The tales of Joseph, appealing to the romantic imagination, were less in vogue and of a poorer quality in the rationalistic eighteenth century than in the sixteenth and seventeenth centuries. Even the dramas of Klopstock's talented Swiss disciple Johann Jakob Bodmer in 1754 and of the English religious lyricist and playwright Hannah More in 1782 are mediocre. The Joseph tales evoked a greater interest in the nineteenth century. Throughout Eastern Europe Joseph plays were performed by Yiddish-speaking amateur actors and were exceeded in popularity only by the Purim plays centering about Queen Esther, the biblical character who was elevated to greater heights even than Joseph. Most nineteenth-century Yiddish versions were based on Eliezer Favir's translation in 1801 of the Hebrew drama by the Maggid Hayim Abraham ben Arye Leib Hacohen of Mohilev. The Hebrew original, first published in 1797 and avidly read by the pioneers of Haskalah, experienced eight editions, but the Yiddish version, which retained the Hebrew title *Gdolas Yosef*, and which could be read by the less learned masses, especially women, experienced forty editions and adaptations. All forty are listed by the Yiddish historian Jacob Shatzky in Yivo's *Archiv far der geshikhte fun yidishen teater un drama* (I, 151-158), 1930.

Gdolas Yosef is also the principal source for *Mekhiras Yosef* by the folk poet Eliakum Zunser, published in 1874 and performed before large audiences throughout the Russian Pale by guilds of artisans in the manner of medieval morality plays, just before Abraham Goldfaden ushered in the Yiddish professional theater. In Zunser's version, Asenath is raised as the immaculate daughter of Potiphar and Suleika, and only on the deathbed of the sinful temptress of Joseph does the pure maiden learn of her own true origin. That she is in reality the daughter of Dinah is confirmed by the amulet which Jacob bestowed upon Dinah when he was forced to expose her.

The most important twentieth-century narrative about Joseph, a true fictional classic, the four-volume *Joseph und seine Brüder* (1933-42) by Thomas Mann, is disappointing in its recording of the Asenath episode. Mann devotes an entire volume to the temptress, the wife of Potiphar. He goes into great detail in tracing her many wily efforts extending over three years to break down the resistance of the chaste Joseph. He is most meticulous in portraying the gradual deterioration of her character under the influence of her overwhelming passion. To Asenath, however, Mann devotes only a few pages, and these describe her physical appearance as a typical Egyptian beauty and dismiss with hardly a comment her placid, mirrorlike personality untouched by searing passion, fierce hatred, or other powerful emotions.

Mann puts no credence in the legend of Asenath as the daughter of Dinah. The requirement that the tribes of Manasseh and Ephraim had to be of pure Hebrew stock in order to satisfy the vanity of the biblical people, the doctrine that the marriage of Jacob's son to the daughter of an Egyptian priest constituted racial defilement, reminded Mann of the current Nazi myths that he detested. Besides, even if such a legend had a basis in truth, then Asenath would still be only half-Hebraic, the offspring of a Baal-worshiping father and of Jacob's daughter, even as Mann's own children stemmed from a father who was the son of a Lübeck patrician and a mother who was the daughter of a Jewish professor. Such unions of so-called Aryans or Egyptians and Hebrews were not, in Mann's opinion, misalliances.

Mann, therefore, prefers to accept the biblical statement that Joseph's wife was of Egyptian parentage, the true daughter of the priest of On, whose name, Potiphar, resembled accidentally that of Joseph's early master.

Mann's Asenath is a gentle, kind, obedient child, submissive to the will of her parents and of Pharaoh. Growing up in the vicinity of her father's temple and surrounded by priestly and aristocratic maidens as her playmates, she retains her virginal, immaculate traits until, in her seventeenth year, the messenger of Pharaoh comes to her father and demands that she be handed over to Joseph. The Egyptian marriage customs are recorded by Mann as a sumptous festival, but he loses interest in Asenath after her wedding. She will undoubtedly remain a faithful, pliant, self-effacing wife, accepting her lot as God-ordained and causing no problems for her husband or the seventy members of her father-in-law's family when they descend to Egypt.

Down the centuries the temptation by Potiphar's wife has been depicted as the central test of Joseph's character and indeed as the central experience of his life, leading to his downfall and imprisonment but also to his elevation to power and to his glorious role as the savior of his Hebraic clan. Potiphar's wife, in her ever changing wiles and ever more adroit seductive efforts, has been the favorite heroine and villainess in the many narratives and dramas on the Joseph theme. Immaculate Asenath, on the other hand, pales beside her. Apparently, her goodness of character, her nobility of soul, her impeccable moral behavior, her unquestioning submission to the authority of father, husband, and king failed to inspire the biblical chronicler and most later writers. The romantic fairy princess may be the most desirable mate for which a mere mortal longs, but she does not possess any of the human frailties upon which the literary imagination longs to dwell.

7

Schiller's Moses

For more than a century Friedrich Schiller was widely read and enthusiastically acclaimed by Jewish youth under the spell of the Enlightenment. He was, in their eyes, the supreme poet and dramatist, preaching individual freedom and national emancipation. His hymn to joy, which Beethoven incorporated into the Ninth Symphony, stirred Jewish hearts with its call for universal brotherhood embracing all children of the one God. His revolutionary dramas, from the earliest *Die Räuber* (1781) to his more mature *Wilhelm Tell* (1804), inflamed denizens of the Pale to dream of Jewish national regeneration. His influence permeated the neo-Hebrew literature of the *Maskilim* and the Yiddish literature that appealed to the less learned masses. Yet few, if indeed any, of his Jewish readers and admirers were aware of his personal antipathy toward Jews or familiar with his prose essays dealing with the role of the Jews in world history.

When Schiller was born in 1759, the atmosphere in his native Duchy of Württemberg was still poisoned with hatred of Jews. Two decades had passed since the Württemberg financier Jud Süss had been hanged and his body publicly exhibited in an iron cage in order to appease the anger of the masses, who blamed their ills on this court Jew rather than on their duke. But the memory of the purported misdeeds of the hated Jew lingered on as the oppression of commoners continued unrelieved. Schiller is said to have modeled the Kosinsky episode in *Die Räuber* upon a particularly nefarious deed attributed to Jud Süss and to have conceived the robbers Spiegelberg and Schufterle as villainous Jews. The latter claim, however, is based on insufficient evidence.

It is unlikely that Schiller had any association with Jews during his formative years in his native town of Marbach or in the military academy at which he studied. The first recorded contacts were, at the end of his twenties, with a Jewish moneylender in Leipzig, and, in his thirties, with a Jewish publisher. These were purely business encounters and not happy ones. During his maturer Weimar years, he did meet a few Jews but never developed a significant relationship with them. Hence, his indifference toward the contemporary Jewish scene was undisturbed, and his childhood prejudices remained unchallenged.

Schiller was not only a poet and dramatist; he was also a philosopher and historian. As philosopher, his most lasting contribution was to aesthetic theory; as historian, his most notable contributions were his studies on the Thirty Years' War and on the revolt of the Dutch against the Spanish Crown. But Schiller also made use of biblical material for historical studies. In his lectures, published in 1790, under the long title *Etwas über die erste Menschengesellschaft nach dem Leitfaden der Mosaischen Urkunde*, he let his fertile imagination fill in gaps in the biblical narrative and his dramatic talent vivify myths about biblical characters. His portrait of Moses anticipated the insights and aberrations of Sigmund Freud's work *Moses and Monotheism* (1937-39), and may, indeed, have influenced the father of psychoanalysis. This study, contained in *Die Sendung Moses* (1790), illumines Schiller's attitude toward historical Judaism, for it was the historical role of the ancient people from whom Christianity sprang that interested him far more than did Jewish contemporaries with whom he had little to do and even less sympathy.

Die Sendung Moses, originally delivered as a lecture at the University of Jena, emphasized the founding of the Jewish religious and national entity by Moses as one of the supreme achievements of mankind, one which had a lasting influence throughout the following generations. Schiller held that neither

Christianity nor Islam would have come into existence if not for the innovations of Moses, primarily his popularization of monotheism. While the belief in one God had penetrated into the minds of individual wise men among the heathens, it had not seeped down to the masses, who continued everywhere to worship a multiplicity of gods. It was Moses who, by the power of his charismatic personality, persuaded an entire people, the Hebrews, to be the first nation to accept monotheism. In Schiller's opinion, the Hebrews were not especially worthy to play such a role in world history. He regarded them as a depraved national group, both in ancient times and in his own day. Yet, so strange are the ways of God: this impure vessel contained precious ingredients of truth, which it dispensed to others before it was deservedly scattered and dispersed. Schiller believed that he was being even-handed in his historical judgment when he stated that, though it would be an exaggeration to ascribe to the Hebrew people a significance which it did not deserve, it would be equally wrong to deny it its one meritorious achievement, the acceptance of the religious doctrines preached by Moses.

Schiller accepted the biblical account that the nomadic family of Hebrews, numbering seventy souls, had come to Egypt upon the invitation of a Pharaoh and had settled in Goshen, and that, in the course of four centuries, these nomads experienced a population explosion which aroused the apprehension of a later Pharaoh, who felt that these strangers in the heart of the country could constitute a danger to the realm. Schiller saw political wisdom in this ruler's attempt to make of these unreliable nomads a productive, sedentary group, and to reduce their numbers by ever harsher measures of compulsory toil. The Hebrews, who had increased to about two million, were pent up in such crowded conditions in Goshen that the inevitable result was uncleanliness and recurrent epidemics of contagious diseases which made them abhorrent to their Egyptian neighbors. Filthiness and scabbiness, according to Schiller, have ever thereafter characterized Jewish settlements. Leprosy, which raged among the ancient Hebrews in Egypt, was handed down by them to their progeny, generation after generation, slowly poisoning the Jewish race. Schiller named as his authoritative sources Greek and Roman writers who based themselves, to a great extent, on the no longer extant anti-Jewish diatribes of the Egyptian historian Manetho, of the third century B.C.E.

When harsh servitude and leprosy, the Jewish disease, failed to decimate the Hebrew population, a second and severer measure, which Schiller disapproves of as inhumane, was introduced by Pharaoh. All midwives were ordered to kill the male children born to Hebrews. To make sure that they did so, hired murderers roamed through the dwellings of Goshen and killed any baby boys spared by the midwives. It was hoped that, within a few generations, the abhorred Hebrew group would be exterminated. This would, indeed, have happened, if not for Moses, the savior.

In interpreting the role of Moses, Schiller faced the same problem as did the biblical chronicler—the savior's origin. If Moses was a child of the debased and enslaved Hebrews, where and how did he acquire his knowledge of Egyptian courtly ways so that he could negotiate with Pharaoh, or of religious mysteries so that he could arrive at his monotheistic creed? If, on the other hand, he was an Egyptian, why should he be interested in the loathed and disease-ridden Hebrews, whom the humanitarian Schiller characterizes as the most savage, most malevolent, and most depraved people on the face of the earth, an unheroic people of almost animallike stupidity?

The providential force that guides the universe found the answer: it took a Hebrew infant, removed it from its savage people, and gave it an opportunity to partake of Egyptian wisdom. In this way, a Hebrew, educated as an Egyptian, became the instrument by which his nation was delivered from slavery. Schiller followed the biblical description of the exposure of Moses among the bulrushes of the Nile, his discovery by Pharaoh's daughter, and his being handed over to a Hebrew wetnurse. From her, his true Hebrew mother, he learned the language and ways of the enslaved group and was imbued with sympathy for them. When the boy was returned to the princess, she adopted him as her own child, gave him the Egyptian name of Moses, and provided him with a princely upbringing. At priestly academies, he was introduced to the most advanced learning and to the mysteries of the religious establishment. This wisdom later found expression in his deeds and doctrines.

It was among the Egyptian priests that the concept of monotheism first arose. The original, fortunate discoverer of this sublime idea did not dare to give it wide currency because it would have undermined the theocratic political structure that was based on polytheism. But he did seek out among the members of his circle talented, trusted disciples to whom he could safely transmit his precious new insight about the one God. This insight, bequeathed for many generations from one thinker to another, finally became the mysterious property of a small coterie of priests who were able to grasp its significance and to develop it further. Moses belonged to that select group from whom no priestly secrets were withheld. The wisdom of the Torah is, therefore, Egyptian wisdom.

A century before the hieroglyphic inscriptions on Ikhnaton's religious reformation were deciphered, and a century and a half before Sigmund Freud's theory of an Egyptian Moses, Schiller credited the votaries of the mysteries of Memphis and Heliopolis with the religious innovations embodied in the Torah, such as monotheism, specific priestly rituals, circumcision, belief in immortality, the ark of God, and even the name of the one supreme deity. These doctrines and practices supposedly impressed Moses during his formative years under priestly tutelage, but, like his teachers, he had to be very circumspect in espousing them. When he was forced to flee Egypt because of his impulsive killing of an Egyptian taskmaster who was mistreating a Hebrew laborer, he found the leisure in his desert loneliness to reflect on his people's oppressed lot and on the religious mysteries to which he had been introduced. During the following years, when he was degraded to a drear existence as a herdsman in Midian, he often recalled that he had been a prince in Egypt and an initiate into profound mysteries.

Amidst the silence and solitude of his exile in the wilderness, there arose in him the desire to return to Egypt and to liberate his suffering kinsmen from their slavish existence. But first he had to

Schiller's Moses

awaken in them hope, courage, self-confidence, and enthusiasm. This could be accomplished only by imbuing them with belief in a supernatural, heavenly power that was especially interested in them. If he could only convince them that he, Moses, shepherd and prince, was the instrument and emissary of this divine power, then he could lead them out of bondage and on to freedom. Obviously, the rabble of Hebrew slaves, the scum of Egypt, was incapable of comprehending the universal, abstract deity that he himself had come to accept when he had been initiated into the mysteries that were revealed to but a few priestly sages. But even if he could get the Hebrews to grasp his grandiose vision, they would not believe that an all-encompassing deity would be interested in them more than in any other people. However, if he could identify his philosophical, invisible God with the national God of their ancestors, and if he could convince them that the God of Abraham, Isaac, and Jacob had at long last attained to supremacy and had succeeded in annihilating all other gods, thus becoming the sole and omnipotent Ruler of the Universe, then they would become followers of this Lord of Hosts who could perform great deeds for them and could lead them on to victory against their oppressors. And, so, Moses undertook his educational mission to eradicate the superstitions that had encrusted the national God of the Hebrew slaves and to elevate this God to supreme eminence in their eyes.

To succeed in the great task which he had set for himself, Moses had to perform miracles. Schiller, the deist of the Century of Enlightenment, makes the comment: "There is no doubt that he really performed these miracles, but I leave it to each person to figure out how he performed them and how they are to be understood." At any rate, Schiller feels that the miracles achieved their purpose. Moses did succeed in overcoming all difficulties and in leading his kinsmen out of Egypt. He did implant in them self-reliance, courage, hope, and enthusiasm. Having deprived them of a country, however, he could not leave them in the desert. He had to gain for them a new homeland. This meant that he had to prepare them for the armed conquest of a territory beyond the wilderness of Sinai, a conquest that could be undertaken only by a united people that would not disintegrate into separate tribes but that would be governed by a common will, best embodied in a constitution and a code of laws that would be unanimously accepted. Such unanimous approval was possible only if all the ordinances were presented as commandments emanating from God. Therefore, Moses, the brilliant statesman, grounded them in divine sanction. He took the God of the Egyptian mysteries and unveiled his secret attributes before the Hebrews. Moses was, thus, the first person to disclose to an entire people the religious truths, including the concept of a single Supreme Being, which until then had been the property of a few wise men. He could not, of course, give the Hebrews the intelligence to grasp the new religion with their reason, since their rational faculties had not yet been sufficiently developed, but he did get them to accept this religion blindly because of their faith in his leadership and to make it the basis for the Hebraic theocratic state. And so it came about that the unworthy Hebrews became the impure vessel for the pure truth of monotheism, and the Hebrew Torah, the religious scroll that embodied the best of Egyptian religious wisdom.

In his 1790 essay on Moses, Schiller did not go as far as did Sigmund Freud a century and a half later, when he stripped this prophet and lawgiver entirely of Jewish ancestry by having him born of Egyptian parents and not merely having him reared by an Egyptian princess. Schiller did, however, anticipate Freud by tracing to Egyptian mysteries the monotheism and some of the religious commandments of the Torah bequeathed by Moses to the Jews and, through them, to Christianity and Islam.

8

The Death of Moses

Moses has been reincarnated in every generation, as poets and thinkers have come to grips with his legendary personality. Many are the stories surrounding his birth, his exposure as an infant among the bulrushes of the Nile, his discovery by Pharaoh's daughter, his nurture at the Egyptian court among the princes of the realm, and his ineradicable sympathy with his enslaved Hebrew kinsmen, for whose sake he jeopardized his privileged position, risked his life, fled into the wilderness, and endured privations as a herdsman among the bedouins of Midian. Equally fascinating are the narratives of his rededication to his people when he heard the voice of the Lord out of the burning bush, his repeated confrontations with the ruler of Egypt, his leadership of the slaves who escaped from Goshen to Sinai and throughout their forty years of wandering in the desert. But the legends centering about his final days have also stirred popular imagination during the many succeeding ages and have found repercussions in talmudic and aggadic lore, in Islamic embellishments, in the traditions of the Falashas, in medieval and neo-Hebraic adaptations, and in the recent literature of Europe and America by Jewish and Christian writers. It is this last aspect, some of the recent imaginative reconstructions of the death of Moses in poetry, drama, and fiction, that is dealt with in the following pages.

Two themes dominate the various versions of the prophet's end. They are, in the first place, his reluctance to die after he led his people almost to the successful completion of their common striving throughout decades of desert hardships, and, in the second place, his lonely ascent in his last hour to the top of Mount Nebo, from which he could see the present and foresee the future of the Promised Land upon which his feet were not destined to tread.

The reluctance of Moses to die is motivated by concern both for his immediate family and for the larger family of the Hebrews whom he shepherded so long. His concern for his wife, Zipporah, and his children, whom he will leave behind with nobody to care for them, gave rise to the legend of "Moses and the Worm." According to this aggadic legend, which received wide currency in the poetic version of the eighteenth-century German philosopher Johann Gottfried Herder, God saw the aged prophet weeping as he took leave of his children. The Lord asked him whether he feared the pangs of death or was so enamored of this world that he hated to leave it. The answer of Moses was that he was worried about his orphaned children. Then the Lord told him to lift up his staff and cleave the sea. As he did so and the waters rolled away, a rock became visible. Upon God's command, Moses smote the rock. It was rent asunder and revealed a little worm which lifted up its voice and praised God for not forgetting it. Then the Lord said to Moses: "If I remember the worm beneath the sea, shall I forget thy children, who love and honor Me?"

This tale formed the main theme of the poem "The Death of Moses" by the nineteenth-century American poet Richard Henry Stoddard. By thus assuring Moses that he need not worry about leaving his sorrowing wife and his children unprovided for, God overcame his reluctance to die. Only then did Moses set out to climb the mountain on which he was to expire, kissed by God.

As for the hesitation of Moses to leave the Israelites leaderless, he is charged with the investiture of Joshua as his worthy successor. When Moses becomes aware that the wisdom of Joshua in interpreting the Torah is beginning to exceed his own, he willingly prepares his soul for death, feeling that he would rather depart from life than experience ever-fading understanding. The French writer Edmond Fleg, who based his *Life of Moses* (1925) on talmudic legends, devoted the last two chapters of his imaginative biography to the efforts of Moses in the twilight of his years to avert his doom by prayer and by having all Israel intercede for him. Moses, however, stopped all intercessions and accepted his doom when he realized that the price of further living would be mental deterioration. He preferred to leave this earth while his eyes were not yet dimmed nor his natural force abated.

According to some versions, Moses, after ascending Mount Nebo on the seventh day of Adar, again had a moment of hesitation, shrinking back from imminent death. Then God showed him Israel's future, its victories and defeats, until the coming of the Messianic Age, and revealed to him the divine decree that all persons and all peoples would be subject to mortality but that Israel alone would continue on down the ages until the appearance of the Messiah. If Moses wished this decree to be changed, then "Thou shalt not die, but Israel shall perish and the Messiah shall not be born." The reply of Moses was: "Let Israel live, and let me perish."

Ahad Haam, in his profound essay on Moses (1904), wrestles with the question as to why the prophet had to die before he completed his life's work. This original thinker arrived at the conclusion that reality required compromises with the ideal. A prophet like Moses can give noble ideals to a people, but to carry them out, practical men like Joshua are needed, leaders with greater resiliency and more readiness to accept the actual human situation, which is less than perfect. Moses, the visionary, dies with gladness in his face, not having compromised, not having acepted half-measures, embracing the ideal of the future, the utopian dream to which he consecrated his life, and for which he toiled and suffered till his last breath.

Two years after Ahad Haam, the German playwright Carl Hauptmann ends his five-act drama *Moses* (1906) with the investiture of Joshua as leader of the tribal confederation that is to cross the Jordan into the Promised Land, and with a vision of an idealized future for the Israelites. Modeling the drama's conclusion upon the last act of Goethe's *Faust*, Hauptmann lets the aged Moses, like the century-old Faust, look out upon the land as far as his imagination can reach. He foresees vineyards and golden wheatfields that will sprout in the valleys below and cities that will arise and prosper in peace. He embraces the Promised Land with his eyes. He presses it to his bosom. He experiences his supreme hour of bliss and collapses as he hears the distant singing of his people on the forward march to its ancestral home.

The ascent of Moses to Mount Nebo is the subject of significant nineteenth-century German, English, and French poems. Ferdinand Freiligrath's German lyric "Nebo" (1830) depicts the nomadic offspring of Jacob encamped along the Jordan after their decades of desert wandering, and Moses climbing up the mountain to catch sight of the land where milk and honey flow but which he may not enter. When he sees the fertile land from Dan to Beersheba, he is content and glories in dying upon the heights, with forests, fields, and streams below, and heaven's golden portals above.

In contrast to the German poet, his English contemporary James Montgomery, in the poem "The Death of Moses," has the prophet look out from Mount Nebo upon the lovely land beyond the Jordan and find it bloodstained and abounding in pagan abominations. But his Moses too is heartened by a glamorous vision of the land's future, the overthrow of the idols and the spread of the Law from Zion in every direction.

Only Alfred de Vigny, the French contemporary of Montgomery and Freiligrath, ends his poem "Moses" (1826) on a gloomy note, with the tragic, weary leader of the Israelites begging God for the unending sleep of death. The prophet, though great and powerful, has remained ever alone. What did it profit him that his feet trod on the necks of nations and that he held generations in his hands? "Alas, my Lord! I am great—I am alone. Give me—ah, give me leave to sleep the sleep of earth."

The Irish poet Thomas Moore intoned a singable dirge in four stanzas on the death of Moses, calling upon the children of Israel to weep for the Man of God.

More elaborate is George Eliot's poetic narrative *The Death of Moses*, which she based on aggadic Jewish sources. It depicts his final hours. When God asks Gabriel to bring the soul of Moses to Him, the archangel does not dare to carry out so tragic a mission. Then God asks Michael, but this archangel also pleads to be spared the performance of such a task. Then God summons Zamael, the terrible angel of fierce death, but the radiance of Moses forces him to retreat. Then God Himself comes down to Moses, draws forth his soul with a kiss, and carries it up to heaven. To orphaned Israel, sunk in mourning, come the comforting words: "He has no tomb. He dwells not with you dead, but lives as Law."

The German poet Rainer Maria Rilke, like George Eliot, also bases his lyric *Der Tod Moses* on the unwillingness of the angels to carry out the death decreed for Moses. Only the dark, fallen angel takes up weapons, steps before Moses, and prepares to fulfill this command. But he staggers back, unable to proceed, as Moses calmly continues to write chapters of Holy Writ, words of blessing, and God's name. Then the Lord, followed by half of heaven, comes down to Mount Nebo, beds Moses within the mountain, reminds the prophet's soul of their friendship, calls upon this precious soul to arise from the body, takes it with a kiss into Himself, and, with the hands that created the universe, closes the mountain so that it will be indistinguishable from other terrestrial mountains.

Among other memorable twentieth-century lyrics on the death of Moses are those of Uriel Birnbaum, the Viennese mystic, painter, and poet; Karl Wolfskehl, the German-Jewish exile in New Zealand; Dietrich Bonhoeffer, the brilliant theologian who completed his poem shortly before he was executed upon Hitler's command; and Karl Shapiro, the American poet, who accepted Freud's psychoanalytic insight into Moses.

Uriel Birnbaum, the younger son of the Zionist ideologist Nathan Birnbaum, was fascinated by the charismatic personality of Moses. He completed, in 1924, fifty colored lithographs of the Man of God. He published a monograph on the life of Moses in 1928 and continued with four long poems on *Die Berufung Moses*.

These poems dealt with the call of Moses to the leadership of his people and were followed by nine sonnets on his later career. Four of these sonnets were devoted to his final moments after he reached the Jordan, his homecoming to God after shedding his human limbs, and the guarding of his grave by angels with flaming swords that dazzle passing caravans, so that no wanderer ever discovers his exact burial spot.

Karl Wolfskehl's poem "Vom Nebo" consists only of seventeen lines depicting the end of Moses on Mount Nebo after he has bequeathed the Law to his successor. Looking at the distant land upon which the strange destiny of his people will be further unrolled, he wants to be spared knowledge of the future. Sated with life, he is ripe for his final rest, bedded in the mountain. In these verses, the Jewish poet, who claimed descent from the patrician Kalonymus family of Mainz, and who loved Germany with all his fervor, mirrored his own tiredness after he was uprooted from the Central European province in which his ancestors had been rooted for more than a thousand years and was forced to flee to Italy, Switzerland, and ultimately to distant New Zealand.

The death of Moses also preoccupied the thoughts of Dietrich Bonhoeffer, another victim of the Nazi regime, and was portrayed by him in a profoundly moving poem shortly before his own death. Throughout the Hitler years until his imprisonment on April 5, 1943, this outstanding Protestant theologian was involved in underground activities to topple the totalitarian regime. When proceedings against him were delayed for more than a year, and the tide of war had turned against Germany, he hoped to survive the war and to enter upon the better moral order that he had dreamed of and fought for and that would follow Germany's defeat. However, when the attempt on the life of Hitler failed in July 1944, and the wide-ranging plot was discovered in which his friends were involved, he realized that he, as well as his co-conspirators, was doomed. Like Moses, he would not live to enter upon the imminent new order that would tolerate liberty of conscience. Also like Moses, he was comforted in his last days by the knowledge that his struggle had not been in vain, and that he had kept his vision of the Promised Land alive before his people during their years of straying in the desert.

In the fall of 1944, Bonhoeffer completed in his prison his most poignant poem, "Der Tod des Mose," one of the last poems to be smuggled out of his Tegel cell before silence gathered about him. The motto of the poem was taken from Deuteronomy 34:1: "And the Lord showed him all the land." As Moses looks out from the summit of Mount Nebo upon the land so near and yet so unattainable to him, he praises the Lord, who delivered the Israelites from slavery, who accompanied them in their desert wandering, and who patiently put up with their murmuring and waywardness. God's kindness, however, has had less influence upon them than God's wrath. As a result, the desert sand now covers the bodies of those who experienced the divine miracles and nevertheless revolted against God. Bonhoeffer, remembering his own impatience with the Nazi regime and his own rash conspiratorial efforts to hasten its downfall, portrayed Moses as the prophet who also had become impatient with the long delay in the fulfillment of God's promise to Israel. The prophet, who was chosen to preach the sacred message to the stiff-necked people, is being punished for his impatience and momentary doubts by dying before the Israelites' entry into the land beyond the Jordan. Nevertheless, he who bore the burden of being an intermediary between God and God's people is granted the privilege of dying on the mountain peak and not in the lower depths among the human dwarfs. In writing these verses, Bonhoeffer was reconciling himself to his fate of martyrdom for preaching God's word rather than the Nazi-imposed creed. Even as the lonely Moses from Mount Nebo, so too the German poet from his solitary Berlin cell foresaw salvation nighing for his people, God's grace transforming the desert-born generation into a rejuvenated community. Speaking through the voice of Moses, he predicted the coming of days when neither arrogance nor envy would prevail, when each person would call his neighbor brother, when justice and mercy would reign, and when God's word would point the way to freedom and virtuous living. No matter how guilty the people still were, they would recover as soon as they would follow God's commandments. The bitterness of death was turning to sweetness for Bonhoeffer, as for Moses, now that he had peered through the veil and had seen his people on the road to freedom. "O God, I loved this people. It is enough for me that I bore its burden and disgrace and foresaw its salvation. Hold me! My staff is falling. God, prepare my grave for me."

On April 9, 1945, as the American and Russian armies began to close in on Berlin, and three weeks before Hitler's suicide, Bonhoeffer descended the last steps to the scaffold and calmly met his end.

Echoes of the years of Nazi oppression and longing for a Messianic Age also resounded throughout all three parts of Sholem Asch's postwar novel *Moses*, published in 1951, a novel in which the author sought rehabilitation with his Jewish readers whom he had unintentionally wounded with his Christological novels during the Hitler period. In the first part, the ever severer restrictions against the German Jews are symbolically reflected in the ever harsher enslavement of the Hebrews by a Pharaoh who knew not Joseph and who had forgotten the contributions made to Egypt by Joseph's kinsmen. In the second part, Nazi cruelty and injustice toward Jews is portrayed in the mask of Amalek, who falls upon the Israelites in the desert without any provocation, merely lured by the lust for plunder. The novelist comes to the gloomy conclusion that in every generation a new Amalek would arise to renew the war against Jehovah and to torment in a thousand ways the people who adhered to Jehovah's commandments. In the Sinai episode, Asch lets Moses catch sight of the vast panorama of the future, including the Nazi era when the suffering of the Jews would far eclipse their travail in Egyptian bondage. "He saw blazing ovens and forever the cry of *Shema Yisrael* going up from them. And with this cry on their lips, they surrendered their bodies to the flames."

In the third part of the novel, Asch deals with the final days of Moses. Though ripe for death like a fruit about to fall from the tree in its season, he yet rebels against death like a mother whom death has called while her child is at her breast, still unweaned.

Israel is the unweaned, suckling child of Moses, and he does not want to leave it. But then God again unfolds for him, as at Sinai, Israel's future, its long march through history, its exaltations and degradations, its aspirations toward the heights, its hideous lapses into the abyss, its exile and dispersion, and its ultimate ingathering on its ancestral soil in the fullness of time, when each of the Bnai Israel will sit peacefully under his vine and under his fig tree. As Moses climbs to the peak of Mount Nebo and then ascends ever higher and higher, he no longer knows where his feet tread or whether he has passed the boundary between life and death. The heavenly gates are opened to his vision. Heavenly Jerusalem is revealed to him, and the Holy Temple which will be built on earth by the Bnai Israel and in which King Messiah, the son of David, will dwell. When Moses wants to know when that will be, the answer comes that it will not be realized until the children of Israel have been scattered and sown among all the peoples of the earth, bringing the Torah to all the four corners of the earth. "For the End cannot come, and the Kingdom of Heaven cannot begin until the Law of Mount Sinai shall have been accepted by all the peoples of the earth." Moses continues to climb until he has passed beyond the clouds to the summit of the mountain, which reaches into heaven and becomes one with heaven. He marches on, a solitary figure on the celestial landscape, until he enters heavenly Jerusalem. "A smile rested on Moses' face, for on his lips hovered the kiss of Jehovah, the kiss wherewith God had taken the soul of Moses, our teacher, to rest with Him."

In contrast to all the versions that stress the ascension of Moses and his gentle end when kissed by God, the American poet Karl Shapiro assigns a violent end to the Jewish leader. He includes, in his *Poems of a Jew* (1958), a lyric of ten stanzas under the title "The Murder of Moses." The theory that Moses was murdered in the wilderness by the Hebrews he had liberated from Egyptian oppression was first broached by the German archaeologist and Bible scholar Ernst Sellin in 1922, but it was not until Sigmund Freud accepted this theory and made it one of the pillars upon which he based his essays on *Moses and Monotheism* (1937-39) that it was given wide circulation. Although Sellin's conjecture received little credence among theologians and biblical researchers, the authority of the father of psychoanalysis sufficed to leave an impact upon anthropologists and was accepted as a fact by Karl Shapiro.

According to Freud, Moses was an Egyptian, probably of noble birth, perhaps even the son of a princess. He was, therefore, raised at Pharaoh's court, and he imbibed Egyptian learning. Myth transformed him into a Jewish child that was found by Pharaoh's daughter in a casket of bulrushes at the brink of the Nile. The casket, in Freud's interpretation, was the mother's womb, and the myth thus symbolized the acceptance of the child by its Egyptian mother as her own. As additional evidence of the Egyptian origin of Moses, Freud pointed to this name's occurrence among Egyptian rulers. Furthermore, Freud held that the monotheism imposed upon the Hebrews by Moses was the monotheism of Ikhnaton, a Pharaoh who reigned from 1375 to 1360 B.C.E. This monotheism was uprooted by the succeeding Pharaohs. Moses, who became the political leader of the Hebrews enslaved in the Egyptian province of Goshen, remained an adherent of Ikhnaton's rigid monotheism even after its decline and forced his followers to accept the proscribed religion, with certain modifications based upon his Midianite experiences and his contact with the desert god of his father-in-law, Jethro. Freud assumed the Exodus to have taken place between 1358 and 1350 B.C.E., during the decade of unrest that followed the death of Ikhnaton and the restoration of polytheism in Egypt. Moses wished to make a holy people out of the Hebrews whom he led out of Goshen and who wandered with him for many years in the wilderness. They often rebelled against his severe religious yoke and finally killed him. Thereafter the tribes who had come out of Egypt combined with other related Semitic tribes who had never been in Egypt to form a single people. The united tribes invaded and settled Canaan, but after a period of political unity they again broke asunder into two parts, the Kingdom of Israel and the Kingdom of Judah. Moses, who was not alive at the crossing of the Jordan, did not participate in the conquest of the fertile land he envisaged for the Hebrews. However, the Levites, his tribal adherents, remained faithful to his teachings and, as the culturally superior group, were able to bring about the ultimate victory of the monotheistic Mosaic religion.

The Freudian hypothesis, rejected by almost all Jewish, Protestant, and Catholic scholars, was the source for Karl Shapiro's poem. The American lyricist presented the Exodus as an act of despair. Moses, the leader who imposed his will upon reluctant followers, was of a different character than Joseph, who had made himself a prince and who was beloved for his skill in management and his sense of propriety. Moses was feared when he came down from Sinai, broke the tablets on the rock, and overthrew the Golden Calf. Finally this lonely leader was murdered by the people who had gossiped about him, hated him, and rebelled against him. Only after his death did they realize his greatness. They then confessed:

> At the end of it all we gave you the gift of death.
> Invasion and generalship were spared you.
> The hand of our direction, resignedly you fell,
> And while officers prepared for the river-crossing,
> The One God blessed you and covered you with earth.
>
> Though you were mortal and once committed murder,
> You assumed the burden of the covenant,
> Spoke for the world and for our understanding.
> Converse with God made you a thinker,
> Taught us all early justice, made us a race.

Israel's lawgiver and supreme prophet still exerts his spell over creative minds. His birth, life, and death are still being illumined and elaborated upon in literary works by contemporary writers and will continue to do so as long as the Torah he brought to Israel casts its spell upon mankind. From the dawn of history and from the banks of the Nile he arose to start Israel on its historic odyssey, and after more than a hundred generations, his spirit still serves as the chief inspiration to his people scattered in lands of freedom and oppression and also now ingathered as a rejuvenated nation in the Promised Land he viewed from Mount Nebo before death enveloped him. The poet Heinrich Heine best summed up the supreme achievement of Moses in these words: "Unlike the Egyptians, he did not form his artistic works out of bricks and granite. He rather built human pyramids. He carved human obelisks. He took a poor tribe of herdsmen and made of it a people that was to defy the centuries, a great, eternal, holy people, God's people, that could serve as a model for all other peoples, indeed for entire mankind. He created Israel."

9

Rahab of Jericho

Rahab of Jericho is the sole heroine of the Book of Joshua. As the strongest fortress barring the incursion of the Hebrew nomads into Canaan, their Promised Land, Jericho had to be captured by the invaders from across the Jordan. Failure to do so would hurl them back into the desert among whose oases they had wandered for forty years since their escape from Egyptian enslavement. With the charismatic leadership of Moses no longer available to them since his disappearance at Mount Nebo, they would face the danger of disintegrating into contentious tribes and might vanish from the historical scene upon which they had just entered.

It was Rahab who facilitated the conquest of Jericho by harboring the two spies that Joshua, the successor of Moses as commander-in-chief of the Hebrews, sent ahead on a mission to discover the strength and weakness of the town's fortifications and to report on the morale of the town's inhabitants. Rahab saved the lives of the spies by concealing them while the search for them was on and by helping them to escape to the hills, where they could hide out for three days until they were able to return safely to camp. Once back in the Hebrew camp, they could join in planning the strategy for the decisive campaign against the Canaanite stronghold.

What sort of woman was Rahab, and what was her motivation

in betraying her own gods and in bringing down destruction upon her own people?

The Bible calls her a *zonah*. This word has generally been translated as "harlot." However, a minority of commentators has translated it as "innkeeper." Since Jewish tradition saw her as the ancestress of distinguished prophets, including Jeremiah and the seeress Hulda, she could serve to illustrate the moral that no person, not even a prostitute, was beyond redemption, if such a person repented and undertook to walk in righteous ways. On the other hand, if Rahab's calling was that of an innkeeper, then she might be rehabilitated as a more respectable woman, and no disgrace attached to her putting up two strangers for the night. Her generous deed in saving her imperiled Hebrew guests not only made her worthy of being spared when Jericho's entire population was put to the sword, but, according to some authorities, even endeared her to Joshua, the head of the Hebrew host, who married her, after she converted to his God and threw in her lot with his people.

According to Matthew (1:5), Rahab was the mother of Boaz, who married Ruth of Moab, another convert to Judaism. Rahab thus became the ancestress of King David and the royal Judean family, as well as of the Christian Messiah.

While Paul in his Epistle to the Hebrews (11:31) and James in his Epistle (2:25) accepted the version that viewed Rahab as a harlot, Josephus Flavius in his *Jewish Antiquities* (Loeb Classics ed., V, 5) saw her as the keeper of an inn to which the spies came toward the end of the day in order to have supper before undertaking the return trip to the Hebrew camp. Their immediate return was frustrated, however, when the king of Jericho learned that these strangers, who seemed to be anxious to escape detection, were at Rahab's inn near the town's wall. He ordered them to be arrested for questioning. If necessary, they would be tortured in order to ferret out from them the real reasons for their coming. Rahab was in the midst of drying flax upon the roof of the inn when she learned of the approach of the king's men. She quickly concealed the strangers and then told the royal messengers that unknown strangers had indeed supped at her inn but

Rahab of Jericho

that they had left before sundown and could be easily caught if pursued immediately. Without wasting time to search the premises, the king's men rushed out and sped along the roads leading toward the Jordan. When they found no trace of the strangers, they gave up the pursuit. After the tumult subsided, Rahab told the Hebrew spies that she had risked her life to conceal them and expected them to keep this in mind. She exacted a promise from them that, during the assault upon the town, they would spare her from harm and those of her kin who would take refuge with her at the inn. Only then did she help them escape by letting them down the wall by a rope in the darkness. Joshua kept the compact made by the spies. He presented Rahab with land as compensation for her brave deed and showed her every consideration.

Talmudists and Jewish commentators laid great stress on Rahab's loveliness. There was no lord or patrician who did not seek her company. She was listed as one of the four most beautiful women in the world, the others being Sarah, Abigail, and Esther. Nevertheless, she did not attract the attention of literary men, as did heroines of the succeeding period of the Judges—Deborah, Delilah, and Jephthah's daughter, or the heroines beloved by David—Michal, Abigail, Bathsheba, and Abishag, or those that Solomon favored most—Sulamith and the Queen of Sheba. It was not easy for writers to transform a lovely harlot into a penitent savior of a foreign people or to find adequate moral reasons for her betrayal of her own people. Only a few modern writers centered their attention upon her and overcame all the psychological obstacles to depict her as a good human being, pure at heart despite all temptations and pressures, wiser and more independent than other women of her age and environment. During the past century, attempts at idealizing her were made in the German drama of Rudolf von Gottschall, in the American novel of Frank G. Slaughter, in the Hebrew drama of Matityahu Shoham, and in the Yiddish historical romance of Shmuel Izban.

Rudolf von Gottschall (1823-1909) began as a revolutionary poet during the efflorescence of the German political lyric in the 1840s, but after the failure of the Revolution of 1848, he abandoned radical agitation and turned to the writing of historical novels, romantic epics, and poetic dramas. The Egyptologist Georg Ebers, who is today remembered far less for his archaeological studies of the Ebers Papyrus than for his authorship of a romance which became the basis for Giuseppi Verdi's opera *Aida*, published a biblical novel, *Joshua*, in 1890, in which the exploits of the young hero in Egypt and Sinai were stressed, but in which no mention of Rahab appeared. By contrast, Gottschall undertook, in his biblical verse drama *Rahab*, which was published eight years later, to center attention on this heroine who became entangled in the Hebraic war against Jericho, but he does not include Joshua among the characters in the dramatic plot.

Gottschall introduces Rahab as the high priestess of Astarte, the goddess of love, who is served both by temple harlots and by virginal priestesses. The dramatist models Rahab's character upon that of Goethe's classical heroine in the drama *Iphigenia in Tauris*. Just as the Greek priestess Iphigenia is dedicated to the service of Artemis, a service from which the ruler of Tauris seeks to release her by offering to share his throne with her, so too the Canaanite priestess Rahab can only be released from her priestly office by the king of Jericho and by no one else. In a moving scene, reminiscent of the wooing of Iphigenia by King Thoas, Rahab is wooed by Jericho's monarch, and like Iphigenia, she evades a positive response. She too thereby provokes the king's wrath. The roles of Orestes and Pylades, the two strangers in Goethe's drama, who are to be sacrificed at the altar of Artemis, are taken over by the two Hebrew spies, Joab and Ruben, who stumble upon the holy grotto of the goddess Astarte, a grotto which may be entered only by priestesses. Intrusion by others is punishable by death. Joab creeps along the grotto and catches sight of the beautiful priestesses as they perform the ceremony of the ablution and investment of Astarte and also glimpses her unveiled high priestess in a cove of the Jordan. Fascinated by this vision, his thoughts circle about Rahab rather than about escaping from the dangerous, forbidden grotto. While Ruben sets out in search of an escape route and is caught by the guards of the sanctuary, Rahab comes across the overtired Joab, who has fallen asleep and who appears in her eyes as the reincarnated Adonis, beloved of the goddess of love. She undertakes to save him. He, however, refuses to escape without his companion.

Rahab's plan to intercede with the king to pardon the captured Ruben is frustrated when she turns down the king's proffered hand. In the climactic third act, she is surprised with Joab in her chamber of the priestly palace by the suspicious monarch, who now realized that she has spurned his own love not because of her priestly oath to remain a virgin but because of her infatuation with this second Israelite spy. She is, therefore, degraded from her position as high priestess to that of a temple harlot. At the ensuing royal feast, which she is forced to attend along with other temple harlots, to strike the cymbals, and to dance before the carousers, she revolts against her humiliation and hurls curses upon the decadent city and its tyrannical king. From the harsh punishment awaiting her, she is saved by the storming Israelite army. However, her will to live is broken. Before dying, she comes to the realization that all gods, Canaanite or Israelite, bring death and destruction upon mortals. Only love can defy heaven's might and confer moments of happiness. Among all the characters, conquerors and conquered, she emerges as the purest and wisest.

A no less idealizing portrait of Rahab, pure at heart despite her body's degradation, is painted by Frank G. Slaughter in his novel *The Scarlet Cord*, published in 1956. Compared to her kind, sensitive, wise personality, Joshua emerges as a strong-fisted boor, of extraordinary bravery but little wisdom. The successful strategies for the campaigns against the Amorites and for the conquest of Canaan are devised by the physician Salman, who has traveled far and wide, and who, therefore, knows the habits and weaknesses of peoples. The novelist, who served as a surgeon with the American army during the Second World War, emphasizes battle scenes and their aftermath in carnage and in the healing of the wounded. Joshua is always in the thick of battle and needs a surgeon's skill when the fighting is over. Winning victories against King Sihon of Heshbon and King Og of Bashan and against the Canaanites after crossing the Jordan, he becomes ever more arrogant and self-centered. It is Joshua who seduces the priestess Rahab and who bears primary responsibility for her ensuing misery.

Rahab is first introduced as the guardian of the shrine of Yah or Yahu in the cave on the slope of Mount Nebo. She is not an Amorite but belongs to the offspring of the Habiru, who came with their leader Abram from Ur of the Chaldeans. Only the main body of the Habiru nomads left for Egypt in the wake of the Hyksos invasion and were enslaved by the Egyptians after the expulsion of the Hyksos. A minority remained in the lands of the Amorites and the Canaanites. As the only child of a scribe, Rahab is highly educated and skilled in healing. She wins the love of Joshua when he is wounded by a poisoned Amorite spear in the battle against Sihon and is nursed by her. On her way from her shrine in order to bring to her father the *mohar*, or betrothal money, that Joshua has given her, she falls into the hands of a passing caravan and is dragged off to the slave market of Memphis, where her extraordinary beauty is expected to fetch a high price for her as a harlot. She is bought by the prince of Jericho, who has come to Egypt to solicit Pharaoh's aid against the Hebrew invaders. She becomes the royal concubine when the prince ascends the throne on his return to his native land. However, when he is assassinated a few months later, she is degraded to the keeper of a brothel near the town wall. She saves the two Hebrew spies sent to Jericho and is herself saved from her horrible fate when the town falls to Joshua's army. Joshua, however, will have nothing to do with Rahab, the notorious harlot. While he goes on from victory to victory, she finally finds peace and happiness as the mate of the gentle, understanding physician.

Rahab is also the central figure in Shmuel Izban's Yiddish novel *Jericho* (1966). Though not as well known as the author's earlier historical novel *Jezebel* (1960), which attempted an imaginative reconstruction of Israel's culture during the reign of King Ahab, it too calls into life a decisive period of early Jewish history.

The author, who lived in mandated Palestine for fifteen years before settling in the United States, was familiar with the terrain of Jericho and the Jordan Valley. He was also able to draw upon the new discoveries of biblical archaeology in his narration of the daily life and the religious rites of the Canaanites. But his greatest asset was his historical imagination. Unfettered by the scholar's need to stick closely to verifiable facts, he could expand on the adventures of Caleb and Pinchas, the Israelite spies, who found in the wise and beautiful Rahab a protectress who helped them to accomplish their dangerous mission. Despite her ill-repute, she is idealized in this novel. As the daughter of a rich but later impoverished wine-merchant, she is filled with a thirst for vengeance upon the corrupt oppressors who ruined her family. This is her chief motivation for wanting to aid the invading Israelites. But her love for the upright and fearless Caleb also plays a role. Her inn beside the town wall is visited by the most prominent aristocrats and warriors, from whom her true feelings are hidden. Stronger than the sword is the web of charm in which she entangles Jericho's corrupt king and courtiers, until she brings about their downfall. And when the hour of destruction comes upon Jericho, her family alone is saved because of her wiles and courage. Caleb, who owes his life to her, then hopes to win her, and her heart too yearns for him. But it is Joshua, his commander-in-chief, who takes her as mate, despite her foreign origin, even as Moses took the Midianite Zipporah. The loyal Caleb and the Canaanite Rahab cannot gainsay Joshua's wishes. The harlot or innkeeper thus becomes the ancestress of illustrious heroes and prophets.

While novelists could paint on a wide canvas the historical conflict between the two civilizations and the two religious systems of the Hebrews and the Canaanites which led to the fall of Jericho, dramatists who were attracted by this biblical theme were more limited. Dramatic economy necessitated their focusing attention on a single climactic moment of this conflict. They could do so best by making Rahab the central figure and concentrating the dramatic action on the last hours of the doomed town. In Rahab, the sacred harlot and chief priestess of Astarte or Ashera, goddess of love, the splendor and voluptuousness of the pagan world could find its most glamorous personification. Furthermore, in Rahab's discontent with her decadent environment and in her longing for the simpler, purer Hebraic world, the new religious revelation could best be expressed.

What the German dramatist Rudolf von Gottschall, who modeled his Rahab upon Goethe's classical heroine Iphigenia, priestess of Diana, failed to achieve, was successfully achieved by Matityahu Shoham, the pioneer of modern Hebrew drama, in his neoromantic verse-play *Jericho*, written in 1923. While Gottschall was more at home in Germanic lore, and Rahab was the sole biblical theme treated by him in a literary career that spanned more than half a century, Shoham was steeped in biblical lore since his childhood in Warsaw and chose only biblical subjects for his plays. His biblical characters ranged from Abraham and Balaam to Elijah and Jezebel. But none of his heroines was as attractive as Rahab.

Jericho was Shoham's first play. It was completed in his thirtieth year. His source was not only the Rahab episode in the third chapter of Joshua, which paved the way for Israel's victory at Jericho, but also the episode in the seventh chapter about Achan, whose transgression brought about the defeat of Joshua's three thousand warriors before Ai. Shoham combined both episodes by making Achan one of the two men sent by Joshua to spy out the defenses of Jericho and to report on the morale of Jericho's defenders. While the older spy, Othniel, who remembers Egyptian luxury before the Exodus, is unimpressed by Jericho's wealth, Achan, who grew up amidst the austerity of the desert, is overwhelmed by the splendor of this Canaanite citadel and dazzled by the beauty of Rahab, the hierodule of the pagan goddess of love. Upon Rahab's invitation, he attends the sumptuous banquet in which priests and dignitaries participate. The merriment is rather restrained because fear of the ascetic desert hordes and their invisible God hangs over the assembled guests. Rahab derides her townsmen as cowards and weaklings, soft-willed, schooled in luxury, lacking the desert's force and flaming passion. She lures the daring, virile stranger Achan until, enraptured by her spell and overcome with burning desire, he remains with her when the sounds of battle are heard and all the other guests leave to man the ramparts. Locked in her enchanting arms, he betrays his people by staying away from the fray. He protects Rahab and guards her valuables against Israelite looters. After the fall of Jericho, he is tried as a traitor and condemned to be stoned. He defends himself by claiming that God made Rahab so lovely that she was irresistible. Hence, God is to blame for his behavior far more than he himself.

In Achan, the dramatist portrayed the struggle within the heart of man between the alluring, sensual world of paganism and the more spiritual, ascetic world of Hebraism. This struggle also raged in the heart of Rahab. It reverberated in Shoham's poems and later plays.

In the Rahab ballad of Börries, Freiherr von Münchhausen, included in his volume *Juda* (1900), this German poet has the heroine of Jericho pass harsh judgment upon herself for betraying her people. She it was who unlatched her door and let a spy sent by Joshua hide in her house when he was in danger of being discovered. She it was who, after a night of bliss in his arms, let down the scarlet cord from her window and helped him to escape, after exacting a promise that the Jewish victors would spare her when they stormed the town. However, her conscience troubles her when she sees Jericho go up in flames. It is her homeland that she has betrayed for a night of love. When the battle is over and silence descends upon the smoldering town, her Jewish lover seeks her out and finds her hanging dead on the scarlet cord.

Rahab, whose behavior has been subjected to condemnation and exoneration by writers down the centuries, will undoubtedly continue to fascinate the creative imagination in coming generations even as in our own.

10

Jephthah's Literary Vogue

Jephthah, one of Israel's great judges during the premonarchical era, was a charismatic figure. Though stigmatized by his illegitimate birth, harried by his more reputable brothers, driven out into the desert, where his associates were outlaws and brigands, he yet overcame all handicaps, won the respect of his Transjordanian tribe, and was called upon in an hour of Israel's need to assume the leadership of his people in war, a leadership he succeeded in retaining throughout the following, more peaceful years until he was gathered to his fathers.

Many were the stories that must have circulated about him and that were handed down the generations by word of mouth and by priestly scribes. Fragments of these stories survive in the succinct written version available to us in Judges 11 and 12.

We learn of his negotiations with the elders of Gilead, who had acquiesced in his being driven forth into exile, and who, when they later sought him out in the land of Tob, had to accede to his severe conditions and hand over to him supreme authority over all the inhabitants of their endangered province before he would budge from his secure place of refuge.

We are apprised of his apparently long-drawn-out diplomatic exchanges with the king of the Ammonites, during which he displayed much subtlety and in the course of which he tried to refute the Ammonite claim for sovereignty over the disputed territory bordering on the Arnon River. And when his diplomatic efforts failed to avoid war, we are told of his heroic exploits in repelling the invaders and in capturing twenty of their cities.

The dispute with the tribe of Ephraim that followed his decisive victory over the foreign foe gives us an insight into his domineering nature. His testing of the defeated, fleeing Ephraimites by means of their mispronunciation of "Shibboleth" as "Sibboleth" provides us with an additional clue to his craftiness, a trait that helped him to overcome the intrigues and snares he must have encountered from his own people after the danger from the Ammonites subsided and tribal dissension reasserted itself.

The most memorable tale of Jephthah, however, concerned his sacrifice of his only child. This tale of his personal error, rashness, grief, and remorse left the strongest impact upon later creative spirits who were inspired by the biblical narrative. Though this episode in the career of the valiant warrior and judge encompasses only nine verses in the Book of Judges (9:30 f., 34-40), there are innumerable literary, musical, and artistic interpretations of it.

Of the more than one hundred musical compositions based upon it, the most famous is the oratorio of George Friedrich Handel, composed in 1751, just as he was turning blind. It is true that the text of this oratorio by Thomas Morell is not of a very high literary standard, but the music is magnificent and has delighted audiences for more than two centuries. Jephthah's daughter was often depicted in medieval and Renaissance illustrations, mosaics, and tapestries, and more recently appears in the nineteenth-century paintings by William Blake and Edgar Degas and in the twentieth-century sculptures by Enrico Glicenstein and Naum Aronson.

In drama, significant reinterpretations of the Jephthah theme go back to the sixteenth century, when George Buchanan, the Scottish humanist and reformer, composed his Latin version in 1542, and Hans Sachs, the Meistersinger of Nuremberg, his German version in 1555. This theme was especially popular among the humanists, who were spellbound by the rediscovery of the classical dramatists, since it resembled the Iphigenia theme as treated by Euripides in his play *Iphigenia in Aulis*, a tragedy translated in 1506 by Erasmus of Rotterdam from the original Greek into Latin. The translation of this Dutch humanist had a large vogue in university circles throughout Europe. Melanchthon's students staged a performance at the University of Wittenberg. In Cambridge, John Christopherson, the English humanist and later bishop, wrote a Jephthah drama in Greek in 1544, explaining that he had chosen this subject because of its similarity to the Euripidean play.

Just as Agamemnon, the leader of the Greek expedition against Troy, had to sacrifice his daughter Iphigenia to a Hellenic deity so that the Greek ships might sail and ultimate victory over the Trojans be achieved, so too Jephthah feels compelled to fulfill his rash vow to sacrifice his daughter if God will grant him victory over the Ammonites. Jephthah, like Agamemnon, is a tragic hero because he is caught in an inner conflict between his duty to God and his fatherly love for his daughter, a conflict which involves him in immense suffering both before arriving at his final decision and after carrying it out. Indeed, his tragedy is even greater than that of Agamemnon, for the latter had other children, such as Electra and Orestes, to carry on the family line, while Jephthah has but this one daughter and no sons.

Structurally, the Jephthah theme lent itself to dramatic treatment consistent with the classical rules as promulgated by Aristotle and interpreted by Renaissance scholars and literary critics. More than half a hundred Jephthah dramas are recorded between the sixteenth and the eighteenth century and are listed in Johanna Porwig's dissertation *Der Jephtastoff in der deutschen Dichtung* (Breslau, 1932) and in W. O. Sypherd's more comprehensive study *Jephthah and His Daughter* (University of Delaware, 1948). Of these dramas, the most enduring was the verse tragedy *Jephta*, completed in 1659 by the Dutch dramatist Joost van den Vondel.

In accordance with the Aristotelian insistence on unity of time, the entire action of Vondel's play takes place on the day of the sacrifice, immediately after the daughter's return from the mountains. As in the analogous Euripidean tragedy, the father seeks to keep the mother away by means of a ruse so that she will not learn of the sacrifice and so that her plea for her child's life may not weaken his resolve. Clytemnestra, wife of Agamemnon, does discover her husband's intent in time, but her intervention is in vain. Jephthah's wife does not learn of her husband's bloody deed until it is too late.

Vondel held that Jephthah's tragic fault stemmed from his sincere but erroneous belief that God demanded the fulfillment of a vow once made and that the offering of a human being was pleasing to Him, as proved by the fact that He continued to bestow victories after the vow was made, victories not only against the Ammonites but also against the Ephraimites. Only after Jephthah carries out his vow do doubts assail him. He realized his error and is ready to atone. At the conclusion of the drama, he undertakes to make his way to the priests in Shiloh, the chief sanctuary of the Israelites, and to do penance for his rashness and his stubborn faith in his own judgment.

Shakespeare, who steered clear of biblical subjects for his dramas, was acquainted with the Jephthah theme. In *Hamlet*, he called Polonius an old Jephthah and echoed verses of a current English ballad on this Israelite judge who, like the father of Ophelia, had "one fair daughter and no more, the which he loved passing well."

A generation after Shakespeare, the English poet Robert Herrich composed "The Dirge of Jephthah's Daughter" (1647). The dirge is sung by the maidens who recall the daughter's martyrdom and was based upon the biblical verse that the young women of Israel went annually to lament her for four days.

The century of Enlightenment was less interested in the Jephthah theme than the preceding centuries. For the romantic generation of the early nineteenth century, however, it again proved attractive, as is evidenced by the lyrics of Lord Byron and Alfred de Vigny, among others.

In Byron's poem of 1815, included in his *Hebrew Melodies*, the Hebrew maiden's nobility of soul and her unquestioning acquiescence in her fate were emphasized. In five stanzas, she expresses her love for her father as she bids farewell to him in her final hour. Having just returned from her two months in the mountains—the period of mourning granted her—she is ready for the sacrifice, since her country, her God, and her sire demand it. She comforts her father by pointing out to him that his vow has brought him success in battle and has assured freedom for her people. She begs him to bless her and to note that she will die pure in thought and with a smile on her lips.

Isaac Nathan, the Jewish composer who set the lyric to music, suggested to Byron that perhaps the tragic end might be modified, since the biblical text did not necessarily mean "a positive sacrifice of the daughter's life but may have referred to a sentence of perpetual seclusion, a state held by Jews as dead indeed to society, and the most severe infliction that could be imposed." Byron replied that he was not guilty of her blood and would not incur censure from the world by killing her in his poem.

Five years after Byron, the French poet Alfred de Vigny wrote the biblical lyric "La Fille de Jephté," a chant of the maidens of Israel. They sing of the Hebraic deity as a jealous God, a God of vengeance, a God who demands innocent blood as compensation for Jephthah's failings. They idealize his daughter, who bowed her head in submission and who placated the deity by her death.

In *A Dream of Fair Women* (1833), Alfred Tennyson included among the world's outstanding fair women not only Helen of Troy, Iphigenia, and Cleopatra but also the pure Gileadite maiden who died to fulfill her father's wild oath. In his dream, the poet hears her recount how from the bliss of life she was lowered down to a silent grave. She had no regrets for her forfeited years, for having given up joy, dance, and song. It was comforting to submit to a father's will. It was beautiful to die for her God. It brought a glow of pride to her face to know that through her sacrifice she assured Israel's victory over Ammon.

The Victorian poet also touched upon the Jephthah theme in the verse narratives *Aylmer's Field* and *The Flight*. In the latter poem, he compared the tyrannical father of the heroine, who would force her into a hated marriage and thus shorten her life, to the godless Jephthah, who because of an impulsive vow forced his meek daughter to yield up her heart, soul, and life.

Not all biblical commentators were convinced that the carrying out of Jephthah's vow necessitated his daughter's untimely death. To be sacrificed to the Lord might be interpreted as being condemned to eternal virginity and unfruitfulness. The German dramatist Ludwig Freytag was aware of this interpretation but rejected it as inadequate. In his verse drama of 1871, entitled *Jephthah*, he went much further in changing the ending. He had a prophet of the Israelite God intervene at the last moment to save the willing victim and to bring about a completely happy conclusion: her being wedded to her heart's beloved. He held that, while heathen deities such as Moloch and Ashtoreth did require human beings as burnt-offerings, the Israelite God would not let such horrible sacrifices be carried out, even if He might test His followers by subjecting them to extreme trials, as in the case of Abraham and Isaac and in that of Jephthah and his daughter. The Jewish God was not only just but also merciful. Hence, when Freytag's play reaches a climax in the submission of father and daughter to God's apparent will for absolute, unquestioning obedience to a vow once undertaken, the prophet Eli is introduced to pronounce God's true, compassionate will. Human burnt-offerings must be ever shunned. They are heathen abominations. Israel must serve God in other ways, by performing righteous deeds.

The Jephthah theme was not as popular with Jewish writers as with Protestant and Catholic writers, even though the Bible was for the biblical people its "portable fatherland." Jewish writers were estranged by Jephthah's behavior in seeking to bribe God with a burnt-offering and in his carrying out his vow despite its involving the unanticipated death of his innocent child. However, the submission of the pure maiden to the will of her father did appeal to the exiled people that prized filial piety as a supreme value in the struggle for ethnic and religious survival. This aspect was, therefore, emphasized in the Hebrew and Yiddish adaptations of the Jephthah legend.

Thus, the trilingual poet S. S. Frug, who fascinated readers during the closing nineteenth century with his poems in Russian, Hebrew, and Yiddish, ended his long Hebrew poem "Bat Yiftakh" with the daughter's descent from her mountain retreat to meet her end, pure, without wailing, meekly submissive to an adored father who means more to her than life itself.

Similarly, Yehoash, whose supreme achievement was the translation of the Bible into Yiddish, and whose lyrics and ballads abounded in biblical subjects and characters, limited himself in his poem "Yiftakh's Tokhter" to an elaboration merely of the last sentence of the biblical narrative, the lament of Gilead's maidens as they made their yearly pilgrimage to the grave of the martyred girl. There is a curse upon the mountain where she lies buried. No grass ever grows there, and no birds ever sing there. The loneliness and silence hovering over the scene are disturbed only during the four days each year when the women of Gilead come to lay a wreath on the ancient grave, to sing their song of lamentation, and to dance their macabre dance. Then it seems to them that the maiden long dead joins them in their song and dances among them with invisible steps.

In 1910, the same year as Yehoash's dirge, I. I. Schwartz, the American Yiddish poet, also idealized the meek daughter who joyfully accepted the tragic fate her father decreed for her. A sacred fire is kindled in her heart as she prepares for her end. While her comrades kiss her hands and the hem of her robe, she stands calm and pensive as she awaits the eternal night that will cut short her young life.

The strangest Yiddish version of the Jephthah theme was Sholem Asch's drama in two acts with a long prologue and a longer epilogue. Asch had visited Palestine in 1907 and 1910, and his creative imagination had been stimulated by its landscape and its people. Nevertheless, though he characterized his work as a biblical drama, there is little of the biblical spirit in it. It rather depicts a struggle over Jephthah's daughter between prehistoric man in search of a suitable mate and the one-eyed, bestial god Moloch, who rules in the rugged mountains on the edge of human habitation. When Jephthah is driven forth from his own, more civilized land of Gilead after the death of his father, he found refuge in the desolate region of the god Moloch, from which his mother stemmed. To this god of fire, it was customary to offer up the firstborn child immediately after its birth. Jephthah, however, withheld his only child from the ravenous deity. Now that his daughter is grown-up, Moloch claims her as a desirable mate.

When Gilead's elders, in their distress, find their way to Jephthah's lonely abode in the mountains and implore him to return to the land of his father and save it from the ravages of the Ammonites, he agrees and prays to the God of his father to grant him victory in the coming struggle. His prayer meets with silence. He then turns to Moloch, the god of his mother, and vows that, if victorious, he will sacrifice whatever comes forth from his house to greet him on his return from battle, even if it is his most precious possession, even his only daughter. After the victory, Jephthah feels obligated to fulfill his vow. The elders of Gilead implore him to flee from Moloch's domain and join them in their land under the protection of the Hebraic God, who does not desire human sacrifices. The daughter of Jephthah, however, rejoices in her father's vow. She prefers to answer the wild call of her blood for Moloch, the savage sun-god, whose fiery darts warm and irradiate her longing limbs.

Between the two world wars, the much-maligned German-Jewish poet Ernst Lissauer treated the Jephthah theme in his drama *Das Weib des Jephta*, performed and published in 1928, and the prolific American writer of Jewish historical romances, Saul Saphire, concluded in 1937 his series of the 1930s on biblical characters with his Yiddish novel on Jephthah. As in his preceding biblical novels, which dealt with King David (1930), Joseph and his brethren (1931), King Solomon (1931), Queen Esther (1932), Moses (1934), Joshua (1935), Samson (1935), and Ruth (1936), his Jephthah narrative, amidst all elaborations, tried to be faithful to the original text and to the Jewish traditional interpretations. Lissauer, on the other hand, was far more interested in voicing through his Jephthah his own protest against the carnage and vain sacrifices of the war he had experienced, and which had earlier led him astray to pen his "Hassgesang gegen England." This hate-filled poem, his most popular one, had helped to whip up war hysteria against Germany's opponents, and he had come to regret its popularity.

As the title of his biblical tragedy indicates, it was the wife of Jephthah and not his daughter who is at the center of the dramatic action. If the daughter acquiesced so meekly in her fate, as indicated in the original source, might it not have been because she was not fully aware of what the loss of life really meant? The dramatist, therefore, portrayed her as a five-year-old child, interested in playing with her doll, rather than as a strong-willed, mature personality who had to decide whether to accept or to struggle against her fate. The role of Jephthah's antagonist devolves upon her mother. Despite the love she bears for her husband, her maternal feelings lead her to oppose him, the would-be murderer of their only child. She cannot justify the sacrifice dictated by his higher religious and patriotic considerations. She, therefore, attempts to frustrate his intentions by escaping with her child to the mountains. When the cave in which both hide is discovered and the child is indeed sacrificed, she rages at the murderer whom others idolize as the conquering hero. She even attempts to kill him, and failing to do so, she kills herself. Though Jephthah lives on as the revered savior of his country, he is a broken man, crushed by his conscience, which will not absolve him of his guilt in having been the cause of his child's death and his wife's suicide. The right of a person, man, woman, or child, to the precious gift of life was juxtaposed by the dramatist to the claim of God and state for the sacrifice of individuals for the good of society, but no satisfactory solution to the conflict was indicated.

While Lissauer's drama, written under the impact of the defeat of the Central Powers, echoed his disillusionment with the patriotic slogans of the First World War, the most significant literary treatment of Jephthah by a Jewish writer after the Second World War, Lion Feuchtwanger's novel of 1957, sought to shake off the novelist's brooding over the most recent Jewish tragedy. Feuchtwanger sought to flee in his historical imagination to the Bronze Age in which Jephthah lived, but he could not entirely escape the nightmare of the Holocaust. It intruded even upon his attempted reconstruction of the ancient world of the biblical tribes as they emerged from primitive religious beliefs to a new concept of divinity.

Feuchtwanger was the author of more than a dozen historical novels, including bestsellers about Jewish personalities ranging from Josephus to Jud Süss. *Jefta und seine Tochter* was his last work, and it necessitated tremendous creative imagination to bring to life and to depict faithfully events, religious beliefs, family relationships, political conflicts, priests, rulers, and commoners of the remote era and of the borderland beyond the Jordan.

In trying to reconstruct the reality of the ancient land of Gilead, Feuchtwanger utilized the most recent findings of archaeologists, historians, and philologists. He saw Jephthah in the midst of a tribe that was barely adjusting to the sedentary life of agriculturalists after its earlier nomadic existence as shepherds. When Jephthah feels wronged by his brothers, who have denied him his father's inheritance, he flees to the wilderness of Tob with his Ammonite wife and his child. Amidst the boundless liberty of the great open spaces, he gathers about him fugitives and outlaws who join him for mutual protection. These freebooters, scorned and feared, become in time a formidable, armed host. When the Ammonites attack Gilead, Jephthah's band of warriors are desperately needed to save the Gileadites from defeat. As the accepted leader of the entire army, he engages in a fierce battle against overwhelming odds. To wrest victory from the jaws of defeat, he vows his rash vow. When the tide of battle turns, he is hailed jubilantly as his country's savior, but his happiness is short-lived. God, who raised him so high in triumph, casts him all the deeper into misery. The fulfillment of his vow necessitates the sacrifice of his beloved child. "He did with her according to his vow." But his heart thereafter is a desert. Though the men of Gilead revere him, as he rules his people justly, he himself feels like a dead man whose life's blood has drained away.

In Feuchtwanger's novel, as in the biblical narrative, the pure, innocent, submissive daughter faces no inner conflicts. It is rather Jephthah who is presented as torn between his father's tribe, the people of the settlements, and his mother's tribe, the nomads of the desert. After his tragic deed, this strong and solitary leader comes to realize its futility and madness. Its consequences become ever clearer to him in all their grim absurdity and imbecile grandeur. He has shed his best blood, his own daughter's blood, for a God who does not exist. Through the mask of Jephthah, the novelist was voicing his own despair after his disillusionment with the Communist idol Stalin he had previously worshiped as well as his still earlier disillusionment with his countrymen, among whom he had spent his pre-exilic years, and who had brought his Jewish kinsmen as burnt-offerings in Auschwitz, Treblinka, and Maidanek.

The Jephthah theme, embracing a conflict between religious duty and parental love, has had an international vogue from the Middle Ages until our day. Though it resembles the theme of Abraham's sacrifice of Isaac and that of Agamemnon's sacrifice of Iphigenia, it has more tragic overtones. After all, Isaac was spared at the last moment by the substitution of a ram, and Iphigenia was saved by divine intervention and transported from the altar of Aulis to a new existence in Tauris. Jephthah, on the other hand, did actually shed his child's blood, according to biblical and most later versions, a deed that could not fail to trouble his conscience as long as he lived, even if he viewed it as God-ordained. In the contemporary world, the national state has been substituted for the God of primitive tribes and prehistoric centuries. The state still requires human sacrifices. It still justifies the shedding of human blood in war, in the preservation of established regimes, in the defense of social ideologies that later turn out to be mass illusions. Jephthah's dilemma continues and will long continue to occupy creative minds.

11

Samson in the Twentieth Century

The character of Samson in its many contradictions has intrigued not only biblical scholars and theologians but also men of letters ever since the Middle Ages. Samson has been variously depicted in prose and verse as hero and bully, wise judge and frivolous jester, God's champion and sinful weakling, national savior and whining lover.

St. Augustine ushered in the medieval approach, which saw Samson as a forerunner of the Christian Messiah and Samson's carrying off the gates of Gaza as a prefiguration of the bursting open of the gates of hell. The Renaissance failed to resolve the contradictions in Samson's personality. The dramatization of the Samson story in 1556 by Hans Sachs, the Meistersinger of Nuremberg and a contemporary of Martin Luther, merely expanded the biblical text to five acts without deepening its meaning. Far superior in dramatic quality were the seventeenth-century versions of Joost van den Vondel and John Milton. The former's tragedy *Samson of Heilige Wraeck*, completed in 1660, is a masterpiece of Dutch literature. The latter's classical drama *Samson Agonistes*, completed in 1671, is a magnificent expression of the English poet's innermost feelings after he became blind. He then saw in the biblical hero, "eyeless in Gaza," an allied spirit whose inner light at life's end compensated for outer darkness.

The Century of Enlightenment displayed little interest in Samson. Voltaire's *Samson*, which formed the text for Rameau's opera of 1730, was not a distinguished work. Handel's oratorio *Samson*, for which Newburgh Hamilton wrote the libretto and which had its first performance in 1744, was based almost entirely on Milton's poetic tragedy. Nor were the romanticists of the early nineteenth century enthusiastic about Samson's exploits in love, religion, or nationalism. Lord Byron, in his *Hebrew Melodies* and in his drama *Cain*, treated strong, defiant, and tragic biblical characters but made no mention of Samson. Franz Grillparzer, Austria's greatest dramatist of the romantic and postromantic generations, did consider making Samson the principal character of a projected tragedy, but, after sketching an outline in 1829, he abandoned the theme.

Not until Saint-Saëns's opera of 1877 did an artistic rendition of the Samson theme reach out to large audiences. But then it was not so much the text by Fernand Lemaire as the music, primarily the arias of Delilah, that made the deepest impact.

During the early twentieth century, the French dramatist Henri Bernstein, in 1907, and the German precursor of expressionism Frank Wedekind, in 1913, were the more important creative spirits that wrestled with this theme. During the First World War, Hermann Burte, German painter and poet, attempted in his verse drama of 1917 to transform Samson into a Nietzschean superman who is always in search of his identity in relation to God and to his people and who only finds it after he is blinded and humiliated. Then the suffering hero learns to love his tribulations and to serve God and his people by means of his last, shattering, self-sacrificing deed. But it was Vladimir Jabotinsky, in his Russian novel of 1926, who created the finest artistic version of the Samson theme since Milton and who influenced contemporary Jewish thinking by emphasizing the continuity of Jewish striving from the age of the Judges until our own. None of the later novels, such as Felix Salten's German *Simson, das Schicksal eines Erwählten* (1928) and Saul Saphire's Yiddish *Shimshon Hagibor* (1935), have aroused comparable interest.

Salten is today best remembered as the author of the animal classic *Bambi* (1923). His innovation of the Samson story consisted in making Delilah the faithful beloved of the hero and in ascribing Samson's being betrayed to his enemies as the vengeance of her jealous sister. The sister insinuates to Delilah that Samson is merely using his beloved as a plaything and that he will not hesitate to cast her aside when he tires of her. Were his love genuine and enduring, he would confide to her his deepest secret. To test his love, Delilah worms out of him the secret of his strength. She is overheard by her jealous sister, who cuts off his hair as the couple lie fast asleep and thus brings about his capture by the lurking Philistines and his blinding. Delilah, however, clings to him even after his disfigurement and disgrace. She comforts him with her undeviating love and dies with him.

For Salten, Samson's fate symbolized Jewish fate. During the years of increasing anti-Semitism in Central Europe, which were to climax in the rise of the Nazis to power, Salten voiced his pessimistic approach to coming developments through the words of the aging Manoah, Samson's father: "Ever and forever the rope will be about our neck, ever and forever the brutal hand of others will drive us as though we were cattle or scum. It is an accursed blessing that we bear but still a blessing. We bear the light of the world and must hence suffer as long as darkness reigns. We bear the wisdom of the world and must hence endure ill-usage as long as stupidity prevails. We bring liberation to the world and are hence persecuted as long as there is slavery. Wise is the Almighty, unfathomably wise, in burdening us with all these tortures and humiliations. Otherwise, whither would our arrogance lead us?"

A similar submissive acceptance by the Jews of their apparent role as God's chosen whipping boys emerged from the reference to Samson in the poem "Der Jude" by Julius Bab, penned in 1930, as the Nazi tide was threatening to inundate his coreligionists in his native Berlin. To a young Jew who wished to resist, even though he despaired of mustering sufficient strength to defeat his persecutors, Bab gave the reply of an old Jew: don't resist, don't emulate neighbors who put their trust in physical might, discover the virtue of your helplessness. The would-be young activist is reminded that, in the era of Samson, Jews also regarded defiance as a noble attitude. In the millennia since then, however, Jews have outgrown such an approach. The nations now persecuting Jews are so young. They too will mature and will cease to enjoy their bloody pastimes. They too will outgrow warfare some day. Meanwhile, let the Jews continue to create and amass spiritual treasures and remain a shining light for others.

Within a few years after these verses of Julius Bab and after the novel of Felix Salten, both writers became refugees in flight from their Central European homes and in search of an asylum in the New World.

It was against the acceptance of nonresistance as a Jewish ideal that Vladimir Jabotinsky protested ever since his youth. As early as 1905, he saw Russian revolutionary hordes swerve from their struggle against tsarist oppression in order to vandalize and pogromize unresisting Jewish neighbors. Militant Zionism then became the burning passion of his life. Rejecting the spiritual Zionism of Ahad Haam, in whose Odessa circle he mingled, he put his faith in physical power as the principal means of attaining his people's unfulfilled yearning, a free territory for a Jewish state, a homecoming of the Jewish wanderers to their historic soil.

Jabotinsky heard the call of Theodor Herzl for Zionist political action. He foresaw the disintegration of the Ottoman Empire. During the First World War, he was the dynamic force behind the agitation for a Jewish Legion to fight alongside the British and to bring about the defeat of the Turkish overlords of Palestine. After the war, he urged the mandatory power, Great Britain, to let Jews arm themselves during the period of transition while they were still a minority and needed to defend themselves against threatening attacks by the Arab majority. In Samson, champion of the Danites at the height of Philistine domination of the Palestinian coast, he found the biblical hero closest to his heart. He had at first planned a trilogy of biblical novels centering about the loves of Jacob and Rachel, Samson and Delilah, David and Abishag the Shunammite, but his political activities as the leader of the Zionist Revisionist movement left him little leisure for literature, and he only completed the middle piece of his trilogy.

Into this novel about Samson, Jabotinsky was able to pour his own dreams, his deepest thoughts on Jewish national aspirations, his faith in a strong, independent Israel that would arise ere long. This novel, translated into various languages read by Jews between the two world wars and above all into Hebrew, became the text that inspired Betar, the Zionist youth movement founded by Jabotinsky in the 1920s and led in the 1930s by Jabotinsky's disciple Menahem Begin. But this novel also gave expression to its author's zest for life and his admiration for the beautiful manners and the loyal discipline that prevailed among his non-Jewish adversaries, the British, whom he portrayed in the guise of the ancient Philistines. If all the documents relating to Jabotinsky's Zionist philosophy were lost, its main tenets could be reconstructed from this novel, which is at the same time a masterpiece of literary art.

Jabotinsky senses in Samson a charismatic personality who combined wisdom and strength, gaiety and loyalty, a love of life and a readiness to sacrifice his life in the service of his people.

The generation of Samson was the late twelfth and early eleventh century before the common era, when the original Canaanite inhabitants of the land between the Mediterranean and the Jordan had already been ground up between two conquering peoples, the Philistines along the coast and the Israelites in the highlands. The Israelite tribes had not yet coalesced into a national unity. An uneasy truce prevailed between Dan and Philistia during Samson's early years.

In Jabotinsky's novel, Samson is introduced as the young leader of a group of highwaymen whom he nicknamed the Jackals. He is depicted as possessing gigantic strength, extraordinary diplomatic skill, and as alternating between asceticism and licentiousness. In Zorah, among his Danite kinsmen, he is a stern Nazarite who abstains from wine, desists from women, and leaves his unshorn hair tied in braids. But in Timnah, the neighboring town of the Philistines, he carouses with drunken Philistine companions, loves Philistine women, gambles, laughs heartily, and lets his hair flow down his broad shoulders. When a Levite upbraids him for sinning, he replies that there is a time for waking and a time for sleeping. In Dan he was awake and subject to moral restraints. In Philistia he has found relaxation in dreams and is free of all restraints.

He proves his basic loyalty to his tribe and his high quality of leadership when he appears in Zorah at the popular assembly of his entire tribe. Dan, wedged in between the Philistines and the more prosperous Hebraic tribes of Judah, Benjamin, and Ephraim, is seeking a way out of its overpopulation, impoverishment, and decline. It has to break out of its encirclement. But how? To war against the overwhelming might of the Philistines, who fight with iron weapons from armored chariots, would result in inevitable defeat and annihilation. To engage in a struggle against the other Israelite tribes, the most likely future allies of Dan against the Philistines, would also not solve the problem of survival. In this dilemma, Samson suggests a third possibility, namely, to send out trustworthy men to scout the land north of Ephraim and Naphtali, a land rich in water and forests, a land which could absorb Dan's overpopulation. Then the tribe would have two territories, even as Manasseh has had since the days of Joshua.

Samson's suggestion is accepted by his tribesmen, who are spellbound by his personality. Subconsciously, they yearn for someone in whom to believe, someone who will do the thinking for them, someone on whose shoulders they can pile their worries. In Samson, they have found such a leader, and they are happy to acclaim him, despite his youth, as their judge and the arbitrator of their disputes. He proves to be wise and decisive, qualities that rarely go together. But Samson is more than merely a sagacious and stern Nazarite. He is also a joyous human being, fond of the refined, sophisticated culture brought by the Philistines from their Minoan ancestral land across the sea. He is charmed by their carefreeness and contrasts their lightheartedness with the Danites' solemn bondage to moral laws. He, therefore, seeks out a wife not of his own tribe but from among the Philistines of Timnah. The wedding ceremonies, lasting seven days, begin with lavish feasting and games of skill and endurance. They end, however, with the betrayal of the solution of Samson's riddle by his young wife, Semadar, and with fierce enmity between Philistines and Danites, leading ultimately to the burning of Timnah and the death of Samson's wife.

When a shaky truce is patched up, Samson uses the peaceful interval in order to solve Dan's population explosion by sending part of the tribe to the northern region which the scouts found suitable for settlement and cultivation. He also uses the years of nonbelligerancy to garner iron and to teach the Danites the art of forging weapons such as the Philistines have. Observing Philistine behavior, he notes that their collective might stems in large part from the discipline that prevails among them. Thousands obey the will of a single commanding person. In this trait he senses the most important secret of how peoples are able to found new, stable states. He also notes that the Philistines, unlike his own tribesmen, can relax from discipline during less serious times, that they can enjoy wine, song, dance, frivolous laughter, and love's delights. In Gaza, he is attracted to a Philistine woman. Delilah fascinates him as once had Semadar of Timnah. Indeed, he sees in her a reincarnation of his wife whom he lost, long, long ago. Delilah, however, is overcome with jealousy when she realizes that, in embracing her, he is but reliving his unforgotten, youthful love for Semadar. In her jealous anger, she cuts off his hair and betrays him to his enemies, who then put out his eyes.

The blinded hero's message to his people before his violent end at the temple of Dagon in Gaza consists of but three words: iron, king, laughter. If his people want to preserve their freedom and independence, they must be strong, and iron weapons will make them strong. They must also be disciplined and united. The election of a king will put an end to their disorganization and disunity. And they must learn to laugh as a relaxation from the constant stern demand of their national existence. An optimistic philosophy would dissipate the gloom that weighed upon Jewish hearts as a result of the tragedies Jews experienced.

In reading this novel of 1926, Colonel John Henry Patterson, who had earlier been the commanding British officer of the Jewish Legion, discerned in its pages Jabotinsky's uncompromising revolt against the unorganized, formless Jewish dispersion with no stable organization, no leadership, no discipline, and no national feeling. "He wanted for the Jews what they lacked most: a united nation with a central leadership; a state with an army; iron for their defense in a hostile world."

More than half a century has passed since Jabotinsky embodied his Zionist credo in his novel about Samson. The State of Israel has since become a reality, and Jabotinsky's disciple, Menahem Begin, became its Prime Minister in 1977. For both Jabotinsky and Begin, the Bible was a constant source of inspiration, and biblical experiences, such as those of Samson, furnished an enrichment of their thinking on Jewishness and on Israel in the contemporary world. In the fourth decade of Israel's statehood, Begin, its Prime Minister, as Jabotinsky before him, constantly emphasized the need for a strong deterrent force, for a disciplined consensus, and for the therapy of exhilarating laughter.

12

Ruth and Medea

The biblical story of Ruth and the Greek story of Medea deal with the alien woman who forsakes her god, her people, and her family in order to attach herself to a god, a people, and a family of her own choice. Yet, how different is the fate of each!

Ruth the Moabite, though a mere peasant girl, is received with affection and as an equal in Bethlehem of Judah and becomes the ancestress of kings, the entire Davidic dynasty. Medea, on the other hand, though a princess of Colchis, is received with hostility in Greece, is looked at askance as the racial outsider, is deemed inferior to those born into Hellenic culture, and ends as the distraught murderess of her own children. The contrast between the experiences of these two women after their fateful decisions gives us an insight into the moral approach of the biblical people and the amoral approach of the Hellenic people.

It is an accepted truism that Western civilization owes its concept of beauty to the Greeks but not its concept of morality. The taming of the Occident by moral laws, to the extent that it has been tamed, is in the largest measure an achievement of the Israelite tribes, who were the first to accept the moral codes promulgated at Sinai.

There are many themes and characters in the Bible that find their parallel in Hellenic literature and folklore, and all of them illustrate this basic distinction between the Israelites, whose behavior was grounded in ethical ideals toward which we are still striving, and the Greeks, who were not primarily motivated by ethical considerations. Let us call attention to a few.

The biblical story of Joseph, Jacob's favorite son, has often been compared with the Athenian story of Hippolytus, son of Theseus, best dramatized by Euripides and enjoying worldwide vogue in the versions of Seneca, Racine, and D'Annunzio. When Joseph is tempted by Potiphar's wife, he resists her and flees from her because to yield to her passionate overtures would be adulterous and immoral. His virtuous behavior and his temporary guiltless suffering because of it are ultimately rewarded by God, and he is elevated to the position of royal viceroy at the court of Pharaoh. Hippolytus, on the other hand, who in a similar situation behaves in a similar way, fleeing from the passionate overtures of Phaedra, wife of Theseus, his stepmother, is condemned because of his chastity and suffers death because he refused to pay homage to Aphrodite, goddess of sensual passion, when the opportunity to answer an erotic call presented itself to him. Obviously, the behavior of Joseph would not have evoked admiration among the Greeks. On the other hand, the behavior of Hippolytus, disparaged by the Greeks, would have been regarded by the biblical seers as a model of civilized conduct.

As another illustration of the striking contrast between the moral biblical and the amoral Greek approach, let us consider the contrasting fates meted out to Samson and to Hercules. Both Samson and Hercules are heroes who put their faith in their physical prowess. Samson, the mighty Danite, learns that mightiness alone does not ultimately lead to salvation, when his career comes to a tragic end as the blinded prisoner of the Philistines, but that submission to the supreme authority of God is the more desirable goal of human endeavor. Hercules, on the other hand, who roams through the world performing his heroic tasks with the help of his club and his mighty biceps, is elevated to the rank of a god or demigod on Olympus. Only the aged, disillusioned Euripides dared to differ with the accepted legend of Hercules and, in his play on this subject, showed that faith in physical prowess must lead to megalomania and ultimate disaster. But then Euripides was a maverick who had much in common with the biblical prophets and who was ever at odds with his own generation and his own amoral people.

It is, however, in the treatment of Ruth by the biblical chronicler and of Medea by the Greek narrators of the Argonautic expedition that the contrast is most apparent between Jewish racial tolerance and the Jewish ethical doctrine of the equality of all human beings made in the image of God, on the one hand, and Greek racial arrogance, on the other hand, which characterized all non-Greeks as barbarians and which rejected their acceptance into the Hellenic cultural community on terms of equality.

Jason, the leader of the Argonauts, was able to accomplish his mission and to recover the Golden Fleece because he was assisted by Medea, the princess of Colchis, who fell in love with him. She saved him from danger and death in this most perilous adventure. She followed him to his distant Hellenic homeland. She bore him two children. For him and his countrymen, nevertheless, she remains the foreigner, the racially unequal. He bears with her for the sake of their children and only until a respectable union with a Greek bride presents itself. Then Medea is cast aside, and he acquiesces in her exile from Corinth, the seat of his anticipated bliss with his new mate. He does not understand why Medea should be so unhappy and so unreconciled to her coming fate, since he is prepared to provide magnanimously for her, and since he will also see to it that his children are well cared for. She, however, will not accept her inferior position and her lonely exile while the man for whom she sacrificed everything revels in a new union. To avenge herself for the inflicted hurt, Medea brings about the death of her rival and of the children she bore to Jason.

How different was the life of Ruth after she too chose to leave her homeland for the foreign soil of her late husband's people! She followed her aging mother-in-law Naomi to Bethlehem. She accepted Naomi's people as her people and Naomi's God as her God. The inhabitants of her adopted homeland, in turn, accepted her as an equal. She was deemed by Boaz, the rich landowner, to be a fitting mate, even though she stemmed from Moab. Ruth and Boaz became the ancestors of King David. Her tale reverberated down the centuries as an example of the equality of all human beings, regardless of their racial origin or of their social position.

Medea survived her tragic ordeal and her exile from Corinth, but her later life was of no interest to the many writers who depicted her before and during her hour of crisis. The most elaborate treatment of Medea in modern literature was the dramatic trilogy *The Golden Fleece* by Franz Grillparzer, Austria's finest dramatist.

Like his predecessors since Euripides, Grillparzer too was confronted with the problem of arousing our sympathy for the murderess and of reconciling us with her revolting deed. He therefore devoted the first play of the trilogy to Colchis, the dark home of the heroine, and showed her in her domineering splendor as princess in a barbarian land. In the second play, he brought her face to face with Jason, soon after this hero's arrival to fetch the Golden Fleece, which her father had obtained through treachery and bloodshed. The Greek leader of the Argonauts saw in her the dazzling sun in a land of gloom and horror. She saw in him a god from some happier clime. She therefore could not successfully resist his impetuous wooing, and for his sake she brought down destruction upon her father, her brother, and her people. The final play of the trilogy depicted the aftermath in Greece. There Medea is no longer the reigning princess, but a helpless foreigner whose sole support is her beloved Jason. He must, however, regard her with different eyes, when he now sees her against a background of Greek culture, and he must chafe under the burden of his liaison with the alien mother of his children. When Medea is banished from Corinth and he is allowed to remain and is even offered the hand of the king's daughter, he may for a moment feel that he ought to share Medea's exile, but he is not likely to persist in this feeling. Too great is the lure of freedom and a new love. Medea, scorned by the cultivated Greeks in spite of her efforts to adjust herself to her new environment, repudiated by her mate in spite of all the sacrifices she made for him, abandoned even by her young children, who, when given the choice, prefer her successor, hounded as a criminal and refused an hospitable refuge—Medea can revert to her original savage nature, can avenge and murder, without wholly forfeiting our sympathy. The trilogy concludes with her bitter, resigned insight: "What is joy on earth—a shadow! What is fame on earth—a dream!"

Ruth, too, ceases to attract the attention of creative writers after her marriage to Boaz. The biblical narrative merely adds that, after her marriage, she gave birth to Obed, who became the father of Jesse, the father of David. Indeed, her story may have been included among the biblical scrolls just because of her relationship to David, the founder of Judea's royal dynasty. Later versions of the idyllic tale continue to center about her loyalty to Naomi and to Naomi's God and people, a loyalty rewarded by a happy marriage. Only a single dramatist in our century, Grillparzer's countryman, Richard Beer-Hofmann, went beyond the biblical conclusion and presented her late in life, when the romantic idealism of her early years had been tempered by the experiences of mature decades and she had become the wise ancestress of generations that turned to her for guidance.

Beer-Hofmann was attracted to Ruth because he saw in her a prefiguration of his own wife, Paula, who also came to him from alien hearths and who was renamed Ruth after she too cast her lot with the Jewish people. In his dramatic masterpiece *Der junge David*, completed in the tragic year of the Nazi ascendancy to power as his proud affirmation of his Jewish fate, he included as a prologue the Book of Ruth almost in its entirety and he painted Ruth's portrait in memorable verses in the first, third, and final acts of the play.

The scene of the drama takes place during the critical days before and after the Battle of Gilboa, which resulted in Saul's defeat by the Philistines and David's coronation as his successor. Ruth, David's great-grandmother, is still alive, an object of reverence and a source of strength to her young descendant, who turns to her for advice in hours of indecision and distress. During her long life, she has witnessed many ups and downs, Israel's victories and defeats, Samuel's judgeship, Saul's elevation to the throne of Israel by popular acclaim, and his replacement in popular affection by David, the glamorous slayer of Goliath and the secretly anointed coming ruler.

In the first scene, Ruth is presented as a legendary figure who is rarely seen by day. Only now and then, when the fruit of the field ripens, does she venture out into the open toward evening and walk alone through the high-standing grain, swathed in white linen that glistens in the fading light like the snow on Mount Hermon. "Folks whisper that the stalks bend aside even before her foot skirts them, that the shy birds remain unafraid near their brood, and that butterflies, tired of winging, rest on her hand. Thus Ruth wanders silently through the blessed fields until the silver sickle of the moon comes up in the pale evening sky."

In the third act, David, on the verge of despair, turns to Ruth for guidance. Earlier, he fled before Saul, found refuge with the Philistine king, Achish of Gath, and swore allegiance to this protector. Now a war has broken out between the Philistines and the Israelites. David, as vassal of a Philistine king, is commanded to join the forces ranged in battle against the Israelites. He is thus faced with a cruel choice. To answer the summons of his liege lord means to join in the slaughter of his own people, whom he is later to rule. Not to answer the summons means to be disloyal to his oath of allegiance, an impossibility for one who demands loyalty of his own followers. In this dilemma, it is Ruth who speaks to him with the wisdom of age and who rouses him from his indecision by calling upon him to listen to the dictates of his heart. He must be faithful to the inner voice within him which registers every deviation from right and wrong and which is the moral seismograph implanted in him, as in every human being, by his divine creator.

In the final act, after the Battle of Gilboa has been fought and lost, and after the defeated remnants of Israel turn to David to assume the crown, he is inclined to refuse the proffered coronation because of a personal tragedy. It is then that Ruth makes her final appearance. She impresses upon David not to surrender to despair in an hour of his own grief. To his anguished outcry "What is to become of me now?" she gives the sage reply: "That which becomes of all of us ultimately—dung of the earth, perhaps a song, but this too fades away." And yet, until our end, we must all continue on our assigned course and live out our fate, no more eternal and no less transitory than the stars above us. An individual chosen for a unique destiny, as David has been, a people chosen to be *am segula*, as the Jewish people has been, may well lament: what is the meaning of our chosenness, what sort of blessing does it confer, what happiness does it bring? Ruth's answer is that beyond all blessings there is the supreme blessing of being a blessing to others. Forgetfulness of self, escape from loneliness and personal tragedy, can best come about by immersion in something beyond self, by being faithful to the universal law that rules clouds, winds, creatures, and constellations, and which manifests itself also as the life-force that courses through us.

Ruth's answer to David is also Beer-Hofmann's answer to his own people in their period of national agony. Chosenness is both a blessing and a burden. Happiness ultimately beams as a byproduct of living in harmony with the universal will, God's will, intuitively felt by us in the innermost layers of our complex being.

Medea and Ruth, in their many literary transformations since antiquity, confirm the basic contrast between the Hellenic, pessimistic, amoral contemplation of life and the Hebraic, optimistic, moral approach. This approach is rooted in faith in a divinely inspired order and in the concept of the Hebraic people as *am segula*. This approach contributed to Jewish survival in the generations when Ruth's descendants ruled over Israel, in the two millennia of Jewish dispersion over the face of the earth, and in our century of the Jewish Holocaust and of the Jewish people's homecoming to its ancestral land.

13

Saul's Tragedy

Saul, the first king of Israel, is the most tragic figure of the biblical heroes. As such, he fascinated painters from Rembrandt to Joseph Israels, musicians from Händel to Honneger, writers from Jean de la Taille, the French Huguenot, Grimmelshausen, the seventeenth-century German novelist, and Pierre du Ryer, the forerunner of Racine, to André Gide, the French symbolist, Richard Beer-Hofmann, the Viennese poet of Jewish Rebirth, and Torahiko Kori, the Japanese dramatist.

No amount of justification for David, his adversary and successor, has been able to rob Saul of human sympathy in all ages. Voltaire, as the outstanding representative of the Age of Enlightenment, depicted him as the innocent victim of religious fanaticism in the polemic drama *Saul*, written in 1763. The supreme master of irony leveled such vitriolic attacks upon the foes of the Jewish king, especially upon the priesthood as personified by Samuel, and was so certain of arousing the resentment of the French clergy by his pointed analogies to contemporary events and institutions, that he feared to acknowledge his authorship of this dramatic satire and therefore had it published as a translation from the English.

In Vittorio Alfieri's *Saul*, Italian classical tragedy reached its climax. Appearing in 1784, this psychological drama experienced a European vogue in English, French, and German adaptations and translations. It concentrated on the final hours of a ruler who had to perish because he could not cooperate with his bravest and wisest subject, David of Bethlehem.

Alfieri's David is a selfless patriot. Though he fled to seek refuge among the Philistines in his hour of mortal danger, he returns to Saul, disregarding all risks, in order to join in the struggle for Israel's survival. The need of his people, and not his own future, is uppermost in his mind. He does not hide in the safety of the forests when Saul and Jonathan go forth to battle at Mount Gilboa.

Noble Jonathan sees in David God's chosen champion, while his father pursues David as a rebel and a traitor. Abner is portrayed as Saul's evil spirit. It is Abner who turns the king's heart against David and fills it with envy of the young hero. As the slayer of Goliath, the gigantic champion of the Philistines, David is the new favorite of Israel's masses and is rewarded with the hand of Michal, the king's daughter.

When Michal and Jonathan join in pleading David's cause before their father, and when David himself arrives to place his fate in the king's hand, then the shroud of darkness and suspicion departs from Saul's soul. He is especially moved when he learns that David has never aspired to the crown and that, at the cave of Engedi, David once found him asleep and spared him from harm. In this climactic scene of reconciliation, Saul even appoints the popular hero as head of the army which is to engage in battle against the resurgent Philistines. But hardly has David departed from the court when suspicion again assails the king, and it is intensified by the whispering of the envious Abner until rage against the possible usurper again takes the upper hand. The returning David is once more able, with the magic of his psalms, to soothe the king's troubled heart and clouded mind, but only for brief moments. When the singer ends his songs with a vision of his swinging the sword of Goliath in the coming battles against Israel's foes, jealousy verging on madness repossesses the distraught monarch, who will brook no younger rival. David is barely saved from Saul's drawn sword.

Thereafter, the deterioration of Saul cannot be arrested. Unable to get David again within his grasp, he vents his rage upon David's protectors and orders the immediate death of Abimelech and the priests of Nob. He himself takes command of Israel's army and changes the well-planned battle strategy upon which David and Abner had earlier agreed. He thus brings about Israel's defeat and seals his own doom and that of his sons. His last words are a recognition of his final loneliness and his readiness to atone in death for his disobedience to the inexorable God of Israel.

In Alfieri's drama, we witness the decay of a strong personality who relied upon his own mightiness and who would not submit to the awesome decrees of a tyrannical God as proclaimed by the prophet Samuel and the priest Abimelech. Though ending in tragic loneliness and self-inflicted death, Saul remains a humane figure, a heroic personality driven to his doom by titanic passions beyond his control.

A generation after Alfieri, Lord Byron too was fascinated by Saul as the superior individual who walked to his doom with head unbowed before divine and human adversaries. In two lyrics of the *Hebrew Melodies,* which appeared in 1816, the English poet poured his own disquieted temperament into the soul of Saul. One of these lyrics dealt with Saul's invocation of the ghost of Samuel on the eve of his last battle, and the other was Saul's defiant song before he entered into this battle.

Byron regarded the scene in the cave of the Witch of Endor, which is depicted in I Samuel 28:7-25, as the finest and most finished ghost scene that ever was written or conceived. He repeatedly referred to it in his verses, as in *Manfred* (II, 2, ll. 175-182), in the Dedication to *Don Juan* (stanza 11), and in the *Age of Bronze* (II, ll. 380-383).

In the poem "Saul," Byron has the Witch call upon the apparition of Samuel to appear. The prophet raises his buried head from his shroud. The king looks into the fixed glassy eyes of the phantom seer and sees in him Death personified. He notices the withered hand, the shrunken and sinewless foot glittering in bony whiteness, and the unbreathing frame. Samuel utters a single word; Saul knows himself to be doomed and falls to earth like a blasted oak. As he lies stretched on the ground, he hears additional fatal words emanating from the prophet's unmoving lips, foretelling that, before the coming day has ended, Saul's limbs will be as cold and bloodless as his own. Crownless, breathless, headless, Saul and the House of Saul will lie in the moldering clay. Samuel's ominous words make the same impact as the handwriting on the wall that predicted Belshazzar's end. Nevertheless, Saul is no weak monarch like Belshazzar. Now that he knows the worst, he does not shrink from it. In the "Song of Saul Before His Last Battle," he calls upon his warriors and chiefs to fight on even if he himself falls. Should they falter or look away from the foe, he asks his armor-bearer to slay him. Royally he lived, and kingly he will meet his end. "Bright is the diadem, boundless the sway, / Or kingly the death, which awaits us today."

The French romantic poet Alphonse de Lamartine completed his lyric drama *Saul* in 1818, two years after Byron's *Hebrew Melodies* was published. Though primarily influenced by Alfieri's classical drama, Lamartine's version was yet impregnated with Byronic melancholy, fatalism, and defiance. Saul remains a rebel against God to the very end, even after the battle against the Philistines is lost and his own dying son implores him to mitigate divine wrath by repentance. No, he will ask no boon of the bloody deity who places snares of evil for men and who is therefore Himself the cause and sharer of the very crimes He punishes. Virtue is but a name, and law is but caprice. God is cruel and vindictive. He enjoys making humans suffer. Through death and absolute cessation of sensations, Saul hopes to be snatched away from God's malignant power.

Friedrich Rückert, the German romantic poet, was no less attracted to the character of Saul than were his English and French romantic predecessors. Though born in 1788, the same year as Byron, it was not until 1843, more than a quarter of a century after the latter's *Hebrew Melodies*, that he published his double-drama, entitled *Saul und David. Ein Drama der heiligen Geschichte*. It covers the entire range of the biblical narrative about Saul, from his rise to his fall, and even includes the coronation of his successor.

Rückert was far more deeply steeped in biblical and oriental lore than were Byron and Lamartine, but defiance of God, which characterized their verses, was unthinkable to him. His first drama, *Sauls Erwählung*, makes no mention of David. It begins with the plea of the elders of Israel that Samuel choose a king to unite the Jewish people, which is split into twelve tribes, and to lead it into battle against hostile neighbors. The play ends with the war against the Ammonites, the Jewish victory at Jabesh-Gilead under the inspired leadership of Saul, the newly chosen king, and his generous treatment of his defeated heathen opponent. Acclaimed by jubilant multitudes, Saul leaves for his festive inauguration at Gilgal.

In Rückert's second drama, which deals with the Saul-David encounter and for which the first play served as a prelude, we witness the deterioration of the powerful ruler, his fall from moral eminence, his loss of popularity. Twenty years have passed since his initial memorable victory, but his hopes for peace with Israel's neighbors have not been realized. The tribesmen of the desert are still raiding Israel from the east, and the Philistines are still encroaching upon Israel's borders from the west. The fickle masses have turned from the aging Saul, and his soul is darkened. Young David, the slayer of Goliath, is now the beloved hero of all Israel and has even won the heart of Saul's son and daughter. Small wonder, therefore, that the king sees in David his chief foe and rival.

Rückert follows the biblical narrative faithfully, perhaps too faithfully. He expands but does not deviate in the slightest from the sacred text. His expansion is no improvement. His attempt to include every aspect of Saul's constant wavering between love and hate for David, his repeated shifting from magnanimity to cruelty, robs the play of dramatic effectiveness. Unlike most earlier versions, Rückert's does not conclude with the tragic death of Saul and Jonathan at Gilboa, but continues on to a happy ending, the coronation of David, thus paralleling the happy ending of the first play, the coronation of Saul. Just as Saul ascended the throne as the anointed of the prophet Samuel and with the endorsement of the popular will, so too David is presented to the people as God's chosen ruler by the prophet Nathan and receives the homage of all twelve tribes. Though jubilation is somewhat marred by Joab's murder of Abner, Saul's most loyal supporter, who came to offer no less loyal support to Saul's successor, it reaches its crest with the proclamation of David that Jerusalem, then still in the hands of the Jebusites, is to become, after its conquest, the eternal capital of his united Hebraic kingdom, and that the Temple of God will be built there as the most sacred shrine of the Jewish people. King Achish of Gath, with whom the pursued and outlawed David once took refuge, offers peace in behalf of the Philistines. King Hiram of Tyre offers timber from Lebanon for the building of the projected Temple. Under such resplendent auspices, David enters upon his reign as God's second anointed ruler of Israel.

The anticlericalism that characterized the versions of Voltaire, Byron, and Lamartine is muted in Rückert's version but again comes to the fore in the versions of the radical writers Karl Gutzkow and Karl Beck, who fought the religious establishment of their generation and the reactionary political regimes of the Holy Alliance.

Gutzkow, the uncrowned head of Jungdeutschland, the literary movement of the radicals between the revolts of 1830 and 1848, made the first biblical monarch the champion of tolerance and freedom in a tragedy of 1839, entitled *König Saul*. Having shortly before served a prison sentence because of his "contemptuous presentation of the religion of the Christian communities," Gutzkow saw a kindred spirit in the unhappy king whose fatal end was caused by his refusal to submit to the insolent demands of the priests led by Samuel. Gutzkow's anticlericalism, which had found its first formulation in his early novel *Mahu Guru*, and which was later to attain even more vigorous expression in the drama *Uriel Acosta* and in the nine-volume prose epic *Der Zauberer von Rom*, gave to his version of the biblical subject a contemporary interest and a political significance far beyond its literary value. His example was followed a year later by his admirer and ally, the Jewish-Bohemian poet Karl Beck, whose drama *Saul* also laid great stress upon the Jewish monarch's nobility of soul.

Saul is, for Beck, the compassionate king who cannot kill

captives or women or children, even if they are Amalekites, Israel's implacable foes. For such behavior, he is rebuked by Samuel, the fanatic prophet. Samuel heaps imprecations upon the very king he had himself anointed and threatens that he will now anoint a more obedient king. Saul bitterly tells him to continue anointing king after king and woe to those who are elevated to royalty. He himself was content to be the guardian of his father's flocks and never aspired to be a king. The purple robe of royalty was imposed upon him. He contrasts Samuel's harsh threats in the name of a merciless God with the beautiful sentiments of a kind God which David, the young harpist, is intoning. Samuel's repudiation leaves the king in a mood of depression. In this mood, he overhears the shouts of the populace hailing David's victory over Goliath. Instead of rejoicing, Saul feels envious and fears that David may soon be in a position to wrest the throne from Jonathan. His innate nobility struggles against the suspicions and nightmares that creep upon him. His heart is good, but his spirit is darkened. When David plays before him, the dark clouds vanish. However, the moment the harpist is out of sight, hatred, rage, incipient madness come to the fore. Hurled hither and thither by conflicting emotions, Saul's personality decays but is never unheroic. He is ripe for death, even before the Battle of Gilboa turns against him and he falls upon his sword.

David is the charismatic personality to whom all Israel turns in hours of peril. He matures under adversity but retains the idealism of his early years. In his last meeting with Jonathan, he prophetically envisages the destiny of his people in its long and renowned journey through history. He foresees its wandering over mountain ranges and dark abysses, across glorious and inglorious centuries. His will be a restless people. The entire world will become its home, but everywhere it will be scorned as homeless. Simple and pure since patriarchal days, it will degenerate under oppression and will become a caricature of a people. Like vermin, its descendants will creep along, despised and worthy of being despised.

This gloomy vision of the Jewish future, which Beck has David outline to Jonathan, is completely at variance with the idealized portrait of the charismatic king which the dramatist projects throughout the play. In these verses, Beck was giving expression to his own *Judenschmerz*, the Jewish pain in his own soul, which also burst forth in his lyrics of this period. He, who wrote glowing poems of yearning for freedom and equality, and who was wooing his German compatriots so ardently, found himself rejected by them because of his Jewish origin. He then turned his anger not against those who spurned his advances but against his own coreligionists, for whose biblical past he felt admiration, and whose present he viewed with contemptuous eyes. Three years after the publication of his drama, he severed his ties with the Jewish community. However, his baptism as a Protestant did not assuage his *Judenschmerz*. He continued to suffer from it to the end of his days. Few remember him nowadays, and those who do, remember him not for his impassioned social and political lyrics nor for his drama but for his "Song of the Blue Danube," to which Johann Strauss composed the music and to which millions have waltzed for more than a century.

As late as 1862, the Swabian lyricist J. G. Fischer, like Beck, still walked in the footsteps of Gutzkow, and in his *Saul*, he too centered the dramatic interest upon the conflict between king and clergy. He too presented Samuel as an intolerant, fanatical high priest, who only reluctantly yields to the clamor of the people for a king. He selects Saul because he expects from him absolute obedience to the priesthood, then the real power in Israel. But when Saul seeks to bring about a reconciliation between Israel and its conquered neighbors by sparing the Amalekite ruler and suggesting mutual trade to replace destructive warfare, Samuel, as the extremist leader of the clergy, slays the unarmed captive, King Agag, with his own hand and thus frustrates possible cooperation between Israelites and Amalekites. It is Samuel who then leads the struggle to undermine Saul's power. It is Samuel who secretly anoints David, seeing in him a more pliant tool of the priesthood. It is Samuel who sends David as harpist to Saul's court and who encourages him to fight against Goliath. It is Samuel and his priestly disciples who are responsible for Saul's deterioration and ultimate tragic end. And yet, when David ascends the throne as Saul's successor, he too soon tries to assert his independence of the priesthood, thus presaging a continuation of the struggle for power between king and clergy.

Even in the twentieth century, the anticlerical tradition begun by Voltaire in his portrait of the first Jewish king and continued by Gutzkow and his followers did not entirely die out. In 1920, the Dutch dramatist L. Knappert published his tragedy *Saul, Koning in Israel*, wherein Saul is presented as a tolerant and sympathetic innovator who is opposed by the fanatical adherents of the old order, symbolized by Samuel and the priests, and wherein David is portrayed as an ambitious youth who enters into an alliance with Samuel's party because he wishes to gain the crown for himself.

Robert Browning's *Saul*, published in fragmentary form in 1845, and in completed form ten years later, is a dramatic monologue spoken and sung by David, who recalls the memorable hour when Abner called upon him, the shepherd lad, to solace with his music the stricken monarch. The aging king, whose brow is bent by constant brooding over the errors he has committed during his reign, needs to be uplifted from despair. Abner hopes that David, God's talented youth, can remove with his melodies the pessimism and melancholy that enshroud Saul.

When David enters the royal tent and announces his arrival, no voice replies. However, in the blackness within the tent, he sees a figure gigantic and even more black. A sunbeam bursting through the roof of the tent reveals the figure to be Saul. When David, the shepherd lad, notes the agony of the monarch, who stands erect, drear and stark, blind and dumb, he begins to play on the harp, first a pastoral melody such as calms his sheep, then tunes that attract other creatures of God, then a song of wine that delights human beings and an elegy that accompanies them on their last journey, then a glad wedding song, and finally a song that Levites intone at God's altar. He pauses, as Saul gradually awakens from his stupor and shudders.

Again David tunes his harp and bursts into an exultant song of the wild joy of being alive and giving full expression to all the heart and the soul and the senses. He sings of the goodness of

Saul's Tragedy

boyhood with its friendships, its wonder, and its hopes. He sings of the triumphs that came to Saul in the prime of manhood, when he grew to the stature of a monarch admired by his people. As David continues his rhapsody of Saul's victories and increasing fame, the king's vacant eyes take on a look of animation and sadness. Then the young harpist reminds his listener of the radiance that his deeds have spread and that will cheer and inspire unborn generations as poets and scribes engrave the story of his deeds and his being. As David touches on the praise he foresees from all men in all times for the statesmanship and the prowess of the ailing king, Saul's face takes on a milder and kinder expression.

David then puts away his harp, and words of love break forth from his heart for the fatherly figure in whom new life is beginning to stream. He sings to the still silent Saul of God's work, in which all is love, yet all is law. He sings of the invisible God whose presence is visible in the star, the stone, the flesh, the soul, and the clod. He sings of the need of imperfect man, God's creature, to submit to the all-perfect Creator and to have faith in Him who bestows life and its gifts, of which love is the ultimate gift. God alone can restore decaying, pain-filled Saul to new harmony, intensified bliss, and grant him in the next world repose and reward for the struggles in this world. "'Tis not what man *Does* which exalts him but what man *Would* do!" The power of loving and being beloved can raise man from sorrow and help him to bear life's heavy burden.

With André Gide's *Saul*, the first attempt is made to interpret the ancient struggle between Saul and David in terms of modern psychology. Written in 1896, while Gide was under the influence of Oscar Wilde, and published two years later, the tragedy seeks to win sympathy for a noble individual conquered and enslaved by moribund desires and sexual aberrations. The French symbolist transfers to Saul the religious and moral conflicts which agitated his own soul, and, anticipating Freud's psychoanalytic findings, he explores with literary equipment the twilight zone of man's complex psychic structure.

Gide's Saul is pathological. His will is paralyzed. He cannot resist his desire for David, even though aware that it is David he must fear most. While the Philistines are threatening war, Saul's main concern is with his own longings rather than with the defense of his endangered kingdom. When his son Jonathan importunes him to prepare for battle, he replies that there are things more important to the soul than the victories of an army. He knows himself to be more a man of desires than of action, and he finds no remedy for his desires other than to satisfy them at any price. Hence, even while the battle rages outside his tent, he admits the demons of lust that knock at his tent. "What am I waiting for? Why do I not get up and act? My will! My will! I call it now like a shipwrecked sailor hailing a ship he sees disappearing in the distance—going—going. I encourage everything against myself" (Act V, scene 4). The heroic biblical king is reduced by Gide to a weak-willed Hamlet who is overwhelmed by demons of desire and who makes not the slightest effort to dislodge them from his soul.

What a contrast between the feeble, helpless, pathological Saul and the titanic, royal personality whose tragic fall forms the main theme of Richard Beer-Hofmann's drama *Der junge David*. The Viennese dramatist completed this play in the eventful year 1933, when the Nazis came to power, and when books by so-called non-Aryan authors were set afire in the public squares of German towns. His drama, the first part of a projected trilogy, embraced the critical days which sealed the doom of Saul and which brought his more fortunate younger rival to the throne. Beer-Hofmann, whose attitude to the Bible, as already revealed in his earlier play *Jaakobs Traum*, was one of reverence and humility, did not wish to enter into competition with the biblical chronicler and was therefore generally silent when the biblical narrator waxed eloquent and was most eloquent when his model did not overawe him with too many details.

The dramatist depicts the disintegration of a powerful personality, the pathetic wreck of a gigantic will, the desolate end of a popular idol. The shy herdsman of the tribe of Benjamin, who once went forth to look for his father's she-asses and found a kingdom, has become a harried ruler who for a quarter of a century has had to bear on his broad shoulders the worries of a stubborn little people wedged in between many hostile neighbors. He has had to fight innumerable battles and to wade in blood. In the process, he has developed into a misanthropic despot, feared but no longer loved.

Saul's face, which shone with pride, strength, and kindness at his coronation, has become clouded in the course of time with melancholy, suspicion, hate, envy, and helpless rage. In the end, this master-builder of Israel, who forged twelve discordant tribes into a strong, united people, has to witness the collapse of his proud structure on the bloody field of Gilboa, a collapse hastened by his break with David and David's followers.

Like Beer-Hofmann, Karl Wolfskehl was ever entranced by the Bible, a source of delight to him during his happy years in Germany, and a source of comfort to him in his sad years of exile in New Zealand. He composed lyrics in the spirit of the Psalms and lyrics on the biblical characters Cain, Lilith, Samson, Moses, and Job. His *Saul* is a poetic drama of the decline of a great personality from the moment he loses faith in himself. In his hour of greatest victory over Amalek, he is repudiated by the aged priest Samuel because he spared Amalek's king and herds. Thereupon his mood becomes darkened. David seeks to dispel with songs the ever gathering gloom about the dejected monarch and to cradle him in happy dreams. But soon such a happy dream turns into a nightmare, in which the king sees himself and his son Jonathan prostrate under the wheels of a war chariot, while a triumphant, crowned young successor passes over them. Seizing his spear, Saul hurls it twice at the singer, who barely escapes death. Inexorably, the king sinks ever further into the shadow of melancholy and proceeds ever more precipitously to his doom. Only in the evening before his final battle does the lonely, dispirited Saul reconcile himself to his tragic fate and hail David as his worthy heir, a glorious ruler who will steer Israel's people to victory over the Philistines after his own expected defeat at their hands. The poetic drama ends with David's lament over the fallen monarch, who has at last found rest from a tempestuous life in the sea of eternal night.

The Nazi avalanche, which drove Wolfskehl from his beloved Germany to distant New Zealand, also uprooted Max Zweig from his native Moravia and brought him in 1938 to a new homeland among his Jewish people. There, on the shores of Tel Aviv, he completed his five-act tragedy *Saul* soon after Israel's declaration of independence, and it was his own feeling of attachment to his ancient ancestral soil that led him to speak out through the voice of the persecuted David: "Better to be the most miserable slave, persecuted, restless, embattled, but with the soil of a homeland under one's feet, than to sit on alien soil as a prince at the table of princes."

Max Zweig's *Saul*, like Wolfskehl's poetic drama, also begins with the monarch's victory over Amalek and the capture of its king, Agag. The magnanimous Saul removes the fetters from his proud royal captive and sets him free. He is, therefore, castigated by Samuel, who demands strict fulfillment of the Lord's commandment to extirpate Amalek from the face of the earth. Samuel's God is solely a God of Justice and knows no mercy. When Saul remains steadfast and refuses Samuel's cruel demand, the enraged prophet kills Agag with his own hand and thunders at Saul that the Lord will now take the kingdom away from him and bestow it upon a worthier and more obedient ruler. After this break with the defiant, truculent Saul, Samuel makes his way to the house of Jesse and anoints David, Jesse's youngest son, as the future royal herdsman of the people of Israel. He then sends David to serve at the court of Saul until such time as the hour of revelation strikes. David, however, is no mere servitor of Samuel's will. He is a compassionate human being. At Saul's court, he comes to know and to feel affection for the complex personality of the harried ruler, whose melancholy he lightens with his songs. This melancholy stems from Saul's conviction that he has acted rightly in exercising mercy and that he has been unjustly dealt with by the revered prophet of God.

All the fury and wrath of the dramatist at the world's spokesmen during the years of the Holocaust find expression in the bitterness of the repudiated Saul, a bitterness verging on despair and madness. David understands the torment within the king's soul. In the climactic scene at the end of the third act, Saul at last becomes aware of David's love and devotion toward him. He offers the succession to the throne to the understanding, young, heroic psalmist and begs him to discover the pretender whom Samuel has anointed. When David reveals that he is the person Samuel has anointed, an elevation unsought and even resisted, Saul feels betrayed by the confidant he trusted most and to whom he opened up fully his innermost thoughts. He hurls his spear at the presumed traitor. When the spear misses its mark, he orders Abner to slay the escaped David. Within the aged king's heart, mistrust and jealousy vie with affection throughout the pursuit, reconciliation, and renewed enmity toward the younger rival. Calm finally descends upon Saul's troubled soul only after he learns of his own impending death in battle when he invokes the shade of Samuel at Endor. "Tomorrow I shall be where there is neither splendor of sun nor darkness, neither the vault of heaven nor the realm of earth, neither youth nor age, neither glory nor the pain of bearing a crown. I shall be where remorse does not sear, where old age does not torment, and where love does not slay. One more brief, noisy day of battle, and thereafter eternal sleep, eternal silence. . . . My land! My earth! Once more to drink the fragrance arising from your blessed fields, to stroke you, my earth, with my hands, before I myself become earth. . . . I was sent to begin the task of liberating my people from bondage. Another will complete it. I was the pioneer, he will continue on the road and reach the goal."

In words such as these do Saul and David voice the beliefs and convictions of Max Zweig, the Central European refugee and Jewish pioneer in the land of Israel during the period of Israel's struggle for independence. No wonder that the first performance of the play was greeted with tremendous applause when the Hebrew version was presented in 1949 in Tel Aviv by the foremost Hebrew theater, Habimah, with Prime Minister David Ben-Gurion and members of the Knesset in the gala audience.

In the same year in which Zweig's drama was staged for the first time, the Yiddish writer David Pinski left for Israel, the land of his heart's desire. There, in the eighth decade of his long life, he experienced a new burst of creative activity. In his drama *Shaul*, published in 1955, the impact of the moral dilemmas posed by the Nazi Holocaust is still evident in Saul's questioning of God's ways with man. Did Israel's first king deserve the fate decreed for him by God's spokesman Samuel? Was not Saul more sinned against than sinning? Samuel, as the prophet of God's will, anoints the peasant Saul as king but also demands of him absolute obedience to God's will. If God ordains that Amalek be destroyed utterly, then Saul must not show mercy even to women, children, and the captured young king, Agag. Saul balks at such cruel demands of the prophet. The sins of Amalek were sins of an earlier generation, that of Moses, for which the later generation of Agag could not be held responsible. If Samuel's God is the Lord of Vengeance, Saul's God is the Lord of Mercy. When Saul insists on listening to the voice of his own conscience and on sparing Agag, Samuel, in religious frenzy, strikes down the unarmed royal prisoner and, in God's name, deposes Saul and anoints David.

The drama portrays how the good king Saul, who began his reign by forgiving his opponents and scoffers, gradually becomes hardened and tyrannical in the course of his tempestuous reign. If God sanctions injustice and the destruction of the innocent, then he, the king, may also drug his conscience and commit injustice. He will not relinquish his throne to the young upstart, the singer David. He orders the death of the priests of Nob, who sheltered David. However, when he learns that Doeg, in executing this command, also slew the women and babes of the priestly city, then he is crushed by the burden of this terrific guilt. He is no Hitler. Basically good, he broods incessantly over the need of terror in order to preserve his throne. "I have committed an injustice," he exclaims, and then adds: "Samuel's injustice toward me drove me to this deed." Thereafter Saul knows that retribution will come, sooner or later. He knows that he is doomed. He goes into battle against the Philistines, a broken man, without hope of surviving.

As in former centuries and as in our own century, the fate of King Saul will continue to stimulate writers to wrestle with moral dilemmas, to probe God's ways with man, to confront the religious establishment and inflexible dogmas with the claims of the individual's conscience, and to explore the ramifications of the conflict between age and youth. The biblical chronicler of the Books of Samuel raised questions which have reverberated and will continue to reverberate down the generations. He touched at eternal problems which, by definition, are problems that cannot be solved short of eternity, but with which the human mind must occupy itself so long as man fulfills his destiny as the sole questioning species on earth.

14

The Love of David and Michal

Michal, daughter of Saul and beloved of David, has come down the ages with radiant and tragic legends clinging to her. Pride and dignity, wisdom and bravery characterize her throughout her life. She dares to oppose her father's will, though this father was the king before whom all Israel stood in awe, and she does not hesitate to rebuke her husband at the height of his popularity, when his conduct appears in her eyes to be unseemly.

It was not Michal but her older sister Merab who was offered as a prize to the slayer of Goliath. If David was not enthusiastic about the offer, it must have been because his heart had already been captivated by her younger sister. His excuse for rejecting Merab is unconvincing. "Who am I and what is my life, or my father's family in Israel, that I should be son-in-law to the king." After all, he was by then the victorious champion whose deed resounded in song, and his father's family was no less distinguished in Judah than was the family of Kish, father of Saul, in Benjamin. Saul had been depressed after his break with Samuel and angered by the greater acclaim accorded the young hero, the victor in a single combat, while his own mighty deeds extending over many years were depreciated. "Saul has slain thousands and David his tens of thousands," sang the maidens. Now he was rebuffed when he was ready to give his older daughter in marriage to David. As father and king, he thereupon used his prerogative and married her off to Adriel the Meholathite. Apparently, Merab was docile while her younger sister was more strong-willed. Though aware of the estrangement between her father and David, Michal set her heart upon gaining Saul's approval of her union with the young man she loved. And she succeeded.

It was not customary for a daughter to chose her own husband. But the love of Michal for David could not be frustrated. The promise that a daughter of Saul would be given to the slayer of Goliath was known throughout the land. If the older daughter was already married, the younger daughter was still available as bride to the champion. Saul would keep his promise, but he hoped he could at the same time get rid of David by asking for a hundred dead Philistines as *mohar*, the bride-gift which a father had a right to claim. Saul felt that it was unlikely that David could fulfill this condition and still survive. But David did achieve the seemingly impossible. He slew two hundred Philistines and thus won Michal as his wife. Saul would have wanted her to be a snare to her husband, but she preferred to be a loyal mate to the man she had chosen and who had chosen her. Saul's hatred and jealousy increased even further, and he planned David's death. Michal risked her father's wrath and her own life by helping David to escape.

Though David became a hunted fugitive and the leader of a band of outlaws, Michal remained faithful to him and retained hope of his ultimate rehabilitation and his return to her. But when word reached the Israelite court that David had taken two new wives, Abigail, the widow of Nabal, and Achinoam of Jezreel, then she no longer opposed her father's dissolution of her marriage and submitted to his choosing Paltiel the son of Laish as a new mate for her.

Michal disappeared from the scene. Her life with Paltiel was apparently not unhappy, although she bore no children to him. According to legendary lore, she busied herself with raising the five children of her sister, who may have died young. The apparent contradiction in the Book of Samuel that Michal was childless until the day of her death and that she had five children is resolved by commentators who state that she regarded her sister's orphaned children as her very own. Michal reemerged from obscurity after Saul and all but one of her brothers had died battling the Philistines. David had meanwhile experienced many changes of fortune. He had found refuge with Achish of Gath and had become a vassal of this Philistine king. After the Battle of Gilboa and the rout of Saul's army, he had returned to his tribe at Hebron and had been crowned king of Judah. In his negotiations with Abner, when wishing to legitimatize a claim to the allegiance also of the other tribes over whom Saul had ruled, he insisted upon the return of Michal to join his harem, despite the fact that she had already reconciled herself to her fate as the wife of Paltiel, a husband who was good to her. Abner was too weak to reject David's demand. Heartbroken at losing Michal, the weeping Paltiel followed her as far as he dared.

The years of separation, however, had taken their toll of David and Michal. The love that had flared so brightly in their young days could no longer be rekindled. David was now a monarch in his own right and had a harem with wives and concubines more attractive than the aging Michal. She felt his coolness toward her and knew that she was a pawn in a political deal rather than a longed-for beloved. She was critical of David's undignified behavior when he waxed ecstatic at a public festival, shouting, dancing, leaping with all his might in front of the ark. At such a moment she despised him in her heart and rebuked him for his shameless exposure before the eyes of all the onlookers. He replied in kind, reminding the proud daughter of Saul that he was now looked up to more than her father had been. Thereafter he would have nothing to do with her.

While David's personality underwent colossal changes, moral deterioration as well as moral elevation, Michal's personality, as depicted in literature until the present day, remained unalterably dignified as well as loyal to her own highest concept of morality. In treating the relationship between Michal and David, contemporary writers always condone her behavior while they are often harsh in judging him. Only writers who limit themselves to the couple's budding love present both in an idealizing light. This emerges from the one-act play by the Yiddish dramatist David Pinski as well as from the sixteen scenes of the English novelist D. H. Lawrence.

Pinski's *Michal* was written by him during the two days of April 11 and 12, 1914, as the first in a series devoted to David's wives. Pinski focuses attention upon the young shepherd who is completely devoted to God. For the glory of God he risks his life in his encounter with Goliath, and not for the sake of the rewards that Saul has promised, great wealth, utmost freedom for the House of Jesse, or even Michal, whom he loves and who has loved him from the moment she first saw him. When he slays Goliath, she waits for him to come to her father and ask for her in marriage. But he does not come. It is true that, when the king offers Merab to the victorious champion, he refuses the elder daughter because of his love for her younger sister. Nevertheless, he still does not press his claim for Michal as his prize. Indeed, he shocks her by telling her that he cannot take her to wife. He dares not accept the reward due him, to become the king's son-in-law, since his deed would then be tarnished. His championing the cause of Israel and the God of Israel against the giant who blasphemed the God and the people of Israel must be as pure in the sight of man as it is in the sight of God. Only the love of God gave him the strength and skill to succeed in his dangerous encounter. If necessary, he will sacrifice his love, even as his life, for God. Michal is too proud to beg for his love and too proud to share it even with God. Her father, angry with the Goliath-toppler who has refused Merab, feels that he no longer owes him anything. He is, however, willing to give Michal to him if he topples a hundred Philistines and brings their heads to him. While consternation sweeps through the king's retinue on hearing of this condition, David accepts the challenge. In his new encounter, he will be fighting for Michal. The strength of Samson courses through his veins as he dashes forth. Though Saul hopes and Jonathan fears that he will never come back, David and Michal are confident that their love will triumph.

D. H. Lawrence, in the sixteen scenes of his play *David*, depicts on a wider canvas the rise of the young shepherd of Bethlehem from anonymity to greatness, but he attributes this rise to David's possessing the qualities of prudence and shrewdness, paramount virtues in the new order. Twilight and doom descend upon the House of Saul because its members lack these virtues, all except Michal, who links her fate to David, the upstart. Though she seems to mock the strange young Bethlehemite who delights her father with his singing and playing, she really seeks by this means to draw his attention toward herself. And she succeeds. He finds her pleasant to think of. He feels her chiding voice to be sweet and her eyes upon him like stars shining through a tree at midnight. She is sad at the thought that her royal father, for political reasons, may marry her off to some old sheikh. She experiences court life as dull and dreary when David is sent back to his native Bethlehem. She wishes she had a charm to force him to return. But he is only permitted to return after Saul has married off to Adriel her older sister Merab. When Saul is made aware of the love of David and Michal, he believes he can retain the loyalty of David, whom he does not really trust, by promising him his younger daughter, a promise he may never have to keep by hedging it with an impossible condition. In an intensely emotional scene by the well of Gilgal, David and Michal express their love for each other, with David adoring her as a gift of God, who is a glowing flame and who loves all that glow, and Michal wishing that she were desired for her own self, without the Lord being put between them. Soon thereafter, both learn of the harsh obstacle that Saul has imposed, that he desires as *mohar* neither sheep nor oxen nor asses but rather a hundred slain Philistines. David is confident that this obstacle too can be overcome, since his love was kindled by God and God will not let him down. David does indeed return with the *mohar*. He marries Michal. He goes on from victory to victory. But he thereby increases Saul's jealousy and dislike until his life is endangered and he is forced to flee, aided by Michal. In the gathering darkness of the House of Saul, she retains her brightness. Her light never falters, nor her love for her outlawed husband.

The play of D. H. Lawrence ends with David's flight to Samuel, with Samuel's prophecy that David's cunning will ultimately win him the throne, and Saul's recognition that he, the lion, is no match for David, the fox. Jonathan will remain with his father to the end, despite the covenant of friendship with David, from whom he parts with the sad words: "I would not see thy new day, David. For thy wisdom is the wisdom of the subtle, and behind thy passion lies prudence. . . . Thy virtue is in thy wit, and thy shrewdness. . . . Take thou the kingdom, and the days to come. In the flame of death where Strength is, I will wait and watch till the day of David at last shall be finished, and wisdom no more be fox-faced, and the blood gets back its flame. Yea, the flame dies not, though the sun's red dies!"

Michal appears only in a single act of *Der junge David* by the Viennese dramatist Richard Beer-Hofmann. Her love for David is unfaltering, even though Saul has selected a new husband for her, the slender, boyish Paltiel. She is pale and tired, filled with remorse for not having opposed her father's will more strenuously, whatever the consequences. Saul vigorously defends his annulment of her first marriage. He has waited for two long years after David's flight and has watched his daughter wasting away, bitter and careworn. But, when word reaches him that David has entered into a new marriage and into an alliance with the Philistines, he feels it is time to make her forget the fugitive, and he finds for her a youthful, handsome, vigorous, new mate. Deeply hurt at her father's words, Michal exclaims: "Was I then a hot mare that you had to seek out a stallion for me?" Saul is made to realize that the loyalty he seeks to impose upon his family and subjects comes to his young rival unsolicited. His rage against David then knows no bounds. Proud Michal and gentle Jonathan may be forced to submit to their imperious father's dictates, but they will never extirpate David from their hearts.

While Beer-Hofmann's play, upon which he worked for many years, was being readied for the stage but could not be performed because of the Nazi takeover of Germany in 1933, the year of its completion, Morris Raphael Cohen, the American philosopher, wrote his *King Saul's Daughter* as a book drama and never intended it to be staged. He composed the thirty-six scenes of its five acts almost in a single sitting in August 1938, after rereading the Books of Samuel and being gripped by Michal's tragic fate. His emphasis is on her later, lonely, unhappy years rather than on her carefree girlhood and her early love for the shepherd of Bethlehem.

Cohen is interested in the interaction between historical movements and personal experience. He follows the biblical portrait of a proud personality who is unbendingly dignified, intellectually resourceful, intense in her affections, and bearing her trials with amazing fortitude. Her travails begin when she is married to her beloved, the popular, national hero, and has to part from him soon thereafter, since he is forced to flee from Saul's wrath. She experiences mortification and humiliation when her father annuls her marriage to the fugitive and compels her to marry Paltiel. In time, however, she becomes reconciled to her fate. Memories of the absent David gradually pale, leaving merely painful scars in her heart. But, after the death of Saul and after bearing five children to Paltiel, she is brought back to David against her will, as if she were an inanimate chattel. For twenty-four years she lives on at David's court, proud and true to her character, while his character deteriorates as he grows older, harsher, more unscrupulous, seeking the comfort of his harem, and unloved by his children. Michal has to endure the pain of seeing David decimate Saul's family, including her own five children, who are handed over to the Gibeonites to be hanged. David justifies his cruel behavior by his need to keep Israel and Judah united and at peace. He is aware that, as the ruler of the united kingdom, he is surrounded by sycophants, ruthless and ambitious men, schemers of all kinds, multitudes of deluded fools. But, if he were to cleanse his court of all these forces that surround a potentate, he would be left with a few simple saints and his kingdom would be fragmented.

In the end, however, David is not too sure that he was justified in his cruelties and that he himself was not a fellow victim of his deeds. As the aged, estranged husband of Michal, he wonders whether he did not make a mistake when he fled from Saul. Perhaps with Michal and Jonathan at his side, he should have faced the suspicious, harassed king, and had he outlasted that storm, his life would have been nobler even in his own eyes. He would have remained David the superb poet, and the kingdom might have been built up with less blood and more wisdom. His final conclusion is that we are all but straws on life's currents, veering somewhat to the right or to the left, but unable to change the deep, mighty, and mysterious currents.

Unlike Morris Raphael Cohen, who follows Michal's career down the years from girlhood to old age, the American poet Mark Van Doren limits himself to a single moment in her life, the moment when she was taken from the weeping Paltiel, who followed her all the bleak way to Bahurim until he was ordered by Abner to turn back. What her own expectations were after her long absence from David is not clear. The poet assumes, however, that she came to scorn the aging monarch and that he, in turn, hated her until her dying day.

Mark Van Doren's poem "Michal" is included in "The People of the Word," a cycle which also contains poems on Abigail and Bathsheba, two other wives of David. Gladys Schmitt, in her long novel *David the King* (1946), also deals with these wives as well as with others, from Achinoam of Jezreel and Maacha of Geshur to Abishag of Shunam, but her chief emphasis is on Michal.

The novelist conjectures that, before David appeared on the scene, Saul had intended Michal to be the wife of Agag, the captured king of Amalek, whose bravery and royal bearing he admired. After Agag is slain by the fanatical Samuel, Michal fears that her father might bestow her hand upon a lord of Moab or Philistia or Phoenicia. But when she falls in love with David at first sight, she assures him that she will oppose all efforts to sell her to any ruler even for the price of ten years of peace in Israel. She will fight for her beloved, even though he is then but the lutist of her melancholy father, and she will win through. Later on, when she has succeeded in gaining her father's consent and becomes David's wife, she discovers that she can never reach down to his heart, which is wrapped up in Jonathan, her brother and his blood-brother. Had David also married her for political reasons, to elevate himself to the House of Saul? She sees herself as always the loser. When Saul, in a fit of madness, throws his javelin at David and misses him, and then seeks to apprehend him and have him killed, she resolutely plans her husband's escape, knowing full well that he will not come back again, not to her, and that her years will be spent in bitterness. Her suspicion has grown to certainty that he has never really loved her as she loves him, that he took her to gain a kingdom. Yet, after he becomes king in the course of years, and has acquired four wives for his royal dwelling in Hebron, she still yearns for him, though she is married to Paltiel. After Saul's death, David did ask that she be returned to him. She wonders whether this request was motivated by political policy rather than by desire for her. He was reaching out his hand to add the tribes of Israel to the tribe of Judah, and he needed her to strengthen his claim. At their reunion, she discovers that, though he does not reciprocate her ardent affection for him, he is kind to her. He remains so until the unforgettable day in the third year of his reign when he brings the ark of God to his capital of Jerusalem, the city he has liberated from the Jebusites. On that day, she, the proud daughter of Saul, sneers at him for dancing naked before the ark, gaped at by the crowd. White with anger, humbled and wounded, he shouts at her that he, and not her father, is now the king of Israel and that she shall never more come into his presence. It is a final break, and it quenches the last spark of her love for him. David goes on to further conquests and increasing loneliness, guilt, atonement, and weariness. Ultimately, he is not sure that the trappings of royal power compensate for the loss of the simple joys that might have been his had he remained in his ancestral home in Bethlehem far from court intrigues, and had he not been estranged from all who were dear to him in his young years.

The political novelist Stefan Heym, in *The King David Report* (1972), lets the aged Michal tell her side of the story about her relations to David, and it does not present this monarch in a pleasant light.

Heym began his literary career in Berlin before the rise of Hitler but fled in 1933 to Prague and two years later to the United States. During the Second World War, his anti-Nazi novel *Hostages* (1942) became a bestseller. After the war, he returned to East Germany but was soon disillusioned with its Communist regime. This disillusionment reached its climax in *The King David Report*, which he wrote both in English and in German. It appeared simultaneously in America and in Western Germany, but its publication in the German Democratic Republic, where he resided, was prohibited because the regime, which had earlier bestowed literary awards upon him, correctly sensed that, under the guise of an historical novel, he was castigating mercilessly developments in the lands behind the Iron Curtain. His novel reexamined the biblical narrative of the reign of David and his successor from a Marxist viewpoint, but his satirical portraits of biblical events resembled too closely contemporary trends in Soviet-dominated lands.

The principal character is the historian Ethan, who is summoned to King Solomon's court in order to write for posterity the history of the kingdom of David and Solomon in such a way as to glorify both of these monarchs and to denigrate their opponents. Unfortunately, the official legendary history, which emerges after Ethan's text is revised by the royal historical commission, is contradicted by too many facts still remembered by survivors of the days of Saul and David. The most knowledgeable of the survivors is Michal.

When Michal, interviewed by the historian, asks him how he intends to portray David, she hears the official legend of her husband as the anointed of God, the conqueror of Israel's many foes, the ancestor of a dynasty destined to rule forever and ever. She interrupts this recital by presenting her own image of David as a poor shepherd who knew how to play on the lute and to compose new melodies. The priests of Bethlehem recognized his talent, educated him in their ideology, and brought him under their spell. When Saul fell sick and medicinal herbs, bleedings, sacrifices, and magic incantations did not help, the physicians prescribed soothing music, and David was brought to the court as a talented musician. He charmed Saul, Jonathan, Michal, and others, for he had many faces, and he was not scrupulous in his lust for power. Michal loved him, but she was for him a means to an end, from their early marriage to his later taking her away from Paltiel. Throughout her ordeals, she remained the proud daughter of Saul. In her quarrel with David, after he danced unrobed in the streets of Jerusalem, she did not mince words, upbraiding him as a lump of ice that chilled those who loved him and prophesying that a time would come when he would yearn for warmth and not find it.

From Michal, the historian learns the real facts of court cabals and royal intrigues, but he can use these facts only in a distorted version in order to construct the desired legends of David as the bravest and most God-fearing of monarchs and Solomon as the wisest of mortals.

Heym's satiric, irreverent biblical novel is in reality a devastating indictment of the postwar, East European, political scene. He manipulates biblical events and characters to make them conform to his vision of contemporary events and characters. His archvillains and hypocrites are David, Solomon, and their coteries of priests, prophets, politicians, and generals. Michal is a victim of the corrupt system but is morally superior to it and retains her haughty grandeur to the end.

The contemporary versions of the love of David and Michal, which embrace the entire course of this love from its tender and glowing beginning to its bitter and tragic conclusion, are basically pessimistic in their final insight. They generally show the aging David discovering that wealth and fame and power are but vanity of vanities, a discovery that his successor Solomon would also arrive at a generation later. The affection of Michal and the friendship of Jonathan, gifts that came to David before his ascent to the throne of Judah and Israel, brought him greater happiness than the dazzling splendor bestowed upon him in his riper years by his numerous conquests and his moral aberrations dictated by ambition and lust. The need to maintain himself on his throne led to his decimation of Saul's family, to the alienation of his own children, and to the contamination of his original pure personality. The romantic halo that the love of Michal wove about him faded with the waning of this love. Michal, however, remained the splendid princess and queen, immaculate in her emotions, courageous in her deeds, and unbendingly imperious in her sad old age.

15

Nabal and Abigail

The biblical tale of Nabal and Abigail rarely aroused the interest of creative writers in former centuries, and only a few writers in our century have attempted imaginative reinterpretations of this strange episode which occurred when David sought refuge from Saul's pursuers in the Wilderness of Paran. Is it because the biblical narrative is so unusually detailed and picturesque that writers despaired of vying with the original text? Or is it because they could not find anything heroic in Nabal, the rich, coarse, mediocre, and yet conceited sheepbreeder, whose very name branded him a fool? Or is it because they could not sympathize with Abigail, one of the wisest and most beautiful biblical women, in her subservience and fidelity to her pompous, unloved husband, whose worthlessness she recognized and yet for whose welfare she risked her life and good repute?

It was on the eve of the First World War that the German novelist Arnold Zweig, who was then known primarily as the narrator of the *Novellen um Claudia*, published his three-act tragedy *Abigail und Nabal* (1913), and that the Yiddish novelist David Pinski completed his one-act drama *Abigail* (1914). The American poet Mark Van Doren's poetic portrait of Abigail did not appear until half a century later.

The original source of the story is found in the twenty-fifth chapter of the First Book of Samuel. The outlawed David, who is in great straits while hiding in the desert, sends ten young men to pay his respects to the wealthy Nabal during the sheepshearing season. David's followers have helped Nabal's shepherds to guard the large flock and to ward off marauders. Now he is in need of provisions for his men, and he hopes that Nabal will be generous in rewarding his services. Nabal refuses his request and adds insult to injury by calling David a servant, one of many who have broken away from their masters, a servant who does not deserve bread, meat, or water. David is furious at Nabal's ingratitude and orders four hundred of his followers to gird for battle. He vows to avenge himself by slaying every one of Nabal's men. When Abigail learns of her husband's rude behavior, she decides to ward off the mortal danger threatening him and his household. Without his knowledge, she quickly assembles provisions and sets out to appease David. On meeting the aggrieved leader, she blames herself for not having been aware of his just request and asks him to pardon her husband's foolishness. Her speech is a masterpiece of cunning flattery and an appeal to David's better nature. He accepts her gifts and grants her plea to spare Nabal's household. When she returns to her husband at night, she finds him drunk at a feast. She waits until the morning, when he has sobered up, and then tells him of what she has done. He gets so excited at her disobedient behavior that he suffers a stroke and dies ten days later. When David hears that Nabal is dead, he sends for Abigail to be his wife, and she humbly agrees.

Arnold Zweig, who undertook to dramatize this narrative, could not use as a principal character a Nabal who was merely a fool and completely worthless. Nabal must have possessed qualities of greatness if he succeeded in retaining the loyalty of the beautiful and wise Abigail. He must have been a strong personality if he could treat David's delegation with so much contempt, though aware of David's reputation as the slayer of Goliath. Hence, Zweig projected him as a feudal lord, an adherent of Saul and a possible successor of this monarch to the throne of Israel. Nabal is cold and imperious. He brooks no opposition. He does not need the assistance of the rebel David to protect his sheep, and he will not pay for the unsolicited protection. As a descendant of the mighty Caleb, he does not need to woo the youngest son of Jesse and will not pay tribute to him.

Nabal is an aesthete and an epicurean. In his youth, his father and the prophet Samuel called him a useless person, and he is still happy in being useless, enjoying the good things of life, and contemplating the stars at night. He does not thirst for power beyond what he wields in his own household. He has observed what power does to people, how those who grasp for it are never sated but become arrogant, blinded, distraught. Saul was happy as a guardian of sheep, but his heart became darkened when he accepted the crown offered him by Samuel. Nabal holds David to be foolish in aspiring to the throne. He himself has no such aspiration. Were Saul to offer him the royal succession, he would hesitate to accept it. He likes the indolent life. He is content to let his administrator manage the large estate while he himself makes merry with wine and women and enjoys the products of his servants' toil.

Abigail is one of Nabal's acquisitions. She grew up in poor circumstances. Her father and brothers were laborers. The girls around her, who were richer, had no difficulty in finding husbands, and when she visited them, she wept at night on her lonely couch because of the passing, wasted years. When Nabal, who had a reputation as a wealthy and very wise landowner, asked for her hand in marriage, she looked forward to a life of happiness not only during passionate nights but also as his helpmate, his inspirer, his comrade who would take loneliness from him, for he too was without a friend. But he continues to use her as a thing, a decoration, a bit of jewelry to hang about his life, while she yearns for a human being with whom to share inmost thoughts and feelings. At night he devours her and she finds him irresistible, but during the day she hates him and even comes to hate herself for her weakness. She is his prisoner, his slave, and not the partner of his plans and the confidante of his wisdom. And yet, when he offers to divorce her, she dreads returning to her uncouth father and her brothers who look down upon her. She drags on her years and tends to Nabal's household, while her dreams of meaningful, great deeds recede ever further.

The hour for a deed of tremendous courage comes when she learns that the infuriated outlaw and pretender to Saul's throne has threatened to destroy all of Nabal's men because of Nabal's ingratitude and insults. Though it is unheard of that a married woman, who never leaves her home unveiled and without her husband's permission, should make her way at night to the camp of a stranger, she dares to take such a step in order to prevent David's carrying out his threat. Her beauty and eloquence have a tremendous effect upon him. His hate-filled heart thaws. She convinces him that his vengeance, though justified, will defile him, and that the memory of his massacre, if carried out, will persist to haunt him ever thereafter.

When David learns that she has come of her own free will, unsent by her husband, with whom she has little in common—indeed, that she is protecting her mate, even though her initial love has turned to hate—he offers to put an end to her pain, loneliness, and fettered existence, to shelter her with his love and understanding. She is terrified at his offer, and he finds her reaction incomprehensible. He asks her: "Where did you get the courage to come to me, where your confidence in me, where the magic of your voice and the spell that emanates from you? A person tortures you and you undertake to save him. You don't love him and yet you risk your life for him. Maybe you even hate him and yet you flare up in anger at me when I speak of liberating you from him, from a husband's house which you confess to be shunning. I don't understand you. Why, tell me, did you come to me?"

When she reveals ever deeper layers of her soul that impelled her to her deed, David too opens up the innermost caverns of his heart. He makes her aware of his basic loneliness and his longing for someone to share with him his burden and his spirit's suffering, someone to whom he can confide without reserve the titanic plans that occupy him throughout his days and nights. In Abigail, he has at last found the queen of his heart. Each of them walked hitherto on lonely paths, and now these paths have converged and they can share misery and greatness together. Her answer is: too late, too late. "Had God brought me to you earlier, I would have brought you peace. I would have been of use to you. By now, I have been broken by Nabal. The fragments of me show his mark. I am tired and old—what should you do with me, you who glow with youth and are about to make the leap for a kingdom?" Once she was a seedling that grew ever taller and higher, but inexplicable fate took hold of her and bent her backward until she could no longer grow upward. She has been transplanted into Nabal's garden, and she will always remain his wife, even if her thoughts stray elsewhere.

When David, nevertheless, seeks to embrace her, and she for a moment feels herself weakening under his spell, she opens her eyes and sees in his flaming eyes a sensuality resembling Nabal's. She flees in horror back to her husband.

Nabal meanwhile has been visited by Abner and a disguised figure that he recognizes as Saul. The tired monarch, disappointed in Jonathan, who is prepared to renounce his own claim to the throne in favor of David, offers the succession to Nabal, the Judean patrician. He then learns that the latter prefers his present life of contemplation under the stars and his freedom from responsibilities to a more strenuous life of action, struggle, domination, and destruction, in the full glare of the sun. He would rather remain the undisputed lord of his household than bear the worries of numerous subjects. However, immediately after Saul departs to continue the pursuit of David, Nabal learns from Abigail that he is not even the undisputed lord of his own wife, the creature he formed for his own bodily pleasure and discarded when she wanted a share of his soul. Perhaps there were husbands who could share with woman body and soul, dreams, longings, insights. He could not. His soul was his unique treasure, and his alone. He would always remain what he was, suave, cool, sure of himself, unshattered in his equanimity, a true sage. But then this sage learns that neither he nor any husband can prevent dreams and longings from arising in the caverns of a woman's heart. Abigail tells him of her encounter with David during the preceding hours of the night. His whole carefully contrived *Weltanschauung* collapses about him, and he is ripe for death. Abigail, however, is now free to enter upon a rejuvenated life with David.

David Pinski's *Abigail* is the second of five playlets in the series *King David and His Wives*. These playlets trace the changes in

David's personality as mirrored in his changing attitudes toward the women who meant most to him. His first wife was Michal, the daughter of Saul. He won her in his young days when he championed God's cause against the Philistines. Then his love was pure. He was even ready to renounce it, if necessary, so that all might realize that when he confronted Goliath, he fought solely for God and God's people, and not for any reward, be it the king's daughter or the king's wealth.

In the playlet *Abigail*, David is maturer. Michal was given to him and then taken from him by her father's command. The former carefree harpist at Saul's court is now the hunted leader of exhausted, hungry men in the wilderness of Paran. He is forced to plead humbly for provisions from the wealthy and evil Nabal. When his plea is turned down, he is prepared to kill in order to feed his followers and to avenge himself on Nabal for the insulting refusal. But when Abigail comes to him, her beauty makes him forget his resolve. The hunger of his men is stilled with the provisions she has brought, but his own hunger can be stilled only by her. She, however, insists on remaining faithful to her husband, though he is wicked and hateful to her. To be unfaithful would mean to break God's commandment, which a moral person ought not to do.

David is entranced by her looks and goodness. He is upset that a scoundrel like Nabal should have such a precious jewel as a wife. Nevertheless, he too will not go against the Lord's commandment. He treats Abigail honorably and is prepared to let her return to her home. But at this moment Nabal bursts upon the scene in search of his wife. He reviles David's men as thieves, beggars, hungry dogs, locusts on the field of others, and he abuses David himself as a seducer, wife-chaser, and coward. When Abigail seeks to calm the infuriated Nabal and defends her own action as the desperate effort of a dutiful wife to save her husband from death, and when David's men taunt Nabal with his food that they are now enjoying, he collapses in a rage. His death is unmourned. David praises God for punishing the wickedness of Nabal and delivering Abigail from bondage to an unworthy mate. He asks her to be his wife, and he reads her answer in her eyes even before she drops on her knees before him in humble submission to his will.

The five-act play *Abigail* (1924) by the American dramatist Grace Jewett Austin versified the biblical narrative but added no new insights.

The American poet Mark Van Doren, in his lyric *Abigail*, follows the biblical narrative faithfully but adds a touch of irony, since he is writing in the irreligious generation between the two world wars. The cunning Abigail meets the bandit chieftain David in a wild pass of the mountains. She reveals her sagacity by arguing that her husband, in refusing the request of David's envoys, did not do so out of malice but because he was a fool, as his name clearly indicated, and that, by sparing him, David would save himself from blood-guilt. When David, who is sensitive to beauty, looks at her beauty, he heeds her plea, and he even magnanimously lets her return to her husband unharmed. She, however, has felt the impact of David's loveliness, and when she gets back to her husband and finds him drunk, she tells him everything. Then his spirit sinks in him like a stone, and he does not survive beyond ten days. When David gets the news that Nabal is dead, he sends messengers to tell Abigail that he wants her as his wife. She is ready and "married him forever, and forgot.—Or did you, Abigail, that first one's fall?"

An ironic tone also pervades Itzik Manger's lyric *Abigail* (1935). The Yiddish poet attains original effects by letting his biblical characters think, feel, behave, and misbehave as they might have if they had grown up in an Eastern European Jewish community still steeped in ancient traditions, and if their personalities were shaped in townlets that had just begun to feel the refreshing breath of modern enlightenment.

Manger's Abigail sits in her little room dressed in yellow, silken pajamas and with a hyacinth in her hair. The week of mourning for her late husband Nabal is just over, and she longs, during the warm summer night, to experience the finale of the biblical romance assigned to her in the First Book of Samuel. Free of marital ties, she is ready to answer the summons of David, who is waiting for her in a cave, his hiding place. In marrying him, all her dreams will come true, all her secret longings will be fulfilled. Her eyes are dim with tears as she prepares to play out her biblical role to its happy ending.

The Hebrew novelist Moshe Shamir, in his novel *David's Stranger* (1964), treats the Nabal-Abigail theme as but a minor episode in the harried life of David, while concentrating attention on the Bathsheba theme. He does, however, draw a parallel between Nabal's folly and David's folly.

The narrative encompasses the last days of Uriah, the husband of Bathsheba, after his arrival in Joab's camp, unwittingly bearing the message of his own doom. In recording the story of his early years with David, the faithful Uriah recalls their visit to the wealthy landowner Nabal the Carmelite, who welcomed them with a feast of roast lamb. The feast was interrupted by a grief-stricken vassal, who complained that his one and only ewe lamb had been taken from him and slaughtered for the banquet. David reacted angrily: "By God, Nabal, if I were not your guest, I would not stay my sword. A man who does such a deed deserves to die!" This cruel deed, as the prophet Nathan was later to point out, parallels David's own deed in taking to himself Uriah's beloved wife, even while this faithful follower was risking his life at the battlefront.

In the dramatic encounter between David and Abigail, Shamir stresses her superiority to David's other wives. In those days, women were not the doers and the thinkers and the fighters. They were expected to be humble and modest. But Abigail is different, a woman of action, wise, brave, and magnificent. She asks no man's permission for her behavior and seeks no man's blessing. She alone, by her sharp intelligence, saves Nabal and his household from David's vengeance and, after Nabal's death, rises to become David's queen.

The idyllic biblical tale of Abigail is of questionable morality. It is not as clearly immoral as the tale of David's later wife Bathsheba, a wicked deed of lust which involved him in sin and guilt and afterwards in remorse, atonement, and much suffering. On the other hand, it was not easy, throughout the many centuries when religious establishments had a dominant hold upon human minds, for commentators and imaginative writers to justify a wife's independent decision to act contrary to her husband's will and to set out upon a perilous adventure in hostile territory in order to parley with an infuriated outlaw, even though this outlaw turned out to be a Robin Hood type. It was far easier for a twentieth-century poet or dramatist, after the double standard of morality in the relationships between man and woman was largely discarded, to exalt the behavior of Abigail as noble, self-sacrificing, heroic. Such exaltation was implicit in the biblical narrative, and recent writers were therefore not contradicting the original text when they undertook an imaginative retelling of their biblical source in the spirit of our century, stressing the beauty, wisdom, purity, and fascination of the independently minded woman who defied convention. Abigail, wife of Nabal, and later of David, thus became the symbol of the brave woman who dared mightily, risked tragedy, and won through.

16

Noble Jonathan

The First Book of Samuel is dominated by the tragic figure of Saul. In the earlier chapters, the book reaches a climax in the confrontation between Saul and Samuel, and in the later chapters, it centers about the enmity of Saul toward David. Both of these conflicts have stirred the imagination of sages and creative writers.

None of these three principal figures are flawless. Samuel's unyielding fanaticism, his cruelty toward the royal prisoner Agag, his unforgiving attitude toward his own protege Saul do not endear him to poets and dramatists. In plays by Voltaire and by Karl Gutzkow, he becomes the hated symbol of religious establishments against which they aim their literary barbs. Saul's deteriorating from his early magnificent stature, when he towers above his contemporaries physically and spiritually, his succumbing to alternating states of depression, schizophrenia, and megalomania, his relentless persecution of David, which contributes to his own final doom, arouse pity and awe but do not gain for him love or admiration on the part of later commentators and interpreters. David too suffers from moral frailties. He reaches an abyss of immoral behavior in the Uriah-Bathsheba episode and has to experience intense suffering before he emerges as the chastened forebear of a royal dynasty whose final offspring will be the Messiah.

Noble Jonathan

Alongside the three major figures in the First Book of Samuel—titanic personalities who reveal character deficiencies—there appears a single splendid character whose nobility of soul is untarnished and whose tragic fate is undeserved. He is Jonathan, the firstborn of Saul and the faithful friend of David.

Jonathan is depicted by the biblical chronicler as gentle and brave, pure and kind, swift as an eagle and strong as a lion, devoted to his father even amidst disagreements, true to his friend even at the cost of his own claim to the throne, resourceful in snatching victory out of the jaws of defeat and, at a later time, not shrinking from death on the battlefield at the side of his father when the odds are overwhelming. Nevertheless, though many legends have grown up about his father and his friend, there are none that center about him. Impeccable Jonathan pales beside Saul and David. Always he stands in their shadow. His dilemma, torn between filial piety and altruistic friendship, does not attract as much notice as does Saul's dilemma, when torn between obedience to God's implacable command, as voiced by the prophet Samuel, and obedience to the dictates of his heart, which stir him to be compassionate and magnanimous toward his helpless captive Agag, or as does David's dilemma, when he, the anointed of his people but also the vassal of the Philistine monarch Achish of Gath, his people's foe, has to choose between his conflicting loyalties during the renewed Philistine war against Israel.

Saul does not solve his dilemma satisfactorily, and David skirts around his dilemma. Saul obeys his heart and is condemned as faithless to God. David is spared a final decision, which would have necessitated his being faithless either to the Philistine king to whom he has sworn allegiance or to his people, against whom he, as a Philistine vassal, would have had to enter into battle. Jonathan alone faces his dilemma resolutely and emerges purehearted and nobleminded. He succeeds in remaining loyal to his father in all of the latter's vacillating moods and loyal to his friend David, his father's rival for the throne. In his undeviating, disinterested devotion to David, he, the heir-apparent, has nothing to gain personally and a crown to forfeit.

Jonathan's first entry upon the stage of Jewish history is as the bold warrior in the struggle against the invading Philistines, and it is his daring which brings about the victory at Geba. When the Philistines thereafter mobilize thirty thousand warriors, and when Saul's troops then begin to melt away and are soon reduced from three thousand fighting men to a mere six hundred, it is again Jonathan who turns the tide of battle at Michmas.

Jonathan's last appearance is at the side of his father in the Battle of Gilboa, faithful even unto his final hour. He was lovely and pleasant in his life, and in his death he was not separated from his father.

At the same time, Jonathan is unswerving in his friendship for David. He intercedes for David when Saul, overcome by jealousy at the young shepherd's increasing popularity, seeks to destroy him. Jonathan risks his father's displeasure, an intervention which almost costs him his own life. He warns David to stay away from court. He gives up his own claim to the throne and is prepared to accept a lesser role as second to David.

This princely figure, this pure personality, this chivalrous knight, this unblemished friend has not stirred the imagination of poets, painters, or musicians to the same extent as have the more sinful or more criminal characters. Not until the twentieth century did he find a dramatist who did full justice to him. In 1933, the year of Hitler's ascent to power, Richard Beer-Hofmann completed *Der junge David*, as the first part of a projected dramatic trilogy, and in this masterpiece he assigned a magnificent scene to Jonathan, in whom he mirrored himself, his own spiritual immaculateness, his own traits of proud dignity and wise humility, and, above all, his own loyalty to the Jewish people to whom he owed loyalty.

Beer-Hofmann's Jonathan is in many ways a reincarnation of young Jacob, the principal character of the dramatic mystery *Jaakobs Traum*, completed in 1915 as a prologue to the trilogy centering about David. In Jacob the poet incorporated his own dreams, desires, and ideals. Jacob is ever obedient to his inner voice that bids him to remain true to the fate assigned to him and to bear it amidst all tribulations, not as a yoke but as a crown.

Jonathan too accepts his fate, including its tragic aspects, without quarreling with his Maker.

Beer-Hofmann avoids all references to the romantic final meeting between Jonathan and David, not only because the biblical text is most eloquent in portraying this meeting and the dramatist did not want to enter into competition with the biblical narrator, but also because drama, as a literary art, deals primarily with confrontations between opposing viewpoints, and there are no basic conflicts or even minor differences marring the relationship between the two friends. The Bible does, however, point to a confrontation between Jonathan and Saul when the former intercedes for David and arouses his father's wrath to such a high pitch that Saul hurls his spear at his own son. This confrontation is presented with such brevity that the Viennese Jewish dramatist, whose attitude toward the holy text was always one of great reverence, felt that it would not be impious to go into greater detail.

In Beer-Hofmann's play, Achinoam, wife of Saul and mother of Jonathan, warns her son against interceding for David during Saul's disturbed frame of mind. Normally, Jonathan would have agreed with her. He certainly would have preferred not to beard his father. However, when Saul, expecting a new incursion of the Philistines into the kingdom, wants first to assure himself that the followers of David will not seize the opportunity to join his enemies, and he, therefore, issues a command to seize all of David's kin as hostages, then Jonathan can no longer remain silent. He pleads for a mitigation of his father's hatred, since hate destroys the hater more than the hated. He urges a reconciliation with David in this hour of national peril. He foresees a horrible catastrophe looming ahead unless there is a cessation of civil strife. He tries to move his father's heart by narrating a recent dream in which he foresaw his own little son Meribaal (Mephibosheth) grown up and seated at the royal table (as in II Samuel 9:10-13), with David standing before him, bowed by the weight of suffering, his eyes dripping tears. Saul's bitter reaction is that what Jonathan saw in the dream was indeed nothing more than a dream. Reality points in a different direction. David has apparently become the chief obsession of Jonathan. The fact that he appeared in Jonathan's dream is but additional evidence that he is dominating Jonathan's thoughts and visions by night as well as by day. However, having gotten the disturbed monarch to listen patiently to his dream, Jonathan ventures going a step further and suggests that perhaps an understanding can be reached with David by realistically accepting the political situation and by ceding to the latter the three southern tribes of Judah, Simeon, and Dan. Even if Saul cannot forget what transpired in the past, recriminations must cease in the interest of all the tribes. David has already been anointed with the crown of Judah, the mighty tribe which will never tolerate being subordinate to Benjamin. The other two southern tribes are allied to Judah. Let Saul content himself with sovereignty over the remaining nine tribes. For a moment Jonathan makes a deep impact upon Saul's troubled soul, but only for a moment. When Jonathan, continuing to plead for reconciliation, reveals that he has already sent messengers with overtures to David, then Saul suspects betrayal in his own house and breaks out in tremendous rage, a rage before which his entire family quails. In this uncontrollable mood, he now modifies his former command. He orders that David's kin are not merely to be seized as hostages, they are to be put to death wherever found. Jonathan is aghast at Saul's outburst, but he continues to stand at his father's side. At the same time, as we know from the biblical text, he will manage to warn David of the threatening danger.

In the fourth act of Beer-Hofmann's drama, the moment that David is released from his obligation to fight on the side of the Philistines who distrust him, his first reaction is to send messengers to Jonathan that he intends to link his troops to those of the House of Saul, even if this means subordinating himself to the monarch's command and risking the abandonment of his own royal ambitions. Whatever the faults of David, he too remains ever loyal to his troth with his friend Jonathan. But already it is too late. The battle at Gilboa is fought and lost before David and his men can get to the front.

Although Jonathan does not appear in the later acts of the play, we learn of his death in battle, faithful to his father to the very end, even as he kept his faith with David.

Saul and David are the two powerful adversaries in Beer-Hofmann's play, as in the biblical narrative. Jonathan, who is caught up in their struggle, emerges as the innocent victim of their rivalry. Though he fails in his efforts to reconcile them, his sweet, radiant character remains untarnished. He is truly a noble personality in life and in death.

If painters and composers, poets, novelists, and dramatists, with the exception of Beer-Hofmann, do not display any great interest in him, it is because saintly personalities do not lend themselves as easily to artistic presentation, and apparently do not normally move emotions as deeply, as characters who sin grandly, who have to work their way through error to clarity, and who have to pay by intense suffering the penalty for their moral aberrations.

17

Abishag the Shunammite

Abishag the Shunammite makes her appearance at the opening of the First Book of Kings as the last bed-companion of King David. The aged monarch, who cannot become warm, even when quilted, is advised that if a beautiful, young virgin were to lie in his bosom, her heat would be conveyed to him and he would then feel warm. He agrees to this medical prescription. A search is then undertaken throughout the territory of Israel for the fairest maiden. Abishag is found in the village of Shunam and is brought to Jerusalem to attend upon the king.

The biblical text emphasizes that, though Abishag ministered to David's needs, he had no intimacy with her. When Solomon ascends the throne after David's death, his older brother Adonijah approaches Bathsheba, the mother of Solomon, and asks her to intercede with her son to let him have the pure maiden as wife. This request angers Solomon to such an extent that he has Adonijah put to death.

Because of the phonetic similarity of the Shunammite to the Shulammite who is extolled in the Song of Songs, creative writers were tempted to identify the two and to explain Solomon's wrath at Adonijah's request as prompted by his own love for the maiden, even though this explanation runs counter to the biblical one that Solomon feared that his older brother might presume to claim the throne as well as the immaculate young companion of David.

It was not until the early twentieth century that Abishag attracted wide attention among secular writers. In earlier centuries, religious writers treated her as a mere minor figure in the struggle for the succession to David's throne. In the drama *Adonias* (1661) by Joost van den Vondel, the greatest Dutch writer of biblical plays, she tries to save Solomon's brother from death and fails.

At the opening of the twentieth century, however, Abishag loomed into prominence. The German lyricist Agnes Miegel, who almost never touched on biblical themes, devoted her ballad "Abisag von Sunem" (1901) to this pure maiden, and the more illustrious poet Rainer Maria Rilke included two lyrics about her in his *Neue Gedichte* of 1907.

Miegel's ballad consists of eight quatrains that convey the thoughts of Abishag. She has been brought to the king to be at his beck and call. She entertains him with her pastoral melodies, and he, who had himself once been a herdsman, is moved to tears and is lulled to sleep. She covers him at night with her hair, she strokes his thin, white curls, she warms him with her breast. But she hates him with a fierce hatred and shudders at his praise. Her hot blood yearns for his red-haired son Adonijah, who is now more fit to wear Israel's crown and whom she would exult to embrace.

Rilke's two lyrics are also monologues. The first of them concentrates attention on the unripe shepherdess, and the second on the overripe king. In Abishag's monologue, she is depicted as lying for long hours on the king, shy and a bit afraid, her childlike arms tied by his servants around his withering body. Longing is in her and about her, but not for the old man. She hears the cry of the owl, she feels the trembling of the stars, she smells the fragrance of the royal chamber, she follows with her glance every movement of the curtain. But still she has to hold on to the aged monarch. Virginal and light as a spirit, she arches above him and senses his royal coldness.

Rilke's second monologue gives us an insight into the king's mind. Throughout the empty day, he sits and broods on deeds done, on passions spent, and on his favorite dog. But at night, when Abishag arches above him, his formerly agitated life lies exhausted and desolate beneath her quiet breasts. As a connoisseur of women, he gazes upon her immobile, unkissed mouth and discerns her feeling of indifference toward him. Then a chill overcomes him, and he shivers as his life ebbs away.

Abishag is the central figure in the drama *König Salomo* (1915) by Ernst Hardt and in *Abisag von Sunem*, a less important drama of the same year, by the Sudeten German novelist and playwright Mirko Jelusich, who became the director of Vienna's famed Burgtheater after the Nazis seized power in Austria.

Hardt was at the height of his fame after the success of his medieval drama *Tantris der Narr* (1907). He continued to enjoy popularity with his other plays on German subjects. However, when he completed his only biblical play on the eve of the First World War, and it experienced its première performance in Berlin on September 11, 1915, it found little favor. After the war, he continued to wield considerable influence as a theater director, but with the rise to power of the Nazis, he was removed from public activities and imprisoned. His fame faded, and his works have since remained unpublished and are now rarely read.

In Hardt's play, Abishag is a far more sympathetic character than David, Adonijah, or Solomon, all three of whom seek to possess her and fail. David is a pathetic, helpless, remorse-ridden figure. Jerusalem lies prostrate, stricken by a devastating plague, while his sons maneuver to succeed him. Adonijah is more domineering than Solomon, but the latter is wiser and more unscrupulous. Mephibosheth, the lame son of Jonathan and the sole survivor of the House of Saul, has been spared from the gallows, a fate decreed by David for seven other descendants of Saul, because of the king's remembrance of Jonathan's friendship. But the hatred of Mephibosheth for the usurper of Saul's throne leads him to espouse the cause of Adonijah, who is being egged on by Joab and Abiathar to rebel against the ailing monarch.

When Adonijah catches sight of the lovely Abishag, he is distracted from his imminent rebellion and thinks primarily of possessing her. As a spoiled prince to whom nothing has been denied, he wants her body to satisfy his lust and pays no heed when she rejects his overtures. She has fallen in love with the eighteen-year-old Solomon, and when both brothers contend for her, the dispute is brought before their father. The enfeebled king denies her to both of his sons and wants her for himself. Adonijah flares up. He threatens to revolt, even as did Absalom earlier, if David keeps Abishag from him: "I want this maiden. I am young and you are old. You have no right to her youth. Why do you take from me what I desire?" When David insists on being warmed by Abishag, Adonijah does indeed raise the banner of revolt. Solomon, on the other hand, is willing to renounce his own love for the fair maiden in order to please his aged sire and to be rewarded with the throne. The dying David's last words, as he holds Abishag in his embrace, are a curse on whosoever lays hands on his virginal widow after him. Solomon ascends the throne and would have spared Adonijah's life if the latter had not persisted in desiring Abishag, despite David's curse.

At the end, Abishag does not want to live on after her tragic experiences of having been frozen in the arms of David, of having been renounced by her beloved Solomon, and of having been the cause of Adonijah's death. Solomon, who buries her, will console himself with a harem of a thousand wives taken from the various nations about him.

By belittling the three rivals who desire Abishag, the dramatist lets her radiance emerge more brilliantly as the personification of youth and spring. She alone is selfless in her affection but is treated as a means to an end by the old king and his ambitious sons.

Stefan Zweig, who admired the play, wrote to Hardt on October 21, 1915, that he found the portrait of Solomon too noble, too Germanic. Zweig voiced the opinion that the dramatist understood Germanic characters, with their purity and nobility, far better than oriental-mythical ones. "The Jewish world of the Old Testament is one of hatred, power, sagacity, and sensuality. Morality is foreign to it save in the form of the rigid priestly law. The impulse toward purity and catharsis is unknown to it" (*Briefe an Ernst Hardt*, ed. by Jochen Meyer, 1975, p. 94). Alas, Stefan

Zweig, in his last years, which ended in flight from the Nazis and suicide in distant Brazil, must have regretted earlier pronouncements about superior Germanic purity and nobility such as this generalization.

In the same year, 1915, in which Hardt's drama was first published and staged, the Yiddish novelist and playwright David Pinski completed *Abishag*, the last of his five playlets on *King David and His Wives*. The first four had shown the gradual decline in David's moral stature, as power corrupted him, and as his harem of eighteen wives and ten concubines debilitated him. Unable to arrest the ravages of age, he still wanted passion to flare around him. In his seventieth year, however, he felt coldness creeping upon him.

In the last playlet, David is shown wrapped in layers of clothes. He is tired, spent, melancholy. No longer can war's excitement or religion's fervor revitalize him. Perhaps the force of life could be roused in him if a beautiful virgin were to warm him. Perhaps the presence of youth about him would again make him whole and sound, full of grace and song.

When Abishag is brought to him, he sees in her the ideal love he has always yearned for, and she envisages him as the hero she has adored, and before whom she has stood in awe, since her childhood. Alas, he soon realizes that he has met her too late. He imagined he would be like the burning bush that was never consumed, that youth and vigor would ever abide with him. Now he knows better. Even Abishag's young, splendid womanhood cannot renew his failing strength. Only his unsatisfied desire for her can warm him. She must remain his great, unfulfilled longing. She must stay near him, pure, immaculate, the goal of his aspiration, the eternal riddle which goads him on toward its solution but which, if solved, would cease to be a riddle. He tells her: "You are my riddle. The longing for you will awaken all my powers, will inflame my blood, will cause my heart to beat faster. The desire for you will be a sharp goad that will not let me fall asleep and be congealed. But, if I were to find fulfillment in you as a wife, then you would be for me a riddle solved. What then should warm your king?"

Abishag continued to occupy Pinski's creative imagination for additional years. In the one-act tragedy *Adoniyahu*, written in 1919 and dealing with events that ensued immediately after David's death, the dramatist showed both Adonijah and Solomon inflamed by Abishag's matchless beauty. She, however, insists on remaining faithful to the memory of the king whose flickering life she brightened with her companionship and devotion. Though Adonijah is prepared to renounce all claims to the throne, he is not willing to let Abishag fall as a royal heritage to young Solomon. His plea to be granted this single wish, to let him have Abishag as wife, is refused by Solomon. He then plans to revolt against the young king in order to obtain her. However, when she still resists his advances, his spirit fails him, and he is ripe for death. The play ends with Abishag being dragged off to Solomon's harem and Adonijah slain upon the king's command.

Among Yiddish writers, Itzik Manger, too, was fascinated by young Abishag and devoted four poems to her. When the shepherdess from Shunam is informed of her coming elevation from a village lass to a king's consort, she looks forward to exchanging her simple summer garb for silk and satin dresses. She imagines the king playing on the harp for her on star-studded nights. Her dreams reach a climax on her last night in Shunam when she foresees herself riding like an aristocratic lady in a coach of pure gold, accompanied by the admiring gaze of curious onlookers. She will be meeting the splendidly uniformed king at the entrance to the palace. She pictures David as young and slender, even as he is portrayed in the picture that hangs above her mother's bed. She will be ascending the royal staircase, arm in arm with him, her silken dress rustling and his golden spurs echoing. She will be his beloved not for a single night but for a lifetime.

Alas, the reality upon which she enters is far different. In the palace of the frigid, white-haired monarch, her thoughts and dreams revert to the pine forest of Shunam, her flock of sheep, the miller's son and the shepherd lad she left behind. In a letter to her mother, she describes herself as the king's hot-water bottle that was brought to warm his bed. The king is old and pious. He will undoubtedly reward her with a line in his Psalms, a single line of ink on parchment as compensation for her young body and her wasted years. The tears that drop from her eyes stain her letter. Her heart is heavy. Her tender girlhood dreams are gone. She cannot continue to write.

The Hebrew poet Jacob Fichman, in his lyric monologue "Abishag," penetrates into the innermost heart of the maiden selected for David's comfort. During daylight hours, she is sad that the spring of her life is being wasted and her longing for love's fulfillment unsatisfied. But at night, when she grants all her warmth to the aged king, she does not feel entirely useless, since he converts to song the tears of her life's springtime.

The lyric monologue "Abishag" by the French poet André Spire, unlike the monologue of Fichman, is put in the mouth of the old, old king, who is grateful to his gentle, sweet-smelling, little maid for ministering to him by day and by night. He is aware that her thoughts and dreams are far away from him. He remains lonely, though surrounded by an entourage of guards, prophets, queens, and concubines. All regard him as a relic of a bygone age. Even his beloved Bathsheba yearns for the day when he will die and be replaced on the throne by her son Solomon. It is only the innocent young shepherdess Abishag to whom he can speak of his youth in Bethlehem, when he too tended sheep. She also listens patiently when he recalls his many battles and victories until his kingdom stretched from Dan to Beersheba. But when he asks her to dance before him, she weeps, and he becomes aware of his present age when he can only offer her trembling hands, whitened hair, and a wrinkled face.

The Viennese poet and painter Uriel Birnbaum included a sonnet on Abishag among his *Biblische Sonette*. As the son of the Zionist pioneer and religious leader Nathan Birnbaum, he was steeped in biblical lore since his childhood. His Abishag is a timid maiden who is brought naked to King David. She feels no shame but rather pride in having been chosen as the loveliest bed companion for the royal hero, glamorized in her imagination. However, when she raises her demure eyes, she sees an old man lying near her and gazing upon her with reddened, half-blind eyes. Then pity overcomes her for the silver-haired king, and her feelings toward him are as those of a mother to a sick child.

Of the novelists who wrestled with the Abishag theme, few have found this last beloved of King David as rewarding a subject as his love for Michal, Abigail, and above all Bathsheba. These few include the Austrian novelist Theodor Heinrich Mayer, the Swiss novelist Ernst Zahn, and the American novelist Gladys Schmitt.

Mayer's novel *David findet Abisag* was published in 1925. It concentrated on the king's last days and showed him unable to reconcile himself to his declining vigor and nighing death. He is resentful of the young generation that will soon succeed his own. He notes that, even while he is still alive, the people prefer wise, young Solomon, to whom he has delegated the power to judge many disputes. He feels that God too has already cast him aside, now that his three score and ten years have been fulfilled, and the time has come for his sons to enter upon their heritage. When Absalom seeks to rejuvenate the kingdom by organizing the youth of Israel to revolt against his apparently decrepit father, David is forced to abandon Jerusalem and flee across the Jordan. In the final, critical battle, he emerges victorious after Joab slays Absalom. When Abishag is brought to him after the battle, her radiant youth stirs his darkened soul to new vitality. She sees in him not the victorious king but the human being who is in need of her and whose pain she can alleviate. Only after he strips himself of all his pompous trappings does he find his way to her heart. He then realizes that man's struggle for union with woman is unconsciously a struggle for union with God's essence. Abishag teaches him to lose his fear of aging and death. There is no absolute death, only eternal reunion of life through love, eternal rebirth through reunion. And when the call of death comes to him, he gladly follows the call, knowing that his life is being renewed in the babe being born to Abishag, from whose descendants the Light of the World will one day come to mankind.

Three years after Mayer, the prolific novelist Ernst Zahn, who generally wrote about the Swiss peasants among whom he lived, published his only biblical novel, *Tochter Dodais* (1928), in which he too concentrated on the last days of King David. Abishag, the naive, unspoiled daughter of Dodai, is taken from her idyllic rural home and becomes involved in the intrigues for the succession to the throne of Israel. In the village of her childhood and youth, David is a legendary figure, the anointed of God. When she arrives at David's court, she remains pure at heart. Though she faithfully performs her assigned duties, ministering to the dying monarch, she feels the spell of Adonijah's splendid, impetuous personality. He reciprocates her love and is ready, for her sake, to renounce his claim to the throne and even to risk forfeiting his life. Abishag and Adonijah are contrasted to the scheming Bathsheba and the crafty Solomon. Upon the death of David and the slaying of Adonijah, Abishag returns to her father's rustic home and lives thereafter with the memories of her brief days of aristocratic elevation and the intense suffering that matured her.

The American novelist Gladys Schmitt, in her early novel *David the King* (1947), does not limit herself, as did her Austrian and Swiss predecessors, merely to the monarch's aged period but rather retells the entire saga of the youngest son of Jesse from his adolescent years as guardian of his father's sheep to his final, cold nights when the Shunammite maiden is fetched to bring warmth to him. Only the concluding chapters deal with the last decade of the king's life, when the force of passion wanes within him. However, his imagination becomes ever more preoccupied with visions of an ideal maiden who will come to him in the naked loveliness of youth. When he once gave expression to such a vision that welled up from his subconscious, he did not believe that it would ever become an actuality. But, when one night a precious, living girl is brought to lie at his side, he is shamed in the very core of his being. However, when Abishag's vibrant flesh sheds its warmth upon him, he cannot reject her. He takes her, even as a shepherd takes a ewe lamb to his bosom. At her touch, an inward warmth arises in the aged monarch and is carried to the tips of his icy fingers and the soles of his numb feet. As he clung to the breast of his mother when he was brought into life, so he clings to Abishag before going forth from life. With her, he undertakes a last trip to his birthplace in Bethlehem. He speaks to her of the ebb and flow of human existence and of his final insight into the ways of God. He asks her to mourn for him for a brief while and then to dry her tears and take a husband who will give her children, so that the cycle of life and death might continue down the generations. In his hour of death, with Abishag near him, he concludes that all love, from his childhood affection for his mother to his last love for the Shunammite, is really a striving toward God, a yearning to become part of the Everlasting Being, the Eternal and the Changeless, from whom we issued forth and unto whom we return at the end.

In James A. Michener's *The Source* (1965), a novel of the eternal Israel, Abishag accompanies King David on an inspection tour to a northern fortress. She is described as the marvel of King David's last years, a gentle peasant girl selected to sleep with him on cold nights, a flawless maiden who serves the king with companionship and makes his declining years endurable. She stays faithfully at his side, silent and obedient, when he errs, and she comforts him when he suffers from contrition.

The twentieth century, far more than preceding centuries, has been attracted to the theme of Abishag, to which the Bible devotes but a few verses. She is portrayed in lyrics, dramas, and novels as youth that comes to old age, as the pure child of nature that casts radiance upon declining days, as the dream-love that replaces the ardor of passion, as the warm breath of renewed life amidst the gathering coldness at life's end, as the shield against the terror of imminent death.

18

The Judgment of Solomon

When Solomon ascended the throne of his father David, he was young and inexperienced. To strengthen his hold on the throne, he had been advised by his aged predecessor to take cruel measures. He began his reign with the murder of Adonijah, his older brother, and of Joab, the former commander-in-chief of the army, and the banishment of Abiathar, the sole survivor of the priests of Nob. Yearning for peace with his neighbors and for tranquility among his subjects, he had to maneuver constantly between the powers encircling his kingdom and to settle disputes between contending groups within his kingdom. The problems he faced during the day continued to trouble him at night during his restless sleep. Then, one night, he had a dream in which the Lord appeared to him and asked him what he desired most. Solomon replied that what he wanted most was an understanding heart so that he could judge between right and wrong and discern between good and evil. It pleased the Lord that Solomon preferred wisdom to riches, honor, or longevity, and the Lord granted the king's wish.

How wisely Solomon judged difficult cases that were brought before him was illustrated by the biblical chronicler in the dispute between the two harlots described in I Kings 3:16-28. Both prostitutes lived in the same house, and each gave birth to a child at about the same time, only three days apart. One of the children died at midnight, and its mother exchanged it for the living child. When the other mother awoke and found the dead child beside her, she insisted that it was not hers. Each mother claimed the living child as her own. The dispute came before the king. He ordered a sword to be brought and the living child to be cut in two, with half to be given to each mother. While one mother, spurred on by envy or spite, agreed to the division, the other mother, whose love was enkindled toward her offspring, implored that the child be spared and be given to her rival. Then the king pronounced his final judgment: the living child belonged to the compassionate woman whose maternal affection had triumphed over all other feelings. Her love had revealed her as the true mother. All Israel then acknowledged the wisdom of the young monarch.

According to the Talmud, Solomon was so absolutely certain of the correctness of his decision because a *bat kol*—a Voice from Heaven—came forth and confirmed it.

The repercussions of Solomon's judgment have given rise to important works of art and literature. Paintings on this subject include those of Giorgione, Rubens, Poussin, and Tiepolo, but the most famous is that of Raphael, in the Vatican. It shows Solomon seated on the throne. He has just pronounced his preliminary judgment, and his servant is about to carry it out. The latter has seized the living child in his left hand and holds a drawn sword in his right. But at this moment, as the child is about to be cut in half, the true mother rushes forward to save it. Her face is turned toward the king, begging him to spare it. The false mother, on the other hand, kneels in the foreground near her own dead child and apparently does not object to Solomon's decision being carried out.

In literature, the closest parallel to the sword test of Solomon is the chalk-circle test. The theme itself, before the chalk circle was added, has been traced back to ancient India, from where it migrated to Tibet and China. It tells of two mothers, wives of the same man, who appeared after his death before a king who was an incarnation of Buddha. Both claimed the same son. The king suggested that each mother take hold of a hand of the child and pull. The false mother was without pity and tore it to herself. She was primarily interested in obtaining the inheritance of the deceased husband through her child, since a childless widow could not inherit the family's fortune. The true mother did not want to hurt the child and did not pull. The king then awarded her the child.

This version, current in India, was recorded at a much later date than the Solomonic one, and yet prominent biblical scholars, such as Hermann Gunkel, Hugo Gressman, and Martin Noth, maintain that the former must have arisen first, probably as a fairy tale spread from mouth to mouth. Gressman, who calls attention to twenty-two parallel themes in various parts of the world, does not claim a common source for all of them. However, the similarities between the Indian and the biblical narrative are so profound that he and other scholars maintain it is most unlikely that the two arose spontaneously in such complexity. They must be somehow interrelated. These scholars give priority to the Indian tale, primarily because it is better motivated. The Indian litigants are wives of the same deceased husband. They are not only jealous of each other but they also wish to be recognized as head of the household, since according to custom in India, only the mother of the child can have this status. The harlot of the biblical narrative, on the other hand, had no reason to burden herself with a child not her own and to fight for its possession. Besides, if the Solomonic tale is an adaptation of an original Indian source, then the transformation of the two wives into two harlots can be viewed as more compatible with biblical morality. The biblical narrator did not want such immoral behavior and litigation to arise in a respectable Hebraic family.

By the middle of the fifth century, the Indian tale, whether pre-Solomonic or post-Solomonic in its origin, had reached China. In the fourteenth century, the Chinese version was dramatized by Li Hsing-tao, who added the chalk test. This Chinese play had its greatest vogue in the twentieth-century European adaptations by Klabund and by Bertold Brecht. The most recent narrative of a dispute between two mothers over the possession of one child eschewed all tests. It was based on tragic reality of the Holocaust years. Though its author, Yehuda Yaari, entitled it "The Judgment of Solomon," he left it up to the reader to render final judgment.

The Chinese play *Hui-lan-ki*, by Li Hsing-tao, has the child placed on a chalked line, not a circle. The judge then calls upon each of the two mothers to take hold of a hand and pull it toward herself. The true mother should have the greater strength. However, the true mother lets the child's hand go. Though the test is repeated, the compassionate mother still refuses to pull hard upon her beloved, tender offspring. The wise judge then recognizes her as the rightful mother.

This play did not reach Europe until the nineteenth century. It was translated into French by Stanislas Julien in 1832, and from the French into German by Wollheim da Fonesca in 1876. It became the basis for Klabund's play *Der chinesische Kreidekreis*, which he wrote for the actress Elizabeth Bergner and which was staged in Berlin by Max Reinhardt in 1925. Thereafter it enjoyed wide popularity on many stages and in print until the Second World War. It inspired Brecht to compose in 1944 and 1945 his more original drama *Der kaukasische Kreidekreis*, the last great work of his American exile.

Brecht had earlier used the theme in his short story "Der Augsburger Kreidekreis," which he wrote at the beginning of the Second World War and whose action he transferred from China to Germany of the Thirty Years' War. His more important dramatic version has the prologue take place in Soviet Georgia, while the main action is transposed to an earlier era of feudal Georgia.

There, long ago, the despotic governor of a provincial capital is killed in the course of a revolt, and his wife is forced to flee precipitously. She manages to save her wardrobe but not her little child. Her maid Grusche is left with the baby. As sole heir to the governor's estate, the infant is in great danger, as the rebels seek to lay hands on it. Grusche, overcome with pity for the helpless, abandoned infant, escapes with it over the icy mountain pass. Her affection for the child increases as she experiences hardships for its sake. In order to care for it better, she passes it off as her own child. When the rebellion is crushed and the former regime is finally restored, the governor's wife returns to town and wants to reclaim the child. But Grusche refuses to give it up. When the case is brought before the former vagabond and newly reappointed judge Azdak, he draws with chalk a circle on the ground and places the child in it. He then tells each woman to pull it out. Since the child is the sole heir to the family's wealth, the greedy biological mother pulls at it with all her might, while the loving foster-mother lets go. Though the judge has become aware that Grusche did not give birth to the child, he nevertheless awards it to her as the true mother.

The judge upholds the author's view that biology should not be the determining factor but rather humaneness. The humble maid who loved and preserved the child in perilous years behaved with greater maternal affection and will undoubtedly be a better mother to it in coming years than the egoistic, aristocratic lady whose only claim is the claim of blood-relationship.

By switching the ending and making the welfare of the child a more important consideration than the accident of birth, Brecht is reaffirming his own adherence to the humanitarian philosophy he always espoused and his belief in the doctrine that truth is socially conditioned.

The Hebrew novelist Yehuda Yaari, in his story "The Judgment of Solomon" (1942), presents the struggle of two mothers over the custody of their one son as basically insoluble from the human point of view, even if it can be resolved legally. The author presents both sides of the case fairly, but he himself suggests no answer.

The story is told by a mother who has survived the Nazi terror. As the wife of a Berlin Jewish doctor, she lived a tranquil, prosperous life with her husband and child until the Crystal Night of November 1938, when the Nazis ushered in their more intensified terror against Jews. Before then the family had opportunities to leave Germany but did not do so. Husband and wife felt that they were needed as doctors to treat Jewish patients, since non-Jewish doctors were forbidden to do so. However, after 1938, life becomes unbearable also for them, but by then avenues of emigration are closed to them, as to most German Jews. Perhaps their five-year-old son can still be saved. A family the doctors know has received a certificate of immigration into Palestine. The permit includes the family's three children, but only two are still in Germany. Their boy's name can be added to the passport as the third child. The mother is hesitant to part from him but finally agrees. The boy arrives safely and is entrusted to a generous woman in Jerusalem, a well-to-do widow without children of her own. She becomes a new, loving mother to him.

One day the Berlin Gestapo called for the father and later told his wife to call for his ashes. When the war breaks out, all correspondence with Jerusalem ceases. Consumed with longing for her son, the desperate German widow risks escaping across the sealed border and through other occupied territories. After many hardships, she succeeds in reaching Jerusalem. Three years have passed since the boy left Berlin and his German-Jewish parents. He is now eight years old when the visitor from abroad arrives. He immediately recognizes her as his German mother and says so to his Jerusalem mother. And now the dilemma arises. Both mothers want him and need him. Both are lonely and longing for his affection. When the immigrant mother, who was thought dead for a long time, asks for the return of her son, the foster-mother suggests that the boy be consulted as to whether he wishes to leave his present home where he is now so happy. Upon such a test, the boy's physical mother does not dare to enter, since she is not certain of the outcome. Nor does she want to consider taking him against his will, by resorting to court, since the experience would scar him and might destroy any affection he has for her. What should she do? And how would Solomon have decided the case of these two lonely widows, one his biological mother and the other his spiritual mother, both in need of the child's love?

Variations of the problem that Solomon was called upon to solve have persisted for three thousand years. The dilemma of the child between two mothers, both of whom claim it, became especially acute after the Holocaust. Many a Jewish mother threatened with deportation to an extermination camp entrusted her beloved child to a kind Christian neighbor who undertook to care for it and who faced dangers in doing so. Such a child, for its own safety, was generally raised in the faith of its foster-mother and escaped more easily the horrors and the death that would otherwise have been its lot.

When the Second World War ended, these children were sought out by surviving relatives, even when the mother perished, or by Jewish emissaries who were most anxious to bring back to the Jewish fold the orphans who had not died along with a million less fortunate children. It frequently happened that the foster-mothers had become emotionally attached to their wards and that the children themselves did not want to give up their safe existence and their Christian faith. They were reluctant to return to unknown kinsmen who were residing in strange lands and to the faith of the emaciated Jewish refugees who emerged from the concentration camps. The wisdom of Solomon was needed to unravel the complexities of individual cases, and often even such wisdom did not suffice. Solutions had to be found for insoluble cases, and these solutions were at times heartbreaking. To this day the judgments of contemporary Solomons have left conscious or subconscious scars on mature personalities who have long since outgrown childhood fears of the Nazi period.

19

Solomon and the Queen of Sheba

The encounter between King Solomon at the height of his glory and the Queen of Sheba, who had heard of his fame as the wisest of mortals and who came to Jerusalem to test his wisdom, is narrated in the tenth chapter of the First Book of Kings and again in the ninth chapter of the Second Book of Chronicles. Such an encounter may indeed have taken place, for there existed a kingdom of Saba in the southwestern part of the Arabian peninsula during the tenth century B.C.E., the century of Solomon's reign. Archaeologists are still uncovering fragments of Saba's past from surviving relics long buried under the desert sand. However, the historical or pseudohistorical kernel of the encounter is overlaid with three thousand years of legendary lore.

The biblical narrative already reads like a romance of courtly splendor dimly remembered. It is preceded by the story of an expedition that Solomon sent out from Eilat and Ezion-geber to the distant shore of Ophir in order to fetch the gold wherewith to adorn the Temple then being erected. The sailors, Phoenicians and Hebrews, not only brought back fabulous treasures of gold but they must also have spread to remote peoples tales of the elegance and wisdom of the king who had ascended the throne of David. When these tales reach the ears of the Queen of Sheba in her inland realm, she is rather skeptical and decides to find out for herself whether there was any truth in them. She travels overland to Solomon's kingdom with a very large retinue. Her camels are laden with gold, precious stones, and spices.

Arriving in Jerusalem after her long journey, she tests the king's wisdom with hard riddles. He answers all her questions and solves all her riddles correctly. Then there is no more spirit of skepticism or arrogance in her. She acknowledges that she had not believed the reports that had seeped down to her kingdom. However, after seeing the magnificence of Solomon's court and experiencing the impact of his wisdom, she can state that the reports were not exaggerated, indeed, that they did not reflect even half of his true greatness. But not only has the king of Israel impressed her. She also has impressed him. He gives her all her desire, whatever she asks of him. This emphasis on his yielding to her desire has given rise to many conjectures as to their relations during her visit. Before she leaves, Solomon presents her with royal gifts comparable to the royal bounty she brought to him. Then she returns with her retinue to her own kingdom.

This biblical romance was embellished by popular imagination, as Solomon's kingdom was divided after his death and less glamorous rulers came to the thrones of Israel and Judah. Bedouins transmitted the romance by word of mouth along caravan trails, and merchants brought it across the Red Sea to Abyssinia. It accompanied Jewish exiles to Babylon and returned with them to their Palestinian homeland. It reached Mecca and was incorporated in the Koran. As Islam spread to ever new lands, the Koran made Moslems acquainted with this romance throughout Asia and Africa. Pilgrims and Crusaders who sojourned in the Holy Land brought it to medieval Europe in Christian adaptations.

Lorenzo Ghiberti in 1457 engraved it on a panel of his much-admired Gates of Paradise installed fifteen years later at the Baptistery of Florence, where it is today still a great tourist attraction. Renaissance painters of the sixteenth century, such as Jacopo Tintoretto, Paolo Veronese, and Hans Holbein the Younger vied to put its magnificent episodes on canvas. They were followed by Peter Paul Rubens and Claude Lorraine in the ensuing century.

While Shakespeare preferred nonbiblical subjects for the plots of his dramas, he was well acquainted with the Bible and with the story of the Queen of Sheba. In the last scene of *Henry VIII*, he has Cranmer, the archbishop of Canterbury and godfather to the newly born daughter of Anne Boleyn, eulogize the royal infant, the future Queen Elizabeth, by comparing her to the Queen of Saba:

> . . . Saba was never
> More covetous of wisdom and fair virtue
> Than this pure soul shall be; all princely graces,
> That mould up such a mighty piece as this is,
> With all the virtues that attend the good,
> Shall still be doubled on her. Truth shall nurse her,
> Holy and heavenly thoughts still counsel her.

Spain's foremost dramatist, Calderón de la Barca, adapted the Sheba theme twice for the stage of the seventeenth century. Handel's oratorio *Solomon*, first performed in 1749, Gounod's opera *La Reine de Saba* of 1862, and Karl Goldmark's opera *Die Königin von Saba* of 1875 were the best-known of musical interpretations.

Since the mid-nineteenth century, the encounter of Solomon and Sheba has left its mark upon novels from Gérard de Nerval's *Voyage en Orient* (1851) and Gustave Flaubert's *La Tentation de St. Antoine* (1874) to John Dos Passos's *Three Soldiers* (1921). It has inspired poems by Robert Browning, John G. Whittier, Edwin Arnold, Arthur Symons, William Butler Yeats, Rudyard Kipling, Lascelles Abercrombie, John Freeman, and a host of other poets. Among contemporary artists, Marc Chagall, in 1956, created a most interesting original interpretation.

James B. Pritchard, who edited the authoritative volume *Solomon and Sheba* in 1974, a volume in which six eminent scholars participated, summed up in the opening chapter the conclusions of present-day archaeologists about the economic and cultural level of Israel during the age of Solomon. A second chapter, by G. W. van Beek, surveyed the results of recent archaeological digs in the Arabian kingdom of Sheba or Saba. Both of these scholars are noncommital as to whether a meeting of the two rulers actually took place. They merely do not negate such a possibility. Equally noncommittal is Sir E. A. Wallis Budge, in his introduction to the Ethiopian classic *Kebra Nagast*, which he first published in 1922 and then again in 1932 under the English title *Queen of Sheba and Her Only Son Menyelek I*. But he does call attention to the invasion of Abyssinia, or Ethiopia, by Asiatic Semites during the age of Solomon or soon thereafter. These invaders came from southwestern Arabia and brought a higher form of civilization to the African realm.

Whether fact or fiction, the reputed meeting of the King of Israel and the Queen of Saba had a significant impact upon the human mind during the past three thousand years and gave rise to four major currents of tradition, Judaic, Islamic, Ethiopian, and Christian. Although there were areas of contact between these currents, each developed along distinct, independent lines.

The Judaic tradition devoted much ingenuity to the riddles propounded by the idolatrous queen and the sagacious answers given by the Jewish king, but it was hostile in its treatment of the personal relations that developed between them. The queen who challenged the monarch to a duel of wits was often presented as a temptress, even as an incarnation of Lilith, the demonic first mate of Adam, who left him for a more suitable mate, Ashmodai, the prince of demons, and who has ever thereafter sought to strangle at birth the children of Eve, her successor in Adam's affections. The queen's affair with Solomon, who succumbed to her wiles no less than to the charms of a thousand other women, had as its aftermath the birth of Nebuchadnezzar, either as their son or as a later descendant of their son. This Babylonian monarch destroyed Solomon's Temple and put an end to the First Jewish Kingdom, thus proving that sin leads to catastrophe, sooner or later.

The development of the Judaic tradition can be traced through various stages from Josephus's *Jewish Antiquities* and talmudic and midrashic texts to kabbalistic incantations and contemporary Yiddish folklore and literary references. Its most detailed and picturesque version is that of *Targum Sheni*, an Aramaic commentary on the Book of Esther, which scholars have dated at approximately fifteen hundred years after Solomon's reign.

After referring to the sumptuous feast of King Ahasuerus, the author of the commentary digresses by recalling an earlier feast in the days of King Solomon and then goes on to tell of Solomon's magnificent throne and royal establishment.

To the earlier banquet there are also invited numerous kings and noblemen. When Solomon's heart is merry with wine, he commands beasts, birds, reptiles, and demons to appear and to entertain his guests by dancing before them. One bird, the hoopoe, fails to appear. When it is peremptorily summoned by the angry, impatient monarch, it explains its delayed appearance by the long distance it had to travel. It has flown from a remote land not yet subject to Solomon's sway, a land whose dust is of silver and gold and lies about in the streets like dung, and whose trees, as old as creation, are watered by streams that flowed from the Garden of Eden.

On hearing this report, Solomon orders the hoopoe to return to that fabulous land with a message to its queen to come to Jerusalem immediately. Otherwise, he will destroy her kingdom and its inhabitants. When she consults her councilors, they advise against her going and urge her to prepare for war, but she overrules their advice and sets sail with a great fleet and with precious gifts. She finds the king seated on a magnificent throne in a palace whose floor glistens with crystal. Never having seen such crystal, she thinks he is sitting in the midst of water. As she nighs the throne, she raises the hem of her garment, thereby revealing to the astonished monarch's gaze that her feet are hairy, the feet of a demon. Though fascinated by her beauty, he is repelled by her hairiness and remarks to her: "Your beauty is the beauty of women and your hair is the hair of men. Hair is becoming to a man, but to a woman it is a shame."

Queen Sheba does not reply to this insult and proceeds to propound her questions to him. She is impressed by his answers. Both exchange gifts, and the king gives her what she asks of him. At this point, the episode in *Targum Sheni* ends, as this commentary reverts to other subjects. However, the hint of her demonic nature clearly showed the negative Jewish approach toward the queen. Neither her glamorous beauty nor her royal affluence sufficed to endear her in Jewish eyes because her behavior was basically immoral.

In our own century, the classical Yiddish writer Yitzkhak Leibush Peretz, in his tales of the reign of King Solomon XXVII in the marvelous realm beyond the Sambation, ascribed the long-raging conflict between the men with small bodies and great souls and the men with great bodies and small souls, a war which could have been nipped in the bud by King Solomon I, to the fact that, when the dwarfs came to Jerusalem to appeal to the wise and mighty monarch, the Queen of Sheba was just then visiting him and he gave no ear to more important matters, a behavior that calls into question his reputed wisdom.

The Islamic tradition, as recorded in the Koran, was based not only on biblical sources but also on postbiblical Judaic sources and on oral stories circulated by Arab weavers of tales in pre-Islamic centuries. It has many similarities to *Targum Sheni*. Sura 27 of the Koran relates that Solomon sent for the sun-worshipping queen who ruled over Saba, demanding that she worship the true God. When she asked her nobles for advice, they hesitated and finally told her that she would have to reach a decision by herself and that they would follow her commands. She tried to procrastinate a final answer by sending gifts to the king of Israel, but he spurned her gifts and sent back her envoys with the threat that he would invade her land unless she herself came. When she arrived in Jerusalem, she found that, upon Solomon's command, a djinn had already transported her throne to him. When she saw his palace, whose floor was paved with sparkling glass, she thought that the floor was covered with water and raised her garment, thus baring her legs. According to Moslem commentators, Solomon wished to verify whether she really had goat's feet, as was rumored. The Koran does not mention the result of his inspection. It merely concludes that she acknowledged that she had sinned against her soul and that she would now abandon her heathen beliefs and accept Solomon's God, the Lord of the World.

Commentators expanded upon the koranic verses. Arabic,

Persian, and Turkish storytellers added themes from native folklore and elaborated on the splendor attending both rulers. In the Islamic versions, the queen bore the name of Balkis and claimed to be the offspring of the emperor of China and a Peri. Her throne was identified as her great bed, which measured thirty feet. Solomon had a demon transport it to Jerusalem because he knew that the way to a woman's heart led through her bed. Djinns had slandered her by telling Solomon that her feet were hairy, but when Solomon tested her by his crystal stratagem, he saw the most beautiful ankle without a single hair and a thigh formed for delights. Solomon succumbed to her beauty, and she to his wisdom.

The most glamorous tradition of the encounter between Solomon and the Queen of Sheba, however, developed on Ethiopian soil. This tradition has been thoroughly studied by Edward Ullendorff, professor of Ethiopian and Semitic languages at the University of London. The earliest rulers of the African kingdom of Axum regarded their capital as the Zion of Abyssinia, and the emperors of Ethiopia down the centuries until our own continued to bear the title Lion of Judah. The last imperial constitution, adopted in 1955, stated in Article 2: "The Imperial dignity shall remain perpetually attached to the line of Haile Selassie I, descendant of King Sahle Selassie, whose line descends without interruption from the dynasty of Menelik I, son of the Queen of Ethiopia, the Queen of Sheba, and King Solomon of Jerusalem." Perpetually—lasted less than two decades, when the ancient royal dynasty was supplanted by a revolutionary regime that liquidated Haile Selassie and his descendants.

Ethiopia's national saga, *Kebra Nagast (Glory of Kings)*, recorded in the fourteenth century, seeks to trace back Ethiopia's royal house to Solomon, son of King David, and still further back to the patriarchs Abraham, Isaac, and Jacob. Since the Christian savior was also of Davidic lineage, the emperor of Ethiopia was his kinsman and ruled his Christian realm by divine right. Ethiopia was therefore to be regarded as God's spiritual Israel, since the Jews, God's original chosen people, had become unworthy of God's special trust by rejecting the Christian savior.

The episodes of the *Kebra Nagast* were derived from the Bible, rabbinical writings, traditions current in Syria and Palestine, and oral and written sources from Egypt, Yemen, and Coptic Christianity.

The saga located Sheba not in the Arabian peninsula but in Africa. The Queen of Sheba, who has been apprised of Solomon's wisdom by the captain of her caravan, goes to Jerusalem not under compulsion but of her own free will in order to test his wisdom. Convinced of his greatness after many conversations, she gives up her sun-worshipping religion and accepts as her God the sun's creator, the God of Israel. One night, after a splendid banquet, Solomon takes her to wife and she becomes pregnant. When she returns to her African realm, a son, Menelik, is born to her. After he grows up, he journeys to Jerusalem. Solomon arrays him in royal apparel and seats him on a throne at his side. But when Menelik learns that Rehoboam is to become the heir to Solomon's kingdom, he returns to Ethiopia with many sons of Jewish noblemen in order to establish a second Jewish kingdom. They take with them the tabernacle of Israel's God which contains the two tablets of Moses, the rod of Aaron, and the pot of manna. Since then, the Divine Presence has dwelt in Axum, the holy city of the Ethiopians, and Ethiopia has been governed by the laws of Israel with the later accretion of Coptic Monophysite Christianity.

The Christian tradition of Solomon and Sheba goes back to Matthew 12:30, which reads: "The queen of the south shall rise up in the judgment with this generation; and shall condemn it; for she came from the uttermost parts of the earth to hear the wisdom of Solomon; and, behold, a greater than Solomon is here." This statement is repeated in Luke 11:31. The reference to one greater than Solomon was to the Christian savior, and medieval commentators, therefore, saw Solomon to be a prefiguration of this savior. The Jerusalem Temple built by Solomon was envisaged as an earthly representation of the Temple of God in the heavenly Jerusalem. The Queen of Sheba, who came with her retinue from the ends of the earth to Zion's House of God, was allegorically understood to anticipate the flocking of mankind to be converted to Christianity and to accept the discipline of the Church. This interpretation surfaced in the writings of Isidore, archbishop of Seville, in the seventh century, and of the Venerable Bede in eighth-century England.

The Queen of Sheba also plays a role in the Legend of the True Cross as recorded in *The Golden Legend*, a popular work of the closing fourteenth century by Jacobus de Voragine, archbishop of Genoa. Of this compendium of miracles, more than five hundred manuscripts survived. It experienced about one hundred and fifty printings in the Latin original and in translations during the first century of printing. It included the following tale of the Cross.

When the aged Adam falls sick, his son Seth approaches the Gates of Paradise and asks for a few drops of oil from the tree of mercy as medicine for his father. Archangel Michael refuses to give him the oil but does give him a branch of the tree of knowledge. By the time Seth returns to his father, Adam is already dead. He plants the branch over Adam's grave and it grows into a mighty tree, which flourishes until Solomon's time. Solomon has it cut down in order to use it in the building of the Temple, but the builders find it unsuitable and throw it across a pond to serve as a bridge. When the Queen of Saba makes her way to Jerusalem and is about to cross the pond, she foresees in a vision that the Christian savior will one day hang upon this tree. Instead of putting her foot upon it, she kneels down to adore it. After the cross is later fashioned of this tree, it remains hidden in the earth for more than two centuries, until it is found by Empress Helena, the mother of Constantine, the first Roman emperor to accept Christianity, after winning a battle with the help of the cross.

The modern adaptations of the encounter between Solomon and Sheba are eclectic. They draw upon all four streams of tradition, with the Moslem tradition generally dominant. The first half of the nineteenth century witnessed the height of the vogue of oriental tales in Western and Central Europe. Byron, Shelley, and Thomas Moore in England, Chateaubriand, Lamartine, Gautier, and Victor Hugo in France were winning wide acclaim with their oriental legends in verse and prose. The Viennese poet, historian, and orientalist Joseph Freiherr von Hammer-Purgstall, who spent many years in Constantinople, included among the legends in his fascinating volume *Rosenöl* (1813), an account of the meeting of Solomon and Sheba, which was based on Persian and Turkish stories and may have been the source for Robert Browning's philosophic poem "Solomon and Balchis," composed seventy years later. The French romantic poet Gérard de Nerval, who traveled through Egypt, Syria, and Lebanon in 1843, incorporated in his *Voyage en Orient*, begun during the following year, tales of this exotic area, among them "The Tale of the Queen of the Morning and Soliman, the Prince of the Genii."

For this tale, he used as his principal sources the Bible, the Koran, the Talmud, and the occult lore of Freemasonry. But he also added incidents, myths, and mysteries culled from his own wild and erratic imagination, which often brought him beyond the brink of sanity. His story begins with Queen Balkis arriving in Jerusalem from the land of the Sabeans. It is her intention to marry King Soliman if he is really as wise as reputed. All workshops are emptied of people as the artisans rush out to greet her. Only Adoniram, the master-builder of Soliman's palace and the still unfinished Temple, keeps aloof. This somber, audacious, and mysterious genius senses no kinship with the Hebrews, offspring of Shem, for he is the last of the descendants of the great, defiant Cain and of Tubal-Cain, the forger in brass and iron. From Tubal-Cain there has come down to him knowledge of how to use fire as a means of subjecting all metals to his will.

The queen is far more impressed by this master architect, sculptor, and builder than by Soliman, whose wisdom turns out to be inferior to her own. Though the inflamed monarch offers her half his throne and kingdom, she remains reserved and cautious. Like Adoniram, she too is a creature of fire. She too yearns to reach out beyond human bounds. When Adoniram gets her with child, she flees from Jerusalem back to her kingdom, expecting him to follow. But he is assassinated. The disappointed Soliman tries to overcome his fatal passion for the queen by drowning himself in sensual indulgence with other women who are brought to him from every corner of the world. He grows old and decrepit and meets an inglorious end trying vainly to cling to the shreds of life.

In the short-lived, solitary genius Adoniram, Gérard de Nerval depicted himself and foresaw his own fate. Geniuses, he felt, were spirits of fire. Scorned despite their superiority, they remain unrecognized during their days on earth, they bestow joys upon others and receive sorrows in return. Their tombs alone will be honored. Yet, these giants of intellect, these torches of knowledge, these organs of progress, these instruments of liberty are the supreme benefactors of mankind.

Gérard de Nerval's recasting of the ancient encounter became the basis for the libretto by Jules Barbier and Michel Carré, which Gounod used for his opera in four acts *La Reine de Saba* (1862). Gounod's opera has been far less popular than Karl Goldmark's *Die Königin von Saba*, which the Viennese composer began a year later and which swept the stages of Europe after its première in 1875.

Goldmark was an admirer of Richard Wagner, and the influence of Wagner is all too apparent, especially in the procession scenes and in the tragically moving final scene.

In Goldmark's opera, for which S. H. Mosenthal wrote the libretto, the hero is Assad, Solomon's favorite courtier, and not the king himself. The calm happiness that has characterized the love between Assad and Sulamith, the daughter of Israel's high priest, is disturbed when the Queen of Sheba arrives in Jerusalem with her magnificent entourage, bearing vases filled with gold, diamonds, and precious spices. Assad recognizes in the queen the beautiful, demonic, Undine-like figure whom he once espied arising from a spring in Lebanon and who had intoxicated his senses. At court, however, she disowns any knowledge of him. Later on, in the garden of Solomon's palace, she again lures him during a romantic night, but disappears when dawn breaks in upon them.

At the Temple wedding ceremony of Assad and Sulamith, attended by the king, priests, and courtiers, the bridegroom is about to place the ring on the bride's finger when the queen enters. Assad, reverting to his blind passion for her, stops the ceremony and rushes to her, but she wards him off and again disclaims any knowledge of him.

The final act takes place at the edge of the desert. There Sulamith and her maidens have found a refuge from the world's turmoils, just like Jephthah's daughter and her virgins. There the exiled Assad wanders about, lonely, disgraced, crushed by his guilt, ripe for death. The queen appears before him and for a third time seeks to exercise her spell upon him. But now he can at last resist the flames that emanate from her. He curses her as a demonic temptress who has destroyed his life and rejects vigorously the paradise of passion that she again offers him. She vanishes from sight, while he accepts his nighing death in a sandstorm as atonement for his earlier sin of lust. When the desert storm subsides, Sulamith and her twelve maidens come across the dying Assad, and in a scene reminiscent of the concluding scene of Wagner's *Tristan und Isolde*, he sinks to death in her arms and enters into the heavenly realm of true, eternal love.

The Queen of Sheba as a demonic temptress was also portrayed by the French novelist Gustave Flaubert in *La Tentation de St. Antoine* (1874). The ascetic hermit was the subject of memorable paintings by Salvator Rosa, David Teniers, and Breughel. Flaubert has the Queen of Sheba tempt the saint with sensual visions. The emaciated Anthony dreams of her arriving on a white elephant. She enters his cell and tells him of her great longing for him, which has led her to leave King Solomon in order to be with him. She invites him to join her in her realm of wealth and oriental splendor. When the saint remains adamant, she offers herself to him as the embodiment of all the mysteries of womanhood. A single touch of her shoulder would let a fiery ray course through his veins, and the possession of her body would fill him with more passionate ecstasy than the conquest of an empire. But still he resists her, and she retreats weeping.

Less glamor and greater profundity surround the encounter between the rulers of Israel and Sheba in the philosophic poem "Solomon and Balchis" by Robert Browning. Seated on an ivory throne on Mount Zion, both talk, on a conscious level, of things sublime, and the king solves the queen's hard riddles without difficulty. But, on the subconscious level, emotional streams course between them. Before giving up the intellectual game she began and lost, the frustrated Balchis asks one final question: whom of all mankind would Solomon admit to his palace as his equals? His answer is that he would welcome as his peers the wise, namely, the supreme creative personalities, poets, painters, sculptors, builders. In turn, he asks her whom she would admit as her equals. She replies that she would prefer as her mates the good, be they rich, poor, shrewd, or simple. As she speaks, she jostles the king's outstretched hand, so that his ring, which bears the Ineffable Name, turns from inside to outside, and he is compelled to tell the real truth which lodges in the deepest layer of his soul. He then confesses that he would consider as wise, and would welcome at his court, only those who would flatter him in word and deed, paint his portrait, or sing his praises in verse. Then, turning the ring with the truth-compelling name of God toward her, he makes her also answer truthfully from the depths of her soul. Blushingly, she confesses that by the good she meant young men, strong and tall and proper. The king notes with a sigh that there have just been revealed to them two levels of truth, the truth of the mind that would spread wing and soar to heaven and the truth of the body that must crawl and plod heavily on earth. At one level he yearns for knowledge above everything else, while at another level he enjoys the praise of fools, even if he recognizes such adulation as pure vanity. When he asks the queen whether her reason for coming to him was solely to test his wisdom, she laughs amidst her blushes and remarks that at the so-called higher level mind may commune with mind and seek wisdom, but that down here at the earthly level she would prefer one small kiss. Would he grant her bold wish?

A similar conclusion permeates Arthur Symons's lyric playlet *The Lover of the Queen of Sheba*. The royal couple are presented as ultimately weary of wisdom. Before coming to Solomon's court, the Queen of Sheba seemed to be indifferent to love and rejected all the royal suitors who poured out gold and incense in tribute at her feet. Wisdom alone then had supreme value for her, but after she meets in Solomon the wisest of mortals and wants to share in his wisdom, she discovers that wisdom too, even as fame and dominion, leads not to happiness but rather to sorrow. Solomon has already arrived earlier at the pessimistic conclusion that, whether life be long or short, fair or forlorn, it is far better not to have been born. When the queen persists in inquiring how we who have not yet been laid away under the earth can best use the interval between birth and death, the king replies that we may love. But is not love also an illusion? asks the queen. The supremely sagacious monarch replies that all life is illusion, even as all wealth and state and power.

> Love only is the eternal now.
> When thou art I and I am thou,
> Time is no more.
> Let us forget that we are wise,
> And wisdom, though it be the sum
> Of all but love, is love's disguise.
> Let us forget all else that is,
> Save this that joy is ours to know,
> A moment, ere he turn and go,
> And that joy's moment, love, is this.

Symons, in this playlet, expresses the pessimism and weary disillusionment of his fin-de-siècle circle, which included Oscar Wilde, Aubrey Beardsley, and Ernest Dowson, and sought in momentary passion momentary forgetfulness of the meaninglessness of life.

John Freeman, the poet and literary critic who rose to prominence after World War I, published *Solomon and Balkis*, an epic in nine cantos, in 1926. He distinguishes between true and ephemeral love. Though Solomon has a thousand wives, the only true love he has ever experienced is his love for Balkis, the princess who has come to the throne of Sheba but who is still unloved and unhusbanded. He journeys to her kingdom, woos and wins her. Of their union is Menelik born. However, after the death of

Balkis, Solomon knows only lesser loves and fleeting passions. The many strange women satisfy his lust and lead him to idolatries. In his hour of death, he seeks in vain to enter heaven. Nobody comes to plead for him at heaven's gate because a ruler has no real friends. Then he remembers Sheba's queen. She flies to him and implores God to let them abide together, whether in heaven or hell, since true love survives earth, heaven, and hell.

The Russian novelist Alexander Kuprin depicted in his idyllic romance *Sulamith* (1908) the impact that the Queen of Sheba made upon the eight-year-old Shulamith when she arrived with her camels in golden harness, her mules with bells of gold between their ears, her monkeys in silver cages, and her wondrous peacocks. After Shulamith matures and becomes the beloved of Solomon, she questions the king about the amazing queen, her predecessor in his affections. Solomon then describes Balkis as a magnificent woman of forty who was already beginning to fade. But she knew how to make her body, grown flabby, seem graceful and supple like a girl's, while her face bore the impress of an awesome, inhuman beauty. Solomon, however, was not at all impressed by her wisdom, which he characterizes as the petty wisdom of a woman. He found her riddles easy to solve. All her secret charms of love's passion in the night did not suffice to retain his love. She soon palled upon him. He hurt her cruelly by having her expose to the entire court her crooked, hairy legs, which she had always kept covered but which became visible when, through his stratagem of the crystal and seemingly waterlike palace floor, he caused her to raise up the hem of her garment. She then fled back to her kingdom in a rage and could not be appeased.

In 1954, the British philosopher Bertrand Russell began his *Nightmares of Eminent Persons* with "The Queen of Sheba's Nightmare." This story was to illustrate the saying: "Put not thy trust in princes."

Returning through the Arabian desert after visiting King Solomon, the Queen of Sheba daydreams about her recent experiences. She was impressed by the king's wealth, splendor, wisdom. But for her he was also the supreme lover and poet. On parting, he gave her a jeweled volume of his songs which expressed in language of exquisite beauty the joy he experienced in her company. Though her queenly duties compel her to return to her kingdom, she will always carry with her the knowledge that there was one man on earth who penetrated into the recesses of her soul and who was worthy of her love.

In her reverie, she espies a figure approaching who introduces himself as Beelzebub, a friend of Solomon. The queen flatters herself that, though the king may share secrets of statecraft with this friend, he shared with her more intimate feelings and incorporated them in a precious volume of love lyrics. Beelzebub then disillusions her by telling her that the love verses were sung by Solomon in his youth to a farmer's virtuous daughter whose scruples he overcame by his poetic gifts. The king later gave a copy of the Song of Songs to each of the ladies he wooed and made each in turn think herself supreme in his affections. The Queen of Sheba is but the last in a long series of seven hundred wives and three hundred concubines.

Horrified by such perfidy, the queen vows that she will never again let flattery deceive her. And yet, when Beelzebub entices her with honeyed words, she is again beguiled and agrees to extend her travels by a visit to his dominion. She trusts herself completely to his guidance and ends up being deceived a second time. But now she cannot escape, since the realm of Beelzebub is the abode of the dead. He tells her that she will be his consort until superseded by Cleopatra. At these words, a tumult of rage and despair overcomes her, and she awakes from her horrible dream.

The Yiddish poet Yehoash, who is famed for his magnificent translation of the Bible, also adapted and expanded upon many of its themes. His "Queen of Sheba" is the longest of his biblical poems. It consists of five cantos. It relates that when the news of Solomon's greatness reaches young Queen Balchis in her remote kingdom, it is not his wealth or reputed nobility of mien that impresses her but rather his supreme wisdom. In vain has she searched in Sheba's ancient temples to find an answer to the riddle of existence. Will Solomon perhaps have the answer? And so she sets out with her retinue of slaves and with rich gifts. For weeks she travels through the desert seated on her throne atop a tall elephant and dreams of the all-wise king. When she meets him, she offers him her wealth for a fragment of his wisdom. Overwhelmed by her loveliness, however, he descends from his throne to woo her. His eyes burn with desire. But, as the queen listens to his words of passion, she turns pale. His words fall upon her heart like heavy stones, and her faith in his wisdom collapses.

For three thousand years, the encounter between Solomon and the Queen of Sheba has reverberated in written and oral lore. And today, when the traveler winds his way along Israel's main road from the north and nears Eilat, the gateway to the African continent, he is advised to make a slight detour in order that he might view King Solomon's Pillars and the natural amphitheatrical opening in the mountains fronting the Araba. There, the traveler's guide explains, the legendary queen, who came up with her rich retinue from her southern kingdom of Sheba, first caught sight of her host, King Solomon, who descended from his northern kingdom in order to escort her to his capital, Jerusalem, the citadel of David, and the Temple he had just built for the Lord, the God of Israel.

20

Sulamith Unallegorized

Sulamith is the heroine of the Song of Songs, which is chanted by Jews on the eve of the Sabbath and read in the synagogues on Passover. This song is a passionate expression of a love that embraces body and soul, a love that burns with a most vehement flame and that is as strong as death. Because of its intense erotic components, the song might not have been incorporated into the Book of Books if it had not been reinterpreted allegorically by rabbinical authorities to meet Jewish religious needs and later on reallegorized by the church fathers to suit Christian needs.

The Talmud reflects the Jewish allegorical approach, which prevailed throughout the Middle Ages and which is still dominant in contemporary Orthodox circles. Rabbi Akiva, whose great authority was most influential in bringing about the inclusion of this scroll among the sacred writings, called it the holiest book of the Bible. Though the song, in its literal meaning, hymns the love between man and woman, a love which is aglow with longing and aflame with passionate fulfillment, allegorical interpretations and misinterpretations have reduced the vibrant personalities of this ardent encounter to abstractions devoid of flesh and blood. Jewish commentators saw in this literary work an allegory of the love of God for Israel, His chosen people, a spiritual relationship enduring throughout all ages. God is the sublime bridegroom, and Israel the beloved bride and the recipient of His grace. Christian commentators, on the other hand, saw in the Song of Songs an expression of the love of their savior for his bride, the Church.

Modern poets, painters, and musicians have generally rejected the allegorical abstractions and have reinstated Sulamith in her role as a maiden, young, beautiful, pure at heart, and yet seething with passion and inflaming her beloved herdsman and King Solomon with equally ardent desire for love's fulfillment.

The eighteenth-century German philosopher Johann Gottfried Herder pioneered in the deallegorization of the Song of Songs. In 1778, his translation and commentary had a great impact. He is ironic about his predecessors, who refused to acknowledge that the obvious theme of the song attributed to Solomon was love. He felt that it might be called the Scroll of Love, for it began with a kiss and ended with a tender sigh. It portrayed the affection of an innocent country lass for a young herdsman, a love that was naive, tender, natural, and that embraced their naked bodies and their clothed bodies from the maiden's shoes to her headdress and from the youth's turban to his legs, which were pillars of marble set upon sockets of fine gold.

For Herder, the song was Solomonic, even if not every line stemmed from his hand. It was an echo of Solomon's youthful soul before he came to know women's folly and idolatry. Not since Adam sang of Eve in Paradise, and never thereafter, were such chords struck. Isaac might jest with Rebecca, Jacob might undergo years of servitude for Rachel, but they did not sing of their love. The eras of Moses and of Deborah were filled with songs of triumph in war but not of triumphant love. David's reign was still too much steeped in blood for such love idyls to sprout. Only Solomon's wise, peaceful, prosperous reign could be blessed with such splendid love lyrics. The king himself competed with his court poets in such songs. The idyllic tale of Sulamith was the supreme flowering of his youthful soul, a tale of delicate taste and boundless joy, a tale that followed the course of love from its budding through its various ripening stages until its climax of ecstasy. It was hymned by the king before he became sated with too many strange wives, before this wisest of men was led astray by them and became the biggest fool, undermining his own mighty empire in his luxurious, decaying years.

The influence of Herder, the Protestant thinker of the Age of Enlightenment, has been felt until our own day. Among Jewish thinkers, Max Brod undertook in the second volume of his *Heidentum, Christentum, Judentum* (1921) a similar deallegorization of the Song of Songs. He reconstructed what he felt must have been its original structure as a love idyl by rearranging the verses, without adding or changing a single word. He held that the original order of the verses was scrambled by biblical scribes so that the scroll could be accepted as a symbolic religious tract. He also sensed in this hymn to love an antimonarchical tendency, a rejection of the king in favor of a mere herdsman. He based this conclusion on a passage such as "If one were to give all the treasures of his house for love, it would be utterly scorned (8:7), and on Sulamith's telling Solomon that her vineyard belongs to her and that he may keep his wealthy vineyard with its fruit that brings in a thousand pieces of silver (8:11, 12). Sulamith is not lured to be Solomon's mate in his royal harem. She rather seeks to flee to her beloved herdsman. Though stopped by the town's watchmen and the keepers of the town's walls, she will yet find her way to him and live happily with him ever thereafter.

The German-Jewish poet Heinrich Heine, during his excruciating final period in a Paris garret, which he characterized as his mattress-grave, wrote a poem about King Solomon at the height of his royal glory. This lyric, entitled "Salomo," and included in the cycle *Romanzero*, showed the wise king in restless sleep, escaping from horrible nightmares to a happier dream of Sulamith, a dream which ends with his outcry: "O Sulamith, the empire is my heritage, the lands are subject to me; I am king over Judah and Israel; and yet, if you do not love me, I shall fade away and die."

Micha Joseph Lebensohn, one of the foremost Hebrew poets of Heine's generation, portrayed the love of Solomon and Sulamith in his romantic poem "Solomon and Koheleth." This poem was included in his *Shire Bat Zion*, published in 1851, a year before his death at the age of twenty-four. The young poet, who knew himself to be dying, was aware of the vanity of existence even as he grasped at the flickering embers of life.

The poem consists of two cantos. In the first canto, he depicted Solomon in the exuberance of youth and Sulamith delighting in his all-absorbing passion. Solomon has not yet begun to brood over the meaning of life, and Sulamith is impressed not by his royal diadem but by the glowing magic of his kisses. The second canto projected Solomon as Koheleth, the aged sage seated on his golden throne, sated with experience, disillusioned with life's fleeting gifts, and yet afraid of death. He recalls his early beloved Sulamith, who died so young, and who, in her hour of dying, tried to comfort him with her faith in a reunion among the starry realms after both have shed their earthly frames. Alas, he who has made wisdom his primary goal cannot share her faith. As a skeptic, he doubts that soul can survive body. Searching for absolute truth, he has encountered riddles everywhere. Draining all pleasures, he has found them to be vanities. Final insight only comes to him in his last hour: to forgo hellish doubts and to have faith in God, who will bring everything to its proper conclusion.

A generation after the death of Lebensohn, the German poet and Nobel Prize laureate Paul Heyse wrote, in 1886, the drama *Die Weisheit Salomo's*, which S. L. Gordon translated into Hebrew under the title *Sulamith*. This play brings a confrontation between Balkis, the haughty Queen of Sheba, and Sulamith, the humble seventeen-year-old daughter of the keeper of Solomon's vineyard. Sulamith cannot be torn away from her first love, a young herdsman with whom she has grown up, even though Solomon offers her his hand and throne. The maturer Balkis, on the other hand, who is seemingly far wiser but still unloved, is attracted to the king; though he is indifferent to her, she nevertheless pursues him with intense *Liebeshass*. She comes up to Jerusalem from her remote southern realm after hearing of Solomon's reputed wisdom. She hopes he will be able to solve the riddle of life's meaning. But the best answer he can give her is that a person must first die and then perhaps he can catch glimpses of a higher knowledge than is afforded to the living during their brief moment on earth. As long as we are still alive, each day seems to teach us that all is vanity of vanities. Generations come with their restlessness and then fade away. Even the wisest sink into the grave and are ultimately forgotten. Splendor, power, passion, pain are vanities, and so are good and evil. It is far better not to have seen the light of the sun than to come to the realization that everything upon which the light shines is really without permanent substance. When Balkis asks whether the king would also include love among life's vanities, he replies that, having experienced so much of it, it too is vanity, though of a precious kind, and lasting but for a brief moment. It is like a fire kindled by the wind, only to be extinguished by the rain.

In the course of the dramatic action, however, during which Solomon offers Sulamith throne and splendor and asks for her freely given love, he realizes that he can compel her to become his wife but he cannot compel her heart to love him. When Sulamith and her herdsman insist on being faithful to each other even when threatened with death, Solomon learns that not everything is vanity. True love is more precious than all treasures. It defies death and endures beyond life. He also learns, and impresses this lesson upon the jealous Balkis, whose affections he cannot reciprocate, that the crown of wisdom is to rejoice without envy at the happiness of others. Both king and queen are then ready to bless the young couple who are experiencing a greater love than they themselves, rulers of mighty realms, have ever known or may ever know.

A generation after Heyse, the Russian novelist Alexander Kuprin, though a realist of the Gorky tradition, eschewed realistic effects when he wrote his *Sulamith: A Tale of Antiquity* in 1908, three years after he had risen to fame with his antimilitaristic novel *The Duel*, which depicted the emptiness of life in a remote military garrison, and four years before the appearance of his best-known novel, *The Pit*, a naturalistic narrative of prostitution.

In *Sulamith*, he escaped in imagination from the Russian milieu of tsarist oppression to a distant, glamorous era. In this romantic tale of the last love of the aging Solomon, Sulamith is presented as a thirteen-year-old who has not yet tasted of the fruits of love.

Written in idyllic prose, this tale cemented the passages of the

Song of Songs and the fantasies of Kuprin's imagination into a mosaic whose theme was the cometlike emergence of Sulamith into the life of Solomon and her ensuing death because of the jealousy of his principal wife.

The novelist reveals an aging Solomon upon whom normal pleasures have palled and who has become sated with wisdom. He has already arrived at the conclusion that in much wisdom there is much grief, and that all ambitions, once attained, prove to be worthless and a vexation of spirit. It is then, in his deepest despondency, that he comes to know a love, tender and ardent, devoted and beautiful, more precious than riches, fame, or wisdom, more precious even than life itself.

Sulamith is Solomon's last great experience. He hears this rustic maiden singing in a vineyard to which he has withdrawn for an hour of deep meditation. He sees her walking between the rows of vines and tying up the clusters of grapes. His eyes cast a spell over her and make her head dizzy. Radiant with joy is their love from the moment he meets her among the vines until he brings her into his palace as his newest wife. But there, in his palace, Queen Astis, a daughter of Pharaoh, a worshiper of the goddess Isis, and the most splendid of his many wives and concubines, becomes aware that the king has tired of her Egyptian unbridled sensuality and is displacing her with a new favorite. With all the jealousy of a woman scorned, she plots the death of her young successor in Solomon's affections. On the seventh night of the king's new marriage, at the climax of his new love, Sulamith is struck down in the palace by the gleaming sword of an assassin sent by Queen Astis.

Sulamith's last words are an expression of gratitude for the love, beauty, and wisdom which Solomon has let her share. His last words, before she ceases to be, are: "As long as men and women shall love one another; as long as beauty of soul and body shall be the best and sweetest dream in the universe,—so long, I swear to you, Sulamith, shall your name be uttered through many ages with emotion and gratefulness."

The novelist concludes that many ages have already passed since then. "There have been kingdoms and kings, and of them no trace has been left, as of a wind that has sped over a desert. There have been prolonged, merciless wars, after which the names of the commanders shone through the ages, like ensanguined stars; but time has effaced even the very memory of them. However, the love of the lowly maiden of the vineyard and the great king shall never pass away or be forgotten."

Sulamith lived on in Jewish folklore, especially in the folklore of Eastern European Jewry until the Holocaust. Jewish youths in their daydreams had more radiant visions of her than of any other biblical beauty, visions fed by their repeated exposure at school and synagogue to the verses of the Song of Songs.

It was therefore most appropriate for Abraham Goldfaden, the father of the Yiddish theater, to model the heroine of his musical melodrama *Shulamith* (1880) upon the beloved of King Solomon. The dramatist did not have to picture in detail his heroine's loveliness, for her name already evoked thought-associations and emotional attachments wafted across the millennia. His Shulamith, too, is a simple, beautiful shepherdess. While on a Succoth pilgrimage to Jerusalem, she loses her way and falls into a well. She is saved by Abshalom, a young aristocrat, a descendant of the Maccabees. When he falls in love with the rescued maiden and offers to marry her, she at first demurely wards off his advances. What could she, a villager and a guardian of sheep, offer to interest the sophisticated urbanite who could far better amuse himself with Jerusalem's rich daughters? But Abshalom sees in her a reincarnation of the earlier Sulamith whom King Solomon preferred to all the princesses available to him. The young man, therefore, vows to ask her father for her hand. Soon, however, he proves faithless to his vow and marries Abigail, the daughter of a Jerusalem priest and famed as the pearl of the Orient.

In vain does Shulamith wait a year and then another year. Abshalom does not come to her home. When she learns of his faithlessness, she invokes the vengeance of God upon him. As a result, his two children perish. Then he realizes the enormity of his guilt and returns repentant to his beloved Shulamith, who has remained unswervingly loyal to her only love.

Sulamith Unallegorized

This musical melodrama of Goldfaden's was more popular than his many other comedies, tragedies, operettas, and historical plays. Its lyrics were on the lips of millions of Yiddish-speaking persons, and its opening song, "Rozhinkes mit Mandeln," still resounds in Jewish homes, classrooms, and at folk gatherings on all continents.

Goldfaden's *Shulamith* was being presented on many Yiddish stages of the closing nineteenth century when Yitzkhak Leibush Peretz, the profoundest of Yiddish writers, wrote his tale "Venus and Sulamith," in which he contrasted the Hellenic and Jewish ideals of love and loveliness.

In a dialogue between two Yeshiva lads, which takes place in a study hall attached to a synagogue of an Eastern European townlet, Chaim reads from a booklet that Hannah was as beautiful as Venus, and he asks his companion Zelik to tell him who Venus was. He then learns that she was a Greek goddess of love, that she arose naked from the sea, that she had as husband a god named Vulcan, with whom she had no children, and that, in addition, she had several lovers, including Mars, the god of war, with whom she had two children, Bacchus, the god of drunkards, with whom she also had two children, Mercury, the god of thieves and businessmen, with whom she had two more children, and Anchises, a mere mortal, with whom she had a son, Aeneas.

Zelik further explains that Venus heaped vengeance upon all who did not pay homage to her, and that once she even transformed the inhabitants of an entire city into oxen.

When Zelik ends his description of the Greek goddess of love by comparing her to Sulamith of the Song of Songs, Chaim gets very angry. How dare one desecrate the name of the pure, radiant Sulamith by comparing her to the immoral murderess Venus, who had affairs with so many men! Sulamith was healthy, young, immaculate. She was no gypsy, flitting about from one person to another. She was more fragrant than all meadows, forests, and gardens. She had nothing to be ashamed of and was not the least bit conceited. She had warm, good-natured eyes like those of a dove. When she spoke, honey dripped from her lips. In her presence, no unseemly thought could arise. On the contrary, when she looked with her modest eyes at a person, he lowered his own eyes and a tremor passed through his heart. When she awoke to love, it was a love stronger than death and lasting unto eternity. But it was love for only one person, a young, handsome shepherd. She did not know that, when away from her, this shepherd wore a crown on his head and was the world's greatest monarch. She did not engage in secret affairs. She regretted that her adored herdsman was not her brother, born of the same father and mother, so that she could kiss him openly in the sight of all. She was a true Jewish daughter, who had a respectable father and mother, and not a lewd, motherless creature like Venus, who arose from sea-foam.

Zelik concludes his glowing tribute to Sulamith by suggesting that Hannah of Chaim's booklet might be compared to Miriam, Abigail, Rachel, Delilah, even to Queen Esther or any other beautiful woman, but not to the incomparable Sulamith. No one was as superb as the maiden of the Song of Songs.

Peretz's lifelong interest in Sulamith is reflected in his three translations of the Song of Songs, the last one completed in 1914, a year before his death. In his introduction, of which there are several versions, he stresses that the allegorical interpretation of this scroll was once necessary in order that it be included among the sacred texts, but when the scroll is deallegorized, as it should be, there emerges the true and glamorous picture of natural life in ancient Israel, the beauty of fields, gardens, and vineyards at the foot of Mount Hermon, the loveliness of the naked rocks in the desert landscape of Baal-Hamon, the delight in wine, women, song, and dance, joy without sophistication in the Solomonic springtime of the Jewish people.

Shalom Aleichem was no less fascinated by Sulamith than was Peretz. His vision of the biblical maiden permeates his autobiographic romance *Shir Ha-shirim* (1909-11), the story of a boy's idealization of a girl with whom he grew up. The young hero, who studies the Song of Songs at school and chants it in the synagogue, envisages Buzi, who is a year younger than he, as the contemporary Sulamith. In his dreams of her, he addresses her in verses culled from the biblical scroll, and he experiences their meetings and partings as paralleling the idyllic encounters between Solomon and Sulamith. As he grows up, he leaves the townlet of his birth in order to seek modern learning far from home. He becomes estranged from father, mother, and his playmate Buzi. However, when word reaches him of Buzi's engagement and coming marriage, his suppressed feelings for her, the ideal companion of his boyhood years, well up in him, and he decides to revisit his home during the Passover season, the *Shir-Ha-shirim* season. There he relives with Buzi, for a few brief hours, scenes and memories of earlier years, when he reveled in images of her as Sulamith. He is able to compare the values of the traditional world from which he moved away with the values of the modern world that lured him. At this point, Shalom Aleichem, the greatest of Yiddish humorists, refuses to continue with the epilogue of his youthful romance, a romance that began so happily and that still evokes in him painful memories of what might have been.

A contemporary of Shalom Aleichem, the trilingual poet S. S. Frug, in his Yiddish lyric "Shulamis," reacted to the Russian pogroms of the closing nineteenth century by calling upon his coreligionists to return to their ancient homeland and to a pastoral and agricultural life on the ancestral soil which was waiting to be reclaimed from the desert. He issued his call through the voice of the idealized biblical shepherdess Sulamith. With her new song of Zion, she seeks to arouse from inertia her dejected and insulted bridegroom Israel, to inject new energy into him, and to inspire him to help himself instead of merely waiting for God to deliver him from his troubles. She offers to heal his sick limbs and embittered soul and to bring hope, joy, and strength to him if he will only come to share with her a life in Zion.

At about the same time as Frug turned from lamenting the horrors of the Russian pogroms in lyrics of faith in the coming rebirth of his people in Zion, the American Yiddish poet Morris Rosenfeld, who called himself a tear-drop millionaire, and who bewailed in heart-rending verses the crushing of the Jewish immigrant soul by the sweatshop system, also saw new hope for his people in their return to the soil of Zion. From sad songs of toil in shops and tenements, as slaves to machines, he turned to songs of longing for Jewish national revival. His poem "Shulamis" bore the subtitle "The Golden Love of the Song of Songs." His heroine is the Orient's most beautiful daughter, a shepherdess who helps to guard the flock of King Solomon. When the monarch catches sight of her, his love for her is boundless. However, the love of the ideal Jewish maiden cannot be bought even for a throne. Her love is freely given to a shepherd who waits for her among the cedars. The wise and saddened king has to renounce his unreciprocated love for the unbribable Sulamith. This poem, as well as Rosenfeld's other national songs, belonged to the early romantic period of Zionism and offered an escape in imagination from the proletarian squalor in which Jewish immigrants lived and of which he wrote.

The lyric "Shulamis" of Moshe Broderzon, the popular Yiddish poet of Lodz, had no national overtones, since it was written after World War I, when Zionist romanticism was yielding to a more realistic assessment of what Jewish colonization on the parched earth of Palestine required in daily sacrifices. Most appropriately, the lyric appeared for the first time in the Passover issue of the Lodz organ *Der Folksblatt*, March 30, 1923, since the Song of Songs, of which Sulamith is the heroine, is read at synagogues on Passover. Broderzon's poem was a hymn to the lovely maiden in whose young heart longing has budded and whose childhood innocence is about to give way to a passionate arousal of the blood.

The two lyrics of the Yiddish poetess Kadia Molodowsky, "Shulamis" and "Tsum Melekh Shlome Kumt di Herlikhe Shulamis" ("Splendid Sulamith Comes to King Solomon"), continued the tradition of portraying the biblical shepherdess in the most glowing colors as the genuine maiden whose beauty never fades.

In Sulamith, the rose of Sharon, the lily among thorns, and a well of living waters, the Jewish people personified the ideal maiden, loving and beloved, modest and pure, ardent and faithful, unblemished in body and soul, a source of inspiration to creative spirits, ancient, modern, and in generations to come.

21

Solomon's Humiliation

Many centuries ago there lived a king in a large palace, surrounded by vineyards, gardens, orchards, and pools of water. He was served by a multitude of male and female servants on plates of silver and gold, for the treasures of many provinces were his. He was entertained by a choir of men singers and women singers and was delighted by the caresses of hundreds of wives and concubines. He sat on a throne whose magnificence awed all who came near him. Whatever his eyes desired, he did not withhold from himself. But he was also famed for his wisdom, which supposedly exceeded that of any of his contemporaries. His subjects wove an aura of legends about him. He was reputed to exercise dominion not only over people but also over beasts and birds, demons and spirits of the air. However, because everything he undertook prospered, he was gradually filled with arrogance and lost his moral hold upon himself.

Then catastrophe struck. He was cast down from his high estate and hurled away to a distant land, while a usurper took his place on the throne. The exiled king had to wander from province to province and to beg for bread from door to door. Wherever he mentioned that he had once been a king, he was laughed at and regarded as demented.

It was after experiencing such humiliation that the dethroned king attained to his greatest insight into life, an insight which he expressed in the single statement: "Vanity of vanities, all is vanity." And when, after several years, the usurper was finally driven from the throne and the legitimate king was reinstated, there was no more arrogance in the latter's heart. He realized that all living creatures, man and beast, were of the dust, and all returned to dust, and that a handful of quietness was better than both the hands full of striving after wealth, fame, power, victory, aggrandizement, and other vanities. He then became the prince of peace and truly the wisest of mortals.

The story of Koheleth, king over Israel in Jerusalem, who is far better known as Solomon, reverberated down the ages. It was later told, in a modified version, in the fourth chapter of the Book of Daniel, and retold by Geoffrey Chaucer as "The Monk's Tale" in the *Canterbury Tales*, about the mighty Nebuchadnezzar, king of Babylon and conqueror of Jerusalem, who was driven from his throne and for seven years roamed in the forest and ate grass, as do oxen, until his pride was humbled and he acknowledged the preeminence of a divine power. It was retold about Emperor Julian the Apostate, who tried to restore to the Roman Empire the worship of Venus, Apollo, and other pagan divinities, a version dramatized by Hans Sachs, the Meistersinger of Nuremberg, in his comedy of 1556, entitled *Julianus, der Kaiser im Bad*. It reappeared in the medieval *Gesta Romanorum* as the tale of Emperor Jovinian, a tale that was recast in the nineteenth century by William Morris, "the idle singer of an empty day," in his verse epic *The Earthly Paradise* (1868). His contemporary, the American poet Henry Wadsworth Longfellow, retold it in 1863, on the basis of an old English romance, as the humiliating experience of King Robert of Sicily. It was dramatized at the opening of the twentieth century by Frank Wedekind, the forerunner of German expressionism, as the story of King Nicolo, under the title *Such Is Life* (1902). The contemporary Yiddish novelists Abba Gordin and Saul Saphire, however, retained King Solomon as the central figure of this strange adventure, even as did the Hebrew versions from the talmudic period until Sammy Gronemann's poetic drama of 1942, *Der Weise und der Narr*, and as did also all the Yiddish versions since the *Maase-Book* of 1602 and the *Tseno Ureno* of 1616, both of them bestsellers in their century and frequently reprinted until the present.

The motivation for the Solomonic tale goes back to the early biblical commentators who tried to explain why a sentence in the opening chapter of Ecclesiastes read: "I, Koheleth, *was* king over Israel in Jerusalem," and not: "I, Koheleth, *am* king over Israel in Jerusalem." The commentators reasoned that there must have been a time during Solomon's life when he ceased to reign over Israel and that at such a time, recalling his earlier years of splendor and folly as a monarch, he recorded his pessimistic insight in the *Koheleth* scroll.

A commentary which goes back to the fifth century, *Pesikta de Rav Kahane* (26:2), tells of an angel who came down from heaven, assumed the likeness of Solomon, and seated himself upon the throne in Jerusalem. Meanwhile, the real Solomon found himself outside of the royal palace and went around everywhere trying to convince his listeners that he was the legitimate ruler over Israel. But he was always told in reply that he must be crazy, since King Solomon could be seen seated on the throne. When a pitying woman offered the famished, apparently demented person a dish of boiled grits or ground beans, he realized that all was vanity of vanities.

Rabbinical commentators differed as to whether Solomon ever regained his throne. Thus Rav, the founder of the Babylonian academy at Sura in the third century, said that Solomon was first a king and then ended as a commoner, while Rav's contemporary, Samuel, head of the house of learning at Nahardea, said that Solomon was first a king, then a commoner, and then again a king. Creative writers in later centuries were, therefore, free to choose between two possible endings. Did Solomon, after his humiliation, find ultimate happiness in being a righteous ruler, dispensing justice to all his subjects, without thought of the personal pleasures he had earlier found in wine, women, and song? Or did he attain contentment and greater peace of mind by remaining a commoner, freed from the cares, responsibilities, and intrigues of government, even as did, many centuries later, Emperor Charles V, ruler of the Holy Roman Empire and also of

Spain, the Netherlands, Naples, Sicily, and the New World, who abdicated his throne in 1556 and retired to a simpler life in the Spanish monastery of San Yuste?

The former version was preferred by the medieval narrators who substituted King Robert of Sicily for King Solomon. As modernized by Longfellow, in one of his *Tales of a Wayside Inn* (1863), Robert, ruler of Sicily, brother of a pope and of an emperor, once hears priests chanting the words: "The Lord has put down the mighty from their seat and has exalted them of low degree." He flares up in anger at such a seditious statement. He wants his subjects to know that there is no power that can push him from his throne. Soon thereafter, lulled by the monotonous chants, he falls asleep in the church. When he awakens, it is already night and he finds himself all alone. He has been locked in unnoticed, while an angel in his likeness and royal attire left with the worshipers. Forcing his way out of the church and rushing back to the palace, Robert comes into the banquet hall and finds another king seated there, wearing his robes, his crown, his signet-ring, and looking like him in every feature. Robert rages and storms at the imposter who has usurped his throne. But the angel-king, with unruffled brow, confronts the intruder and suggests that Robert, who claims to be the king, could far better qualify as the king's jester. When Robert's raving and threatening prove to be of no avail, he gradually adjusts to his role as a fool in cap and bells. After three years of humble living as a menial, he is sufficiently chastened to realize the truth of the words that the Lord can put down the mighty from their seat and can exalt those of low degree. Then is he fit to be restored to his throne.

The versions that substituted Emperor Jovinian for King Solomon also have the ruler regain his kingdom after his pride is humbled and he has experienced much suffering. Their main source was the *Gesta Romanorum*, a medieval collection of entertaining stories, each emphasizing a moral. The fifty-ninth tale, which stresses the aftermath of overweening haughtiness, has Jovinian survey his vast dominions and impiously assert that he is more than mere mortals, if not the equal of God. The next day, outriding all his servants while on a hunt, he dismounts at a stream to refresh himself in the water. But when he comes out of the water, he can find neither his horse nor his clothes. Someone has replaced him and ridden off as the emperor. Naked and ashamed, he makes his way to the castle of a knight. When he introduces himself as the emperor, he is flogged for his impudence and driven off. He experiences similar treatment when he tries to make himself known to a duke. There he is imprisoned and fed bread and water before and after a lashing. Escaping from the dungeon, he finally gets to the palace. There he hopes he will be acknowledged as the emperor by his wife. But neither the empress nor his courtiers recognize him. Ultimately, his humiliation brings about a change in his personality. He repents of his arrogance and subjects himself to the mercy of God. Then the pretended emperor, who is an angel sent from heaven, vanishes from the scene, and Jovinian reascends the throne.

Hans Sachs, in a *Meisterlied* of 1549, remained faithful to the version of the *Gesta Romanorum*. However, in his comedy of 1556 on the same subject, he substituted Emperor Julian the Apostate as the haughty monarch who was humbled, mocked, beaten, and chased away from his palace until he repented of his apostasy and returned to the true God.

The Victorian poet William Morris entitled his tale based on the *Gesta Romanorum* "The Proud King," and added his own conclusion that the ruler, thirty years after he is restored to the throne, commands a clerk to write down the adventure, since no man is any longer alive who remembers that the madman once thrust out of the palace had been the king himself. He hopes that what happened to him will be taken to heart by his successor. Yet, like Rehoboam, the successor to Solomon, the new king who fills the throne upon Jovinian's death takes little heed of his predecessor's humiliation, so much do all things feed his swelling pride.

> But whether God chastised him in his turn
> And he grew wise thereafter, I know not;
> I think by eld alone he came to learn
> How lowly on some day must be his lot.

Less popular among poets and novelists was the ending that Solomon never returned to his throne but lived on as a simple commoner far from his sumptuous palace and flattering courtiers. This ending, espoused by the ancient Babylonian talmudist Rav, was preferred by the contemporary writer Abba Gordin in his Yiddish historical novel *King Solomon* (1960). The author, who lived on three continents and wrote in the four languages Russian, English, Hebrew, and Yiddish, adhered to anarchism as his political and social philosophy, and regarded all governments as evil and oppressive. He, therefore, depicted Solomon as sated with orgies, wives, slaves, and palaces, and as disgusted with court intrigues and sycophantic courtiers. Voluntarily he abandons his kingdom and flees incognito from Jerusalem. He has arrived at the conclusion that people do not need a king but only the illusion that behind the portals of a palace lives someone in royal attire who rules over them. A golem could be substituted on the throne and would gain the reputation of a successful monarch, provided that there were competent generals and warriors to fight his wars for him. If all kings were dethroned, life could still go on normally, but if peasants were to stop cultivating the soil, a real catastrophe would result.

In ragged clothes, begging for food and then insisting on paying for his nourishment with hard work, Solomon wanders on and on until, in his third year, he overhears a fantastic rumor that Ashmedai, king of the demons, has usurped the throne in Jerusalem and that the real king has been hurled far away. Solomon's reaction is that only Ashmedai could find satisfaction in ruling, indeed, that every ruler, no matter how benevolent his beginnings, must become in time a demonic Ashmedai. Dominion over others corrupts. Government is a diabolic institution.

The itinerant Solomon finally arrives in Rabbat Ammon and finds honest work as a dishwasher in the royal palace. There he rediscovers Princess Naamah, whom he had earlier known, loved, and lost when she, disguised as a shepherdess, escaped the fate of her brothers, who were slaughtered by the Hebrews after David's victory over the Ammonites. When the king of Ammon hears of the love of his daughter for the dishwasher, he imprisons both and condemns them to death. Before the sentence can be carried out, the queen helps them to escape. They make their way to a remote fishing village. There they live to the end of their days, happy to be far removed from the evil world of rulers and ruled.

The legend of Solomon's love for Naamah, daughter of the king of Ammon, goes back to ancient sources and reappears in the kabbalistic tract *Emek Hamelekh* (*The King's Valley*, 14a-15a) of Naphtali Bacharach, published in 1648. The Bible mentions, in I Kings 14:21, that Naamah was the mother of Rehoboam. Since it also states that Rehoboam was forty-one years old when his father died, after ruling over Israel for forty years, the love of Solomon for the disguised shepherdess Naamah must have occurred before he ascended the throne and not afterwards. However, the novelist had to change the chronology in order to make the story conform to his political and social philosophy. His predecessor, the seventeenth-century kabbalist, also had to manipulate the chronology, and also had to emphasize the saintliness of Naamah, but for a different reason, namely, in order to make her worthy of being the ancestress from whom the Messiah will descend at the end of days.

In the talmudic version of the humiliated Solomon, as related in *Gittin* 68b, the role of the usurper is assigned not to an angel but to Ashmedai, and it is the king's experience with this demonic adversary that opens his eyes to the vanity of all earthly power and possessions.

As the possessor of the ring upon which God's Ineffable Name is engraved, Solomon is able to keep Ashmedai in chains and to get him to complete the building of the Temple. One day, when both are alone, Solomon wants to know wherein the demons are superior to human beings. Ashmedai replies that if the king would remove his chains and lend him the magic ring, this superiority would be demonstrated. Solomon agrees. Then Ashmedai swallows the ring and, placing one wing on the earth and the other on the sky, he hurls the king four hundred parsangs away and palms himself off as King Solomon.

The dethroned Solomon wanders about begging from place to

place and insisting that he is the legitimate king of Israel. When he finds his way back to Jerusalem and comes to the Sanhedrin with his claim, the rabbis inquire of Benaiah whether the king has sent recently for this faithful servant, and the answer is no. They then ask the queens whether the king ever visits them. They reply yes, but that he behaves peculiarly. The rabbis of the Sanhedrin recall that demons have legs like those of a cock and therefore ask the queens to examine their husband's legs. But the queens reply that he always comes in stockings. Thereupon the rabbis give the claimant another ring with the engraved Ineffable Name. When Ashmedai then catches sight of Solomon, he flies away, and Solomon regains his throne.

In Arabic literature, the role of the usurper was taken over neither by an angel nor by Ashmedai but by the rebellious spirit Sakhr. Just as a single sentence in *Koheleth* sufficed to stimulate the creative imagination of Jewish commentators and talmudists, so too did a single passage in the Koran stimulate Moslem commentators and storytellers to elaborate its significance by the addition of illustrative tales. The relevant passage, sura 38:34 f., is as follows: "Certainly we made trial of Solomon, and we placed a phantom upon his throne, then he repented in true devotion. He said: 'O my Lord, forgive me.' "

A typical Arabic tale of the testing of Solomon related that when the king was washing himself, he used to take off his signet-ring, in which his power resided, and ask one of his wives to hold it. Sakhr, the demon who lived in the sea, comes to her on such an occasion in the figure of her husband and asks her for the ring. When she gives it to him, he is able to usurp Solomon's place on the throne. The true Solomon is driven away from the palace as an imposter. For forty days Sakhr rules over Israel, while Solomon roams about as a beggar. These are forty days of humiliation that rid the dethroned king of his arrogance. Toward the end of this period of trial, he is hired by a fisherman as an assistant and is given two fish each day as his pay. On the fortieth day, the demon Sakhr drops the ring in the sea, and it is immediately swallowed by a fish. When the fish is caught and given to the hungry Solomon for his supper, he cuts it open and discovers the ring. Then his power returns to him. He regains his throne and reigns thereafter as a wise and just king.

The final episode of the Solomonic tale reappears in the Arabic collection *A Thousand and One Nights* as the testing of a pious Israelite. This good person gives the money he has received in the marketplace to a friend who is in greater need. Coming home without any money, he finds an old jug and an old cap. He tries to sell them, but nobody wants to buy them except a fisherman who pays for them with a fish. When the fish is split open, a pearl is found in it, which the pious Israelite then sells for seventy thousand drachmas. On his way home with this immense sum, a beggar accosts him, and the Israelite tells him: "Yesterday, I was as poor as you. Take half of my money. The beggar replies: "Keep your money. God bless you. I am a messenger of God, sent to try you." The Israelite praises God and lives happily ever after.

On the basis of Arabic, Persian, and Turkish sources, Joseph Freiherr von Hammer-Purgstall included in his collection of tales, *Rosenöl* (1813), the episode of Solomon's dethronement. According to this account, genii have tried for twenty years to obtain Solomon's magic ring. Finally, one of his many wives, who is secretly an idol-worshiper, finds an opportunity at night to slip it off his finger and hands it over to a demon named Sihrtshin. The demon then impersonates Solomon on the throne. When Solomon asserts his claim as the legitimate monarch, he is mocked, beaten, and expelled. Becoming aware of his helplessness, he keeps from starving by hiring himself out to fishermen. Though the demon is at first successful in impersonating Solomon, his demonic nature soon reasserts itself, and the people become suspicious of their ruler, especially since his decisions lack wisdom. The wives of the harem complain that the king no longer visits them, and the concubines complain that when he does visit them, he behaves in a wild and arrogant manner, unworthy of Solomon. The Hebrew priests and prophets then decide to get at the truth by conjuring. They assemble in front of the throne with Torah scrolls in their hands and begin to chant passages aloud with so much Jewish clamor as can be heard only in a Jewish school. The demon cannot resist such penetrating noise and flees to the depths of the sea, his more congenial element, abandoning his kingdom and throwing away the signet-ring. On the same day, Solomon finds the ring in the fish on which he wants to lunch. He regains his kingdom and reigns for another twenty years.

Shortly after Hammer-Purgstall published his *Rosenöl*, the German poet and novelist August Friedrich Ernst Langbein wrote his verse "Märchen vom König Luthbert." His model for King Luthbert was Napoleon, who had been hurled from his imperial throne and exiled to Elba. Did Napoleon learn the lesson that arrogance and tyranny did not pay, and would he be a better ruler if he made a comeback from his exile?

Luthbert, who only knows how to command others and to wage bloody wars, has to beg from house to house after his dethronement and learns to give thanks for a bit of bread. In his humiliation, he betakes himself to a hermit, who recognizes him as the real king and upbraids him for his tyrannical rule, which has plunged the country into misery, and for his wars, which have resulted in a sea of blood. However, now that the king himself has experienced what it means to be a beggar, remorse at his earlier nefarious behavior assails him, and he promises, if forgiven, to be henceforth a father to the poor and to walk in God's ways. Thereupon he is restored to his former greatness, but whether he then really behaved better, the poet left unsaid. Apparently, it was not clear to Langbein how Napoleon, the model for King Luthbert, would have behaved if he had made a successful comeback and had not been defeated at Waterloo.

There is considerable similarity between the theme of Solomon's dethronement and his return to power and the theme of the prince who exchanges clothes with a pauper and experiences humiliations until he is restored to his princely estate. However, there is no evidence that the latter theme, as best treated by Mark Twain in his novel *The Prince and the Pauper*, was influenced by the former. The similarities can better be explained by parallel patterns of thought operating upon creative minds. Nor can any relationship be established between the Solomonic theme and the theme of the beggar who is elevated to aristocracy and then hurled back into the gutter. The latter theme also went through a considerable development from a tale in the *Arabian Nights* and Shakespeare's *Taming of the Shrew* to Ludwig Holberg's *Jeppe vom Berge* and Gerhart Hauptmann's *Schluck und Jau*. The two themes are, however, combined in Sammy Gronemann's German comedy *Der Weise und der Narr*, which has been repeatedly staged in Hebrew since the first performance by Tel Aviv's Ohel Theater in 1942. After the text was set to music by Alexander Argov in 1965, it became the first successful Hebrew musical comedy, under the title *Solomon and the Cobbler*.

Gronemann, the son of a rabbi, was immersed in biblical lore. Though he had to give up his successful career as a jurist in Berlin when Hitler came to power, he did not give up his optimistic view of the world. In his satiric tales and plays after reaching Palestine in 1936, his wit and wisdom cheered readers and theater audiences both before and after the emergence of the embattled Jewish state.

Gronemann's King Solomon, even at the summit of power, remains a lonely, unhappy person, who flees to books and women. On the other hand, the cobbler Shemadai, whose features resemble those of Solomon, is a happy person, though often wallowing in drunkenness, jeered by his cronies, and scolded by his distraught wife. Solomon, who maintains that a king remains a king even in beggarly clothes, and that a beggar retains the traits of a lowly commoner even if garbed in royal robes, undertakes to prove that the opposite dictum, held by others, that clothes make the man is far from the truth. He summons Shemadai to the palace and exchanges clothes with him. Thereupon the unrecognized Solomon is thrust out of the palace, and the royally swathed Shemadai adjusts quickly to the kingly role. It is this cobbler turned king who unwittingly solves the riddles of the Queen of Sheba and wins ever greater adulation. However, Shemadai's new eminence does not bring him happiness, even as it did not to Solomon. The cobbler finds kingship a lonely, miserable existence. He is bored even when rushed from one festive ceremony to another, and he feels his muscles growing flabby when deprived of physical work. He can hardly wait for his ordeal to end, so that he can return to cobbling. Solomon, meanwhile, acquires deeper insight and greater humility by mingling with ordinary folk on their level. He realizes that man is in God's hands and that much which formerly appeared important is in reality trivial. He returns to the throne, and Shemadai to hammer and last, both to continue their brief span on earth as best they may before death envelops them.

In 1971, the Israeli composer Josef Tal composed the opera *Ashmedai*, based on a libretto by Israel Eliraz. Its theme was a wager between the king, who is proud of the culture, music, religion, and enduring peace he has brought to his people of simple peasants, and Ashmedai, the chief of the devils, who holds that peace is undesirable and that the kingdom's subjects are really yearning for the glory of conflict and conquest. Ashmedai suggests that the correctness of his own view could be tested if the king and he were to exchange roles and he were to take over the conduct of the state for a year. The king, who is certain that the people will not tolerate the rule of a stupid devil, agrees to the interchange. Ashmedai takes over the reins of government. He introduces a military dictatorship. His subjects readily adjust to war, cruelty, murder, injustice, and exciting orgies, even though they see ruin gradually spreading about them. When the year is over and the king, in accordance with the wager, replaces Ashmedai, he finds to his dismay that he cannot end the bloodthirsty system. Officers, soldiers, and the masses of ordinary people, under the leadership of his own son, accuse the king of wanting to betray the regime which has registered victories on many battlefields and conquered much territory, even though final victory has not yet been attained but might be within grasp. Philosophers, musicians, and theologians acclaim the verdict of death pronounced upon the royal pacifist. After the liquidation of the peace-loving monarch, Ashmedai exults and leaves the scene. The people, who are left with the ruins of their kingdom, deny that such a devil had existed, and they are purified by the holy water of the priest. Only the daughter remains at the end as the representative of another world in which the sun shines golden, the fields are carpeted with flowers, and blue peacocks fly on clouds up to heaven.

The opera is obviously a commentary on Germany before, during, and after the Nazi period, with Hitler as the model for Ashmedai and the German people as his willing dupes.

Despite the introduction of comic elements into the story of Solomon's humiliation, the theme is basically pessimistic, proclaiming the final insight of Israel's monarch in Ecclesiastes that all things are full of weariness and that all striving is but vanity, a conclusion well expressed by Christina Rossetti's verses on Solomon:

> He who wore out pleasure and mastered all love,
> Solomon wrote "Vanity of vanities;"
> Down to death, of all that went before,
> In his mighty long life the record is this.
>
> With loves by the hundreds, wealth beyond measure,
> In this he who wrote "Vanity of vanities!"
> Yea, "Vanity of vanities," he saith of pleasure
> And of all he learned set his seal to this.

22

Elijah in Yiddish Literature

During the Passover festival the legendary figure of the prophet Elijah is as vividly alive in Jewish consciousness as is Santa Claus in Christian consciousness at Christmas time. However, unlike Santa Claus, Elijah does not have to steal into homes through the chimneys even when bringing gifts. For Elijah the front door is opened, the cup of wine is filled, and warm hospitality is extended, even if he enters as a beggar and brings no gifts.

The exploits of Elijah have been related from mouth to mouth down the centuries, and his intervention in hours of adversity was envisioned in dreams of old and young. As the forerunner of the Messiah, he stirred the imagination of aggadic sages, poets, storytellers, dramatists.

Already in talmudic and medieval lore, the wrathful prophet of Ahab's reign, the implacable foe of Baal and the wicked Jezebel, was transformed into a compassionate helper and protector of the Jewish people amidst their distress. Kabbalists and Hassidim saw in Elijah the revealer of the hidden knowledge of mysticism.

The Hebraic and Aramaic Elijah legends were made available to English readers by Louis Ginzberg in his *Legends of the Jews* (1928). The folktales of Elijah, transmitted orally by Eastern European, Yiddish-speaking, simple men and women were collected and studied by Shmuel Lehman, Shlome Bostansky, J. L. Cahen, S. M. Segal, B. S. Weinreich, and Abraham Menes. Several fascinating tales in Old Yiddish printed sources have been described adequately. These include the Elijah stories in the *Maase Book* of 1602, translated into English by Moses Gaster and analyzed by Jacob Meitlis, and also an early-eighteenth-century Yiddish variant of the Joseph della Reina legend in which Elijah is a central figure and which Zalman Rubashov, better known as Zalman Shazar, Israel's third president, discussed with great acumen in *Edar he-Yekar*, the festive volume published in honor of the Hassidic scholar S. A. Horodetzky (1947). However, the rich development of the Elijah theme in Yiddish literature of the nineteenth and twentieth centuries still awaits scholarly investigation.

The earliest of the Yiddish classical triumvirate, Mendele Mocher Sforim, reproduced in Yiddish verses the chants sung at the close of the Sabbath about Elijah the Seer, Elijah the Tishbite, Elijah the Gileadite, Elijah the Herald of Messiah.

Shalom Aleichem composed a fantastic story of Elijah for Jewish children but intentionally left it incomplete so as to stimulate their creative imagination. His Elijah, an old man with a wrinkled face, a long beard, soft, kind eyes, and carrying a sack on his shoulders, offers a child who failed to stay awake to the end of the Seder evening a choice of being carried off in the sack or else of remaining asleep forever and ever. Leaning on his staff, Elijah waits for the boy to make up his mind—or is there still a third alternative as yet unexplored? The solution of the riddle posed by Shalom Aleichem is left to his young readers.

More frequently than Mendele or Shalom Aleichem was Peretz fascinated by the legendary figure of Elijah. In the beautiful, romantic novelette *Mesiras Nefesh*, he introduced Elijah as the teacher of Torah to a poor, homeless orphan who lives alone in the desert and nourishes himself on herbs. The young man cannot look at his teacher save from a distance, because the latter's eyes glisten in the dark like stars and his white beard is radiant like pure snow. Peretz also has Elijah pave the way for the redemption of the central character in the narrative, the repentant sinner Hananya.

In Peretz's tale "The Magician," Elijah is introduced as the savior of the believing couple Chaim-Yone and Rivke-Beele, conjuring up for them an unexpected Seder feast when they are unable to provide it for themselves. They are deemed worthy of his extraordinary assistance because, in adversity, they still retain faith in the fundamental justice that must prevail in heaven and on earth, in the realm of God and in the destiny of man.

In a tale written for children Peretz lets the kind-hearted, white-bearded wanderer Elijah come into a home to rest for a while. He puts down his bundle, which is filled with raisins, almonds, and other sweets, and he talks about the rewards available to children who behave properly.

In Peretz's most popular Elijah story, "Seven Years of Plenty," he has Elijah offer the porter Tevye seven good years. These can be taken immediately, but thereafter Tevye will revert to his poor condition, or else the years can be allotted to him at the end of his life, and then he will leave this world as a wealthy person. Tevye and his wife prefer to accept the proferred riches immediately, so that they can pay the tuition fee for their children to learn Torah. When Elijah reappears seven years later and learns that the pious couple have not used the wealth entrusted to them for any other purpose, he feels that they deserve to retain it until the end of their days.

In a one-act play by Peretz Hirshbein, Elijah is shown not only in the role of a bestower of bounties upon the worthy but also as one who takes back his benefactions if the recipients prove unworthy. When Elijah comes as a Sabbath guest to a poor villager and is received with great hospitality, then the winebottle he leaves his host after the Havdala continues to pour out wine into glasses and casks, the cow of the villager continues to give milk unceasingly, and the sack that the guest has seemingly forgotten continues to dispense gold coins until all unfilled vessels in the household are filled to the brim. However, when greediness takes possession of the family and Elijah's gift of Havdala wine is poured out from the casks in order to provide additional containers for gold pieces, then the sack ceases to be a magic purse and the heaped-up gold turns to dross. In pouring away God's wine, the family has poured away God's grace.

In H. Leivick's messianic dramas, from the earliest, *The Chains of Messiah*, written in 1908 during his imprisonment in Minsk for revolutionary agitation, to his better-known *The Golem*, written under the impact of the Russian Revolution of 1917, and *The Comedy of Salvation*, a sequel to *The Golem*, composed between 1930 and 1932, the Yiddish dramatist assigns to Elijah an important role as the forerunner of Messiah. In the first play, when the angel Azriel rebels against God's command to chain the Messiah until the distant era of redemption and prefers to forfeit the bliss of all the seven heavens for the deeper experience of sharing in the woe of earth and of man, Elijah, who once ascended to heaven on a chariot of fire, joins him in descending again to earth. He too is prepared to wander on all roads through the generations of pain, to work for the liberation of the Messiah from chains, and to comfort man with the assurance of glorious salvation as soon as the human heart has been cleansed of evil.

In *The Golem*, Leivick, who could not reconcile himself to the cost in blood and cruelty brought about by the revolutionary golem, has the true Messiah appear as a young beggar in the company of Elijah, an old beggar. Both roam about unheeded, and, when finally recognized by the Maharal, the golem's creator, are chased away by him. For their age has not yet dawned, their love is still unwanted and undeserved, human hearts are not yet purged of evil, suffering has not yet reached sufficient magnitude to renovate the human spirit.

Leivick's *Comedy of Salvation* takes place in the remote future and concentrates on the final struggles between Gog, Magog, the bloodstained, power-hungry, unholy Messiah of the House of Joseph, and the pure-hearted, love-imbued, holy Messiah of the House of David. The latter feels the pain and terror of the tortured and the slain. He embodies the conscience of the world and, as the true redeemer, is, therefore, the last to be redeemed. His companion in his travails is the blind, old beggar Elijah, who guards him from ill and suffers with him during the dominance of Gog, Magog, and Messiah ben Joseph.

The Elijah figure in the poetic cycle of Abraham Liessin has much in common with that of Leivick, as might be expected from the kindred strivings of both poets in prerevolutionary Russia and on American soil. Liessin's Elijah keeps on returning to earth every Passover during the twenty-eight centuries since his ascension to heaven. Each year he hopes for the promised redemption to nigh. He himself is the messenger of a coming salvation, but he cannot hasten the Messiah's arrival. He hears the living call from every house for the Redeemer, and he sees the shades of the dead point to himself as their expected resurrecter. But all he can do is to weep with the living and the dead and to plead with God to answer mankind's prayers for salvation.

For Aaron Glanz-Leyeles, as for other Yiddish poets, Elijah is the messenger of love who seeks to banish fear, to dispel care, and to convert each weekday to a holiday. Amidst the radiance of heaven, he yearns for his people, and they, in turn, yearn for him, trust in his righting of all wrongs and in his revealing the mysteries still concealed from them. In a cycle of sixteen sonnets, the poet describes various situations encountered by the wandering prophet. Passing the hovels of three families, Elijah avoids the first, in which loud anger is the reaction to poverty, and the second, from which vociferous complaints emanate, but enters the third, which is shrouded in darkness, silence, and sadness, to which he brings cheer. Coming to the wedding of a deaf-mute bride and a blind groom, he supplies food, wine, music, he entertains with happy, sweet melodies, he dances with the couple. Seeking to comfort the mother of a dying child, he tells her that it would be unwise to reawaken the child to the miseries of existence, but when she replies, "You are holy, great, divine, but not a mother," he is silent for a moment and then grants her wish to bring back the child to the world of the living.

Elijah, as viewed through the eyes of children, is a favorite figure in Yiddish poetry. Benjamin Bialostotsky, in his songs for children, recalls his own childhood in Lithuania, when he envisaged Elijah wandering through the world as a beggar and succoring the needy. Ever thereafter, the poet waited for Elijah and whenever he encountered a poor man, he wondered whether this seemingly humble person might not be the longed-for savior.

In the lyric "Eliahu Hanavi" by Naftoli Gross, children look out in holiday joy from rooms radiating dazzling light and seated at tables bedecked with golden wine-cups. They hope that the kind-hearted prophet will not forget to enter their home.

The Los Angeles poet H. Rosenblatt, in his poetic volume *Herodes* (1930), recreates the images, figures, and episodes that remained in his memory from his earliest years in a Podolian village. Among these memories, Elijah looms prominently as a white-bearded figure, with eyes like stars and a face yellow like the tallow of Yom Kippur candles. Yet this Elijah could perform all the pranks and deeds that the poet, in his childhood, would have wanted to do but could not.

Kadia Molodowsky, in a poetic tale for children, tells of a poor man who encounters the disguised Elijah on the road and asks him if both of them may not wander on together. Elijah agrees on condition that his companion ask no questions, no matter what they may see or hear. During the first night, they are granted hospitality at the home of a poor widow. After they leave, Elijah prays that the only goat of the widow die. During the second night, they seek lodging at a rich man's home and are turned away. When the house burns down, Elijah prays that the wicked owner might never lack bread. In the presence of such apparent unfairness, Elijah's companion can no longer hold his tongue. Elijah then justifies his behavior. Heaven had decreed an early death for the widow, and, therefore, he prayed that God might accept the death of the goat and let her live on to a prosperous old age. As for the wicked man, Elijah had prayed that he be provided with bread so as not to resort to robbery.

The delightful charm of Kadia Molodowsky's early tale gives way to cries of anguish in a poetic epistle addressed to Elijah in 1942, when her kinsmen in the ghettos were suffering under Nazi oppression. She asks the prophet of vengeance and mercy for news of what is happening behind the wicked walls in the land of her people's pain. A second grim poem of the same year depicts a Seder night in which the table has been set for twelve, but all twelve Jews have perished. Only Elijah's cup shows a diminution of wine, while all the other cups remain full. Will he now answer the annual call to pour out his wrath upon the oppressors? Will he at last bring comfort to the remnants of his people?

Mani-Leib's ballad "The Stranger" resembles Kadia Molodowsky's folktale. Elijah, the ragged stranger, is refused entry at a rich man's palace on a cold, dark night, but is given shelter in a poor man's hovel beside the unlit stove. When he leaves before dawn, the stove warms, a lamp burns brightly, the table is laden with rich food, while in the cold palace servants scurry around in search of a missing lamp.

Mani-Leib also versifies four other tales about Elijah. In one story, Elijah strolls through the forest disguised as a peasant, in another, he feeds the pigeons of the marketplace, in a third, he hires himself out as a servant, with the money for his hire going to a poor Jew who has already pawned everything of value but not *tallit* and *tefillin*. In the fourth story, Elijah sits as an unrecognized beggar in a Beth Hamidrash—a House of Learning—warming his cold feet at an old stove. Suddenly, he hears the wind bring from afar the moaning of a woman in childbirth. He goes out into the snow and storm, and awakens the woman's neighbors from their sleep. When they come to help her, he returns to join the Jews in the Beth Hamidrash, who are still bent over their old, yellowed tractates.

Two ballads of the poet Itzik Manger center about Elijah. In one, the prophet is presented as an aged beggar whose fiddle dispels the fear of pogroms and lulls poor children to happy slumber. In another, Elijah redeems from the pawnshop the silken dress of the poet's mother, so that she can wear it at her daughter's wedding; as Reb Eliahu Hanavi, he then joins the wedding guests in dancing and merrymaking.

The aging Montreal poet J. I. Segal in late lyrics, Yehoash in the fable "Elijah and the Dogs," Alef Katz in his post-Holocaust verse playlet "Good Morning, Alef," Chaim Grade in a cycle of twenty poems, and other Yiddish men of letters find ever new variations on the Elijah theme.

Yiddish writers have a more intimate relationship to Elijah than to any other prophet. They are able to project through him their own sorrows, their own demands for justice, their own longing for salvation. Time does not tarnish his radiant personality, nor do his beggarly disguises and his humble behavior diminish him. He has become the symbol of patience and endurance far more than of fanatical heroism. He exemplifies for the individual Jew, and especially for the Jewish child to whom many Elijah poems, plays, and narratives are directed, the ideal of moral man, good and kind, righting wrongs, comforting with helpful deeds, and ever holding out hope of better days to come, indeed of a Messianic Age when evil and strife shall cease, and universal love and peace shall embrace all things living.

23

The Literary Impact of Jonah

The Book of Jonah has attracted much attention among Jewish sages and Christian theologians. It has inspired numerous artists ever since the beginning of the common era, as is attested by the scenes from the prophet's life in ancient sarcophagi and in illustrations to manuscripts of the early Middle Ages. In literature, however, the subject was never popular until our century.

Since the Book of Jonah is read every year in the synagogues during the Afternoon Service of Yom Kippur, Jews were thoroughly familiar with its contents, which emphasized the prophecy dooming Nineveh and God's mercy extended to this city when its people repented. By recalling on this most solemn Jewish day of repentance and fasting that even the wicked inhabitants of the Assyrian capital were spared when they turned from their evil ways, worshipers were imbued with the hope that their sins too could be atoned for, and that the Supreme Judge of the universe would also be merciful to them and would not carry out any harsh judgment he may have contemplated.

Christian theologians saw in the return of Jonah from the watery abyss into which he had been hurled, and from the bowels of the Big Fish in which he had been entombed for three days, an anticipation of the crucifixion and entombment of their Messiah and his resurrection after three days. In the words of Matthew 12:40, "For as Jonah was three days and three nights in the whale's belly, so shall the Son of Man be three days and three nights in the heart of the earth." Both Matthew and Luke reported that just as Jonah became a sign to the inhabitants of Nineveh, so too will the Son of Man be a sign to a later generation, and just as the Ninevites repented at the preaching of Jonah, so will repentance come to another wicked generation, since someone greater than Jonah has arrived upon the world's scene.

The story of Jonah was often interpreted as an allegory of death and rebirth. The swallowing of the prophet by the Big Fish stemmed from his disobeying God's command and thereby meriting God's severe judgment. However, when he accepted his punishment and prayed to God out of the belly of Sheol, then he was deserving of God's mercy and was liberated from his dark entombment. He was reborn as a willing messenger of God. (See Uwe Steffen, *Das Mysterium von Tod und Auferstehung: Formen und Wandlungen des Jona-Motivs*, 1963.)

Scholars have called attention to Indian and Babylonian myths that bear similarities to Jonah's experiences in the sea-monster. Far better known are comparable myths told of the Greek heroes Herakles, Perseus, and Arion.

When Hesione, daughter of King Laomedon of Troy, was chained to a rock on the Trojan shore and was in danger of being devoured by a sea-monster, Herakles broke her chains and freed her. When the monster poked its head out of the sea and opened its great jaws, the hero leaped down its throat and, after a fierce combat lasting three days, he fought his way out of the monster's belly and emerged victorious in order to continue with his labors of cleansing the world of evil.

Perseus too slew a sea-monster and thus saved Andromeda, a king's daughter, when he beheld her chained naked to the seacliff off Joppa, now Jaffa, and in danger of being devoured by the Big Fish.

Like Jonah, Arion too faced death, during a sea-voyage, at the hands of the ship's captain and sailors. As a final favor, he asked to be allowed to sing a last song. On its conclusion, he leaped overboard with his lyre. He found himself on the back of a dolphin that had been attracted by his music. As he continued his songs invoking the help of the gods, the dolphin bore him over the waves until he landed safely in Corinth.

While Jonah's emerging alive from the Big Fish readily lent itself to artistic reproduction, this theme could not easily attract the literary imagination, for Jonah was no hero performing deeds of great valor. In English literature, the most elaborate treatment of the Jonah theme before our century was that of the religious poet Francis Quarles, who began his literary career in 1620 with his Jonah poem in thirteen sections, or cantos. The poem bore the strange title *A Feast for Wormes*. In an introduction, Quarles asks his readers not to wonder at the title, for his is a song of God's mercy to the inhabitants of this planet. What greater feast could be conceived than mercy? And what are men but quickened lumps of earth, worms and a feast for worms?

As envisaged by Quarles, Nineveh is an ancient replica of sinful London, a city ripe for destruction because of its vices. Each of the poem's thirteen sections consists of two parts, first an elaboration of an event in the Jonah narrative and then a meditation upon its significance for the poet's generation.

In England, king and Parliament were girding in 1620 for a fierce struggle that was to rock the stability of the monarchical system. Quarles was a royalist, a believer in the divine right of kings, an opponent of the Puritans, who were challenging the Church of England. He held that when the word of God came to Jonah commanding him to speak out against the wicked sons of Nineveh, he should have obeyed unquestioningly, as should all who are enjoined to do God's work: magistrates to hand out justice, merchants to deal honestly, tradesmen to act in harmony with their conscience. Jonah, however, objects to carrying out his mission. He cannot understand why the inhabitants of a foreign metropolis such as Nineveh should listen to him when his own people do not. Besides, a gentle and merciful God is apt to change His mind upon the least sign of repentance, and then Jonah will be branded as a false prophet. After much heart-searching, he decides to flee to Tarshish, only to discover that flight from the Lord of heaven, earth, and sea is impossible. The disobedient Jonah ends up in the bowels of the mighty whale. Only after he has learned his lesson is he disgorged upon the land. Then the reborn, chastened prophet betakes himself to Nineveh and pronounces its doom. However, Nineveh, whose people repent, does not fall. This leads the English poet to meditate whether God can unsay what He has said and alter a decree He has once decreed. It is normal for a human being to change his mind and to waver like the wind, but is it not strange for a God not to be steadfast?

The poet gets around this difficulty by asserting that God never threatened absolute perdition. Doom could be warded off by repentance. But then it must be true repentance. It must be more than skin-deep, more than the mere trappings of ashes and sackcloth. It must be repentance of the heart, as was Nineveh's, repentance which brought a remission of its pronounced doom. Jonah, however, is angry because what he originally feared when he fled to Tarshish actually happens. God does change His mind, and the prophet proves to be a messenger of lies. He feels that later on the Ninevites will revert to their earlier, more normal, evil ways, and that they will then scorn any new divine threats. To teach Jonah the supreme value of mercy, there follows the incidents of the gourd and of the worm that devoured the gourd. The poet concludes his history of Jonah's doubts and Jonah's restored faith with a lesson for the reader:

> Here mayst thou see, how prayer and true repentance
> Do strive with God, prevail, and turn his sentence
> From strokes to stroking, and from plagues infernal
> To boundless mercies and to life eternal.

Two more centuries were to pass before the Jonah story again ripened in the mind of a creative writer and was embedded by him in a classic work of fiction. In 1851, the American novelist Herman Melville completed *Moby Dick*, his prose epic of American whalers and whaling. By then it was generally accepted that the Big Fish, capable of swallowing and disgorging Jonah alive, must have been a whale, the Leviathan of the ocean. The novelist, therefore, incorporated in his narrative of whaling a hymn and a sermon on Jonah, as well as a survey of speculations on how Jonah managed to survive for three days within the whale. The hymn concludes with Jonah's calling upon God when in black despair, and his Deliverer answering him and saving him from within the whale's maw. The sermon, delivered in the Whaleman's Chapel of New Bedford, Massachusetts, before a motley congregation of fishermen, sailors, and harpoonists, reinterprets the tale of Jonah in a manner most meaningful for a seafaring audience. The minister, Father Mapple, was himself a sailor and harpoonist in his youth, and he knows how to stir the heart of his listeners. He stresses Jonah's willful disobedience of God's command, his punishment, repentance, and joyous deliverance after the fugitive from God accepted God's dreadful punishment as just. "And here, shipmates, is true and faithful repentance; not clamorous for pardon, but grateful for punishment."

Melville recounted in the course of his narrative several adventures that paralleled Jonah's, including those of the Greek mythological heroes and that of St. George, who marched boldly up to a dragon of the sea, identifiable as a whale. To skeptics who might doubt the literal veracity of the Jonah story, the American novelist, with tongue in his cheek, devoted an entire chapter to various theories explaining Jonah's survival at sea. These ranged from Bishop Jebb's surmise that the prophet might have been lodged in the whale's open mouth rather than in the belly to the commentator who held that when Jonah was thrown overboard, he continued swimming until he was picked up by another vessel with a whale for a figurehead. Melville ironically added to the various theories two of his own. He surmised that Jonah might have been saved by a ship called "The Whale" or by clinging to a life preserver that was inflated with air.

Echoes of such theories resounded in an American courtroom three-quarters of a century later in the course of the sensational Scopes trial in July 1925. The Tennessee legislature had passed a law forbidding the teaching of the Darwinian theory of evolution in the public schools of the state. John Thomas Scopes, a teacher of biology, was accused of defying this law. His trial, which drew national and international attention, climaxed in the cross-examination by Clarence Darrow, the brilliant attorney for the defense, of the fundamentalist orator and earlier Democratic presidential candidate William Jennings Bryan. When Bryan testified as an expert on the Bible and affirmed his belief in the literal truth of everything recorded therein, he was closely questioned on Jonah's experiences within the belly of the Big Fish. Bryan's explanations exposed him to the withering satire of the incredulous Darrow and to the ridicule of the world's press, an exposure which may have hastened his death a few days after he left the witness stand.

It was in the wake of this trial that Robert Nathan published in 1925 his ironic novel, entitled *The Son of Amittai* in the British edition and *Jonah* in the American edition. Nathan presented the prophet as a contemporary of Amos of Tekoa, as a saintly young man who beholds visions and converses with angels, but who becomes tired of life in the desert and returns to the town of his birth. There he falls in love with Judith, the niece of Prince Ahab, but soon discovers that she will not be allowed to marry him because of his poverty and that, despite her love for him, she will readily accept the rich Phoenician merchant Hiram of Tyre, who can offer her a life of luxury. Jonah refuses to go to Nineveh, because he feels that the God of Israel has no power beyond Israel's borders, even as the deities Marduk, Dagon, and Ishtar cannot intrude outside of their territories. Jonah's exposure within the whale, however, teaches him that Israel's God is everywhere, exercising command over the fish of the sea, the hosts of the air, and the creatures of the land. He then obeys God's command and boldly prophesies Nineveh's doom. However, when beautiful Nineveh is spared, he is angry at God. "All his courage was gone, his pride, his hope of glory, all gone down in the dust of God's mercy to others. To him alone God had been merciless and exacting." Jonah then wishes to return to the desert, a chastened, humiliated creature. God, looking down from the clouds, then turns to Moses and says wearily: "You Jews, you don't understand beauty. With you it is either glory or despair." And with a sigh God looks westward to the blue Aegean, where the sunlight lies warm and golden over Greece.

The ironic and irreverent treatments of the Jonah theme declined as the Book of Jonah came to play a significant role in the struggle against the racist theories that arose, flourished, and collapsed during the second quarter of the twentieth century. In Central Europe, the struggle could not be waged openly during the dominance of the totalitarian Nazi regime. Theologians and men of letters then resorted to biblical symbols to cloak their opposition. Jonah, the prophet who was at first indifferent to the fate of a people other than his own, and who hesitated to bring the word of God to far-off Nineveh, was the biblical character ideally suited to bring to a focus the controversy raging around the narrow nationalism of the Third Reich. The Jonah versions of the 1930s were, therefore, permeated with open or concealed anti-Nazi sentiments.

The Danish novelist Harald Tandrup, writing beyond Germany's borders, could be openly satiric about the German racist theories in his narrative *Jonah and the Voice* (1937), but the poet Dietrich Bonhoeffer, penning his Jonah poem in a Berlin prison in 1944, had to be more circumspect. In 1946, after the Nazi collapse, the dramatist Guenter Rutenborn could again pass annihilating judgment upon the Nazi racist theories in his play *The Sign of Jonah*, and in 1965 the anti-Nazi novelist Stefan Andres, who had gone into voluntary exile thirty years earlier, could voice in his prose epic *Der Mann im Fisch* his disillusionment with his generation, which worshiped Mammon while giving lip service to the God of Jonah.

The Danish title of Tandrup's novel was *Profeten Jonas Privat*. When the book was published in 1935, the Nazi wave had already swept over Germany but had not yet inundated Germany's neighbors. Tandrup could poke fun at the Nazis' blaming all calamities on the Jews by portraying his Jonah as a harmless, poor, little Jew completely lacking in physical and moral courage and incapable of inflicting hurt. When such a person is singled out by God to prophesy the destruction of the proud capital of the Assyrian Empire, it is only natural for him to flee in terror from such an assignment. His fabulous sojourn in the whale convinces him that the Lord will not tolerate disobedience, and so he makes his way to Nineveh. There he experiences various changes of fortune and is used by Assyria's king as a mouthpiece to prophesy against the arrogant priestly establishment. At one time, Jonah is exceedingly glad of a gourd that God has prepared to shield him from grief. The gourd is construed as the ideal wife, who loves and protects him. But then there arises a worm which smites the gourd so that it withers and dies. The death of Jonah's wife coincides with the poisoning of the king by the priestly opponents. The priests blame the Jews for bringing down the wrath of the gods upon the Assyrians and for causing the king's death. Sennacherib, the new ruler, gives orders to save the country by killing all its Jews, since Jews are not of pure Assyrian blood and hence strangers to genuine Assyrian ways of thought. The people of Assyria rejoice at the generous royal gift of Jewish lives, Jewish houses, cattle, goods, and slaves. The killing of Jews is turned into a popular entertainment. The mobs surge into the Jewish quarter. The hungry forget their hatred of the well-fed, now that all are permitted to eat their fill at the Jews' expense. Even beggars can become rich by looting Jewish possessions. It is a great day, one which brings out the heroic qualities in men. While the majority plunder, idealists prefer to enjoy the delight of murdering the unresisting Jews. Money can be made at other times, but it is not often that one has a chance of killing people without getting into trouble.

Jonah survives the pogrom, but after this experience at Nineveh, he finds the courage to stand upright before his God. Never will he be one of the lowly of heart who fill the heavens with hymns of praise. He has become one of the great doubters, the untiring questioners.

If the Nazi events of the mid-1930s were mirrored in the Jonah novel of Tandrup, the aftermath of Nazi dominance was reflected in the Jonah poem of the Lutheran theologian Dietrich Bonhoeffer, written on October 5, 1944, in his prison cell at Tegel, half a year before he was hanged upon Hitler's command as the Russian army closed in upon this district of Berlin. Since efforts to save Bonhoeffer's life were not yet exhausted when he wrote the poem, he had to veil its anti-Nazi thrust in obscure metaphors, hence the difficulties in interpreting the stanzas. The storm-tossed ship that sailed from Joppa to Tarshish is the German ship of state, and the desperate sailors who cry out to the enraged gods for salvation in the hour of distress are the German people. When a contrite Jonah accepts his share of the guilt and is thrown overboard, the storm is allayed and the sea is again calm.

While Bonhoeffer's poem was written just before the imminent end of the Third Reich, Guenter Rutenborn's surrealistic play in nine scenes, *The Sign of Jonah*, appeared in the original German a year after the war's end. It was rewritten in 1955, and the revised version was published in English in 1960.

The dramatic action is set in a theater in West Berlin. The Judge calls upon Jonah to appear before the postwar audience, but Jonah, like his biblical namesake, hesitates, because he does not believe that the Germans can be converted to change their evil ways, as were the Ninevites. When German cities were heaps of rubble, the people seemed different, but with their cities being rapidly rebuilt, they do not want to remember the recent past. Jonah must remind them of the days when fire and destruction rained from the skies. He must talk to their conscience. He then appears before them not in the role of the prophet Jonah, who was swallowed up by a whale and survived, but as himself, Jonah, the commander and sole survivor of a submarine that crashed to the sea-bottom after an attack by a bomber. Whether whale or submarine, hell is always one and the same. Having emerged from the bowels of the submarine, he is ready to present God's case against contemporary Ninevehs. Actors representing the three archangels appear upon the scene: Gabriel, who was buried alive for ten days after the American bombardment of Dresden and was taken out alive; Michael, who carried out mass executions of inferior races in the East, and who, though otherwise innocent, was punished by the Americans when they reached Dachau; Raphael, who was caught by the Russians in Pomerania and barely missed death. Jonah, as prosecuting attorney, calls attention to these German archangels, who combine in their faces so much cruelty, self-righteousness, and emptiness. He compels each of them to testify to additional aspects of their past. The real Michael, not the pseudoarchangel, had been a clerk in the marriage license bureau and took it upon himself to inspect documents and to certify who had a non-Aryan grandmother, so that such persons could be assigned to the furnaces. Gabriel was a bombardier who dropped bombs on London, Coventry, and Rotterdam. Other unmasked characters include the Average Man, who as a German tortured Poles and murdered Ukrainians, as a Pole expropriated Germans, as a Ukrainian served as a murderous partisan, as an American pulverized Dresden, as a Russian raped and pillaged; and also the Average Woman, whose justification for denouncing others was that she wanted to improve her family's circumstances and get her husband a better position. All have excuses for their monstrous deeds, which brought about the death of millions of people of another denomination in gas-chambers. Having been denazified, they do not want their past dug up. After all, not they are guilty but the Judge and Supreme Ruler of the world. The Judge accepts this verdict and condemns Himself. Jonah, God's witness to Nineveh and Berlin, voices the conclusion that, just as the guilty Judge of the Universe condemned Himself and accepted suffering as atonement for fashioning an imperfect world, so too God's human creatures must also condemn themselves and atone for their viciousness. Let them stand in awe before the chastened God, for the fear of the Lord is the beginning of wisdom. Let them repent before an atomic conflagration overtakes them. Let them atone for their sins. Then they can expect to be spared, as were the people of Nineveh.

The contemporary relevance of the Jonah theme, stressed by Rutenborn, also emerges from the religious novel *Der Mann im Fisch* by Stefan Andres. Like Bonhoeffer, Andres contemplated a theological career. He was educated in a cloister school. During his university years, however, he discovered his literary talent and thereafter devoted himself to writing novels. These delve into the inner consciousness of modern man. His Jonah novel of 1963 reflected his long immersion in biblical studies. He found many parallels between his own generation in Germany and that of Jonah in ancient Israel and sinful Assyria.

Andres presented Jonah as a popular hero during the reign of

King Jeroboam of Israel. He correctly prophesied Israel's victory over the Syrians at Hamath, but after the victory, he is shocked by the brutal decapitation of thousands of captives to the accompaniment of hymns of praise to God. He flees from the adulations of the court and the masses. For twenty years, he lives incognito. His son Jochanan becomes a follower of Amos of Tekoa, who preaches that all peoples are equal in the eyes of God, that the Lord who brought Israel out of Egypt also brought the Philistines out of Caphtor and Aram out of Kir. Jonah cannot accept such a doctrine. He, therefore, resists the call to bring God's message to Nineveh's cruel inhabitants. Why should he cry out to the Assyrian murderers to repent and live, when they deserve to perish because of their misdeeds? He decides to flee to Tarshish. After being hurled overboard during the storm at sea, he sinks into the watery abyss and is swallowed by the fish of timelessness. On stepping out of *Nichtzeit* on one of the droplets of time, he finds himself in the twentieth century and meets his counterpart, the preacher Dr. Jonas. The latter tells him of our contemporary pills against unrest, fear, loneliness, and despair, pills of forgetfulness that enable us to flee from the voice of conscience, the demanding voice of God within us.

The prophet Jonah realizes that, after a hundred generations, war still rages and heads are still being decapitated. If man may be blamed for wars and not God, then is man also to be blamed for earth's pestilences, famines, and other catastrophes? On the other hand, if God is responsible, then He must be a cruel, unjust tyrant, and one is justified to flee from Him, as did Jonah. The twentieth-century Dr. Jonas had also preached God's word until one day when winged monsters rained down bombs from the sky and in a single moment transformed an entire city, the size of Nineveh, to dust and ashes. Then his faith in God, who cared so little about His creatures, collapsed. It is true that a flying man dropped the bomb, but if God is really interested in the world, should He not have stopped such a monstrous act? The rebellious Jonah does not want to be a mere puppet in the hands of the Supreme Puppeteer. He does not want to undertake voyages and engage in activities whose meaning eludes him. Jonah, like all elect personalities, poets, and prophets enmeshed in time, faces God with deeply probing questions. On returning from timelessness to his own generation of ancient Israel and Assyria, he rages on and on. And yet, he must continue to Nineveh and do God's bidding. The prophet of a hundred generations ago ends by bowing in submission to a God who is inconsistent and incomprehensible but who is also almighty, all-righteous, and all-merciful. However, Dr. Jonas of our generation, who is unsure of God's essence, righteousness, or mercy, still waits for an answer to his skeptical questions.

The German-Jewish writer Schalom Ben-Chorin, no less than the Protestant poet Dietrich Bonhoeffer and the Catholic novelist Stefan Andres, wrestled with the meaning of the Jonah theme for contemporary man. Driven from his German fatherland by the Gestapo, after his ancestors had sojourned there for many generations, Ben-Chorin found refuge in Palestine in 1935. His book *Die Antwort des Jona* appeared twenty years later and was republished in 1966. It was directed primarily to German Christian readers, since the author's activities after the fall of the Third Reich were concentrated on a reconciliation between the Germans and the Israelis, between Christians and Jews.

The biblical Jonah, who tried to reach the gold coast of Tarshish, while the divine word commanded him to betake himself to Nineveh, is for Ben-Chorin the symbolic precursor of contemporary man in flight from God to gold. Jonah is, at the same time, also the symbol of the everlasting Jew, who entered into a covenant with God to serve Him in the unending struggle against the world's wickedness, and who tries in vain to evade the fulfillment of this covenant. Jonah-Israel is unable to escape from the deity even when on the storm-tossed ship of state and even when he pretends to fall asleep. Jonah, the stranger and eternal outsider, cannot assimilate to others. He cannot successfully conceal his identity and claim to be a German, Frenchman, Englishman, or American. He must acknowledge to the ship's captain that he is a Hebrew. Nationally, he remains a Hebrew, even though religiously he is a believer in a universal God who rules over all peoples, including the people of Nineveh. He sinned in fleeing from the destiny assigned to his national group, but suffering has taught him to accept his burden of being a witness of God to other nations from his old-new national home in Israel and from all the lands of the Diaspora.

While the literary impact of the Jonah theme in our century was most intense in Germany, other literatures also felt repercussions. Laurence Housman's English Jonah play in five scenes, included in his *Palestine Plays* (1942), continued the irreverent, ironic approach of an earlier period. And so did the South African poet Lewis Sowden, whose long poem *Jonah*, embracing seventy-seven quatrains and included in his last lyric volume, *The Jaffa Road* (1974), traced the career of the humble and hesitant seer, whom experience has taught that no prophet can stand the world for long, and that neither can the world stomach him but must spew him out. When Sowden's Jonah cries out in anger that all his life he has been a servant of the Lord, but that, as a reward, he has ended as a castaway deprived even of the shade of the locust tree, it was the angry poet giving expression to his own frustration that, in his South African homeland, he had fought for moral causes and was rewarded by being exiled and muted. Nevertheless, Sowden concluded with undimmed faith in the ultimate fulfillment of his prophetic vision and in a doomsday for regimes like Nineveh.

> It took a hundred years or more,
> while Heaven's patience held,
> to fetch a sword for Nineveh
> as Jonah had forespelled.
>
> Then was that city ripped with flood
> and raked with hammer and hook.
> The only monument to stand
> is Jonah and his book.

The Yiddish poem *Jonah*, by Kadia Molodowsky, included in her volume *Likht fun Dornbush* (1965), continued the Jewish approach of Ben-Chorin. Her Jonah is the symbolic Jew, and her

Nineveh symbolizes the non-Jewish world. Though Jonah may disguise himself, change his language, and prefer restful ease, God will ferret him out and send him on to Nineveh. Though he would rather care for his own apple trees and date trees, God will tear him away from his hearth and orchard, since he is chosen for pain and compassion and for purifying Ninevehs, old and new, of their sins.

The Book of Jonah has continued until the present to stimulate reflections and reinterpretations in literature as well as in art, music, and theology.

24

Job and Faust

The Book of Job and Goethe's *Faust* are classics of world literature and rank among the finest expressions of the human mind. Structural similarities between both have often been noted, but the basic differences between the older work, a profound product of the Hebraic attitude toward life, and the more modern work, a profound product of the occidental attitude, have rarely been stressed.

What are the structural similarities? Both classics begin with a "Prologue in Heaven." In both, the heavenly hosts present themselves before the Lord. Among them is also the Spirit of Negation, the skeptical, critical, contradictory force, God's shadow that God casts across the universe: Satan in the biblical version, and Mephistopheles in Goethe's philosophical drama. Roaming about the earth and coming in contact with homo sapiens—the crown of creation—Satan and Mephistopheles have lost all respect for the human race and doubt whether even superior individuals, such as Job or Faust, would remain faithful servants of God if severely tested. A wager is entered into by the Lord of the Universe and his dark adversaries, the Lord insisting that a good human being, despite all temporary aberrations, cannot be permanently deflected from the right path, while the Spirit of Negation doubts that even a Job or a Faust can survive testing if it is carried far enough.

The drama initiated in heaven is then enacted on earth, and this forms the main content of both literary classics. In the end, after many ups and downs, God wins the wager. Job is rewarded for his steadfastness by being healed of his afflictions and by being restored to prosperity. Faust is snatched from the claws of the hellish emissaries of Mephistopheles and is transported by angels to the Abode of the Blessed.

The basic differences between Job and *Faust*, despite the structural similarities, are those that distinguish the Hebraic approach and Hebraic values from the occidental approach and occidental values. Job, but not Faust, is content to live out his life within the limitations set by God. He avoids evil and is blessed with health and riches. When both are taken from him, he does not abjure God and seek death, as his wife advises. He retains his faith. He is prepared to accept suffering no less than joy. But what he will not countenance is injustice. What he does not understand is why he, who led an apparently decent life, has been singled out for so much pain. What he does demand of God is a reaffirmation that righteousness reigns on earth as in heaven. While his comforters insist that his afflictions are punishment for his sins, he insists on his guiltlessness. In the end, however, he submits to his tragic fate, not because he has been persuaded that he is indeed a sinner, but because he has become convinced that neither he nor any other tridimensional creature can fathom the intent and the ways of the infinitely dimensional deity. He accepts his assigned place in the pattern of the universe on the basis of faith and trust rather than on the basis of logical reasoning. He thus vindicates God's faith in him as in Abraham before him and in the descendants of Israel down the millennia after him.

Faust, on the other hand, is not content to stay within the limits set for the human species by the divine creator. Nor does he care whether a just or unjust moral order permeates the universe. He tries to break out into unexplored dimensions of reality. His will to experience knows no bounds. Heaven and hell do not affright him. Forever striving, he does not shun wrongdoing, seduction, murder. Striving is for him an end in itself and not a means toward an ideally envisaged objective. "Whosoever strives everlastingly, him can we save" ("Wer immer strebend sich bemüht, den können wir erlösen")—in these words Goethe saw the key to Faust's salvation.

In entering into the contract with Mephistopheles, Faust therefore exchanges a life of contemplation, the life of a scholar, for a life of restless activity. He seeks self-realization, intensification of his sensations, rather than forgetfulness of self and immersion in a goal beyond self.

If Job is tested by suffering, Faust is tested by joy, by being tempted with sensual pleasures and earthly satisfactions ranging from drunkenness in Auerbach's Cellar and love in the arms of Gretchen to power in the Emperor's realm and dominion over a magnificent estate of his own. Passion and reason war in the breast of Faust, while Job steers clear of passionate involvement and strains toward universal justice. Passion leads Faust to sin and crime. Reason is perverted by him into a refined instrument to gratify his desires. Up to the end, Faust countenances pillage and destruction to gain his goal, namely, to convert sand dunes into a flourishing estate as far as his eye can reach. His victims include the aging, pious, unoffending couple Philemon and Baucis, who do not wish to part from the little piece of land on which they have spent their lives and which Faust covets in order to round out his possessions. Faust does not have the moral sensitivity of Job. He does not really care, as does Job, whether righteousness or unrighteousness rules the universe. His ideal is the Viking, Germanic ideal upon which a Christian superstructure of redemption through love has been grafted.

The Germans have prided themselves on being Faustian, the people of Faust, and have appropriated as their own the Faustian ideology and Faustian characteristics. The German Brockhaus dictionary defines Faustian as "zu immer neuem Erleben drängend, niemals satt-zufrieden," a definition which may be translated as "an everlasting striving for new experiences, never sated or satisfied." According to Goethe, this insatiable, aggressive dynamism is desirable, and yet it must lead to damnation unless it is tamed by the Eternal Feminine—"das ewig Weibliche"—and buttressed by God's grace and Christian love.

Hence, in the end, the heavens are opened in order to admit the ever aspiring individual, despite all his errors and guilt, because of the intercession of the saintly, forgiving Gretchen, whose tragic fate on earth stems from his seducing her under the tutelage of Mephistopheles. Faust is, indeed, in need of Christian forgiveness in order to escape eternal damnation and to attain salvation in heaven, whereas Job is restored to renewed, desirable existence on earth, because there is justice in the terrestrial realm.

If the people in the heart of Europe often refer to themselves as the people of Faust, the Jews may rightly claim to be the people of Job, the sufferer who clings to his God, aware that amidst almost unbearable loss and bodily torture, he has not been cast off by the Lord of Justice, the righter of wrongs, the creator of a universe in which truth overtops falsehood and morality reigns supreme.

25

In the Days of Job

The Book of Job deals with the experiences of the righteous man of Uz, his suffering, his outcry to God, his disputations with his comforters, and his final acceptance of God's answer, which comes to him out of the whirlwind. Among the literary works of our century inspired by this biblical masterpiece, from Leonid Andreyev's *Anathema* to Archibald MacLeish's *J.B.*, none probes deeper than does the poetic drama *In the Days of Job*, completed in the post-Holocaust decade by H. Leivick, the Yiddish singer of Jewish martyrdom, glory, and messianic hope.

Leivick does not vie with the Bible by attempting to restate the events and the arguments that are stated with such perfection in the original Hebrew text. He rather steps in where the Bible is silent and dramatizes the impact that Job's affliction and outcry must have had upon his contemporaries. For Job's case was not unique. His questions as to the reasons for the existence and persistence of undeserved suffering must have been asked by innumerable victims in his day, even as they were still being asked by victims of Leivick's generation, the Holocaust generation, and are indeed asked in every generation.

In Abel, who fell under the murderous hand of Cain, in Isaac, who was led to the altar on Mount Moriah upon the command of a superior will, as well as in Job, who was upright and eschewed evil and who nevertheless suffered far more than did the wicked,

Leivick saw biblical figures who presaged the Jewish martyrs of all ages, including his own. The questioning of Jewish destiny had occupied the poet ever since his youthful years behind tsarist prison bars and in Siberian entombment. It had ripened in him from decade to decade until it widened into a questioning of God's ways with all mankind, indeed with all living creatures.

In his Job drama, completed in 1953, just before he himself was afflicted with years of bodily agony, for which death in 1962 was a welcome relief, Leivick reached the apex of his creative career and fought his way out of the darkness of doubt to a reinvigorated faith. He saw that, after the deluge of blood, after the Nazi effort to exterminate the Jewish people, and after Stalin's measures to liquidate the Jewish spirit, a rainbow was appearing in the heavens, a Jewish state was arising, the remnants of Israel were beginning again the rebuilding of their lives. Perhaps, after all, a moral balance did operate in the universe. Perhaps there was meaning to the swing of the pendulum from apparently unmerited suffering to unexpected joy.

With Job, whom God had chosen for testing and who had cried out against such election, Leivick had felt, during the Hitler years a stronger bond of sympathy than with Abraham and Isaac, who had also been tested severely and who had accepted their lot without protest. To rage against a God whose justice or injustice remained inscrutable did at least offer emotional relief amidst great anguish. But soon Leivick realized the inadequacy of mere lamentations and protests. Was Job's frenzy really to be preferred to Isaac's silent resumption of a dutiful existence after the experience on Mount Moriah? Did not Job himself later arrive at a similar conclusion to resume normal activities?

Leivick was struck by a talmudic passage (*Bava Bathra* 15) that Job may have lived in the days of Isaac. This passage gave the dramatist the possibility of bringing together these two victims of God's testing.

Leivick's Satan, a magnificent personification of the spirit of skepticism by which faith is tested, does not relish his assigned mission as negative executioner of God's will. The radiant deity, who directs his satanic counterpart to subject Job to the cruel ordeal, seems to be unmoved by the victim's woe and expects the pious, saintly man of Uz to endure without whimpering. Satan's sardonic laughter, on the other hand, stems from his basic sadness, a sadness growing out of his sympathy with all the pain that he has witnessed while roaming over the face of the earth. He was at Mount Moriah when Isaac lay on the altar gazing with horrified eyes upon the knife that played about his neck. Was not such a deed, commanded by God and to be executed by a father, more reprehensible even than his own more recent mangling of Job's healthy body? Moreover, even if Isaac's flesh was miraculously spared at the last moment, would not his soul ever remain affected by this agonizing experience? Leivick had seen many scarred souls among the survivors who had been miraculously redeemed from Auschwitz and Treblinka. They had relived Isaac's ordeal.

Leivick felt that such persons, the Isaacs of all eras, could not remain aloof when they heard of Jobs who writhed in pain. A person who was as severely hurt as the son of Abraham had been must ever be sensitive to the plea of all living things, even of the moth and the blade of grass, when these begged him not to mutilate or crush them. The distance that separated him from Job would not shield him from sharing in the latter's pain.

When, therefore, the biblical Job opens his lips after seven days of silence and curses the day that he was born, then Isaac has to leave Abraham's peaceful tent in Beersheba and join the blind, the lame, the crippled, and the leprous, as they make their way to the afflicted crier in the night who is demanding a reckoning of God.

Job, in his agonized protest, does not blaspheme God. Conscious of his own innocence, however, he wants the Supreme Overlord to justify Himself. All the misshapen, underprivileged, beaten creatures find a spokesman in him. They bless his courage in questioning God's ways with man and join in his protest against God's universal order or disorder.

If all their suffering is punishment for guilt, then God is equally guilty, perhaps more so, for subjecting them to temptation and leading them on to guilt. If God's omnipotent will rules the world, then God also wills sin, cruelty, misery, and bloodshed. Job wants to know why. Once the question, which Isaac had not dared to ask when bound on Moriah, is opened up by Job, others join in, from the sick and the disabled of the human species to the overburdened camel and the becudgeled donkey. The sacrificial lamb, whose throat was slit in lieu of Isaac's throat, asks the son of Abraham how it was possible for one who had just been dragged to the altar himself to drag joyfully another living creature to be sacrificed. How could one who had felt the knife poised at his own throat himself become an executioner a short while later? Must not each of us feel responsible not alone for the pain we have caused but also for the pain that inheres in all existence and whose author is God?

The dramatist repeats these questions in many variations through the mouths of diverse characters, and he refuses to accept the facile answer that, in the long run, the Lord requites all pain with joy and atones for all seeming wrong that He has caused. For not even God can undo what has once been done, or make the past disappear as if it had never been. Assuming that He could bring back to life children who were hurled into the flames and reduced to ashes, could He also obliterate the agony they experienced as they were being consumed in the fire?

God's answer in the whirlwind awes Job, the temporary doubter, but it does not satisfy Satan, the eternal critic of God's ways. The Lord's recital of the grandeur of natural phenomena does not refute weighty rational arguments and powerful accusations directed against the moral structure of the world He created. Perhaps there is no answer logically supportable. However, beyond the realm of logic and beyond the spirit of skepticism, personified by Satan, lies the realm of faith and the spirit of trust.

The dramatist, therefore, has Satan in the end bow before the Lord and plead for his own annihilation, thus leaving the field to Abraham and Isaac and Job, three righteous persons who have been seared but not broken by pain. They are prepared to bind up each other's wounds, to rebuild their lives on the basis of faith and love, to plow and to sow the desolated earth so that it might bear more wholesome fruit for less turbulent generations.

In the final scene, wherein Abraham advises Job to return home and to plant anew vineyards and fig trees, the patriarch also has a vision of his own descendants wandering over the face of the earth, enduring patiently all privations, and returning ultimately to their native land, purified by their tragic experiences and ready to resume their creative existence as a great and unique people. This vision of a bright future for God's elect people was meant to infuse confidence in the generation that had emerged from the struggles for survival in the 1940s, both in Europe and in Israel.

26

The Cult of Moloch

Moloch, the better-known form of Molech, which is derived from *melech*, the Hebrew word for "king," was an idolatrous god to whom children, especially firstborn sons, were sacrificed by being burned alive.

The worship of Moloch was introduced into the Kingdom of Judah by Ahaz, who reigned from 743 to 727 B.C.E., even though Solomon had already earlier permitted his Ammonite wife to retain her religious allegiance to this idol of Ammon when she joined his harem in Jerusalem.

This worship reached a climax during the long reign of Manasseh, 698-643 B.C.E., and the short reign of his son Amon, 642-640 B.C.E. It was abolished by Amon's son, King Josiah, when he undertook the purification of the Jewish religion from foreign excrescences. But the cult of this idol was not completely eradicated. It must have lingered on to some extent until the Jews were exiled to Babylon, for Jeremiah continued to thunder against it. There is no evidence of its later persistence among the Jews who returned from exile. In neighboring Phoenicia, however, and in the Phoenician colonies of North Africa, the Moloch cult continued to thrive until the Roman destruction of Carthage in 146 B.C.E.

As a literary theme, Moloch has often occupied the imagination of writers. The worshipers of the fiery idol that received children as sacrifices in its cavernous, glowing mouth found successors in our century in the heart of Europe among those who stoked the fires of Auschwitz, Mauthausen, and other extermination camps in which thousands upon thousands of children were incinerated. However, these modern worshipers preferred more fashionable appellations for their resurrected Moloch and an ideology of racial purity more appealing to their impure minds.

The injunction against the worship of Moloch was already pronounced in Leviticus 18:21, which stated: "And thou shalt not give any of thy seed to set them apart to Moloch, neither shalt thou profane the name of thy God. I am the Lord."

The prohibition was repeated with greater emphasis in Leviticus 20:2-4, and was applied to all who dwelt in the Promised Land: "Whosoever he be of the children of Israel, or of the strangers that sojourn in Israel, that giveth of his seed unto Moloch, he shall surely be put to death; the people of the land shall stone him with stones. I also will set My face against that man, and will cut him off from among his people, because he hath given of his seed to Moloch, to defile My sanctuary, and to profane My holy name. And if the people of the land do at all hide their eyes from that man, when he giveth of his seed unto Moloch, and put him not to death, then I will set my face against that man, and against his family, and will cut him off, and all that go astray after him, to go astray after Moloch, from among the people."

The strict injunction was again stressed in Deuteronomy 18:9 f. "When thou art come into the land which the Lord thy God giveth thee, thou shalt not learn to do after the abominations of those nations. There shall not be found among you any one who maketh his son or his daughter to pass through the fire." In warning the Israelites, who were soon to enter into the Promised Land, against taking over the abominations of the Canaanites, Moses gave as a monstrous example of Canaanite aberration that "even their sons and daughters do they burn in the fire of their gods" (Deuteronomy 12:31).

The stern, often reiterated prohibition of sacrificing children to Moloch was violated by King Ahaz when he ascended the throne of Judah. It was said of him that "he made his son to pass through

The Cult of Moloch

the fire, according to the abominations of the heathen, whom the Lord cast out before the children of Israel" (II Kings 16:3).

It was not long afterwards, in 722 B.C.E., that the ten tribes of Israel were driven from their land by an Assyrian conqueror. The inhabitants of the surviving Kingdom of Judah were warned that a similar fate might befall them unless they mended their unrighteous behavior. They were charged not to worship the host of heaven, not to serve Baal, and not to cause their sons and daughters to pass through the fire (II Kings 17:17). Nevertheless, King Manasseh rebuilt the high places which his father, Hezekiah, who succeeded Ahaz, had destroyed. Manasseh even made his own son to pass through the fire (II Kings 21:6).

Baal was the general name for the Canaanite and Phoenician idols against whom the prophets declaimed with great vigor, while Moloch was the specific Baal who was appeased by the burning of children.

A few biblical commentators since Rashi (1040-1105) have held that in Jerusalem, the capital of Judah, unlike Sidon, the capital of Phoenicia, or Carthage, the capital of the Punic Empire, the passing of children through fire should not be interpreted literally but rather figuratively, as a rite of initiation into the religious community of Moloch. This initiation took place at Tophet, which is in the valley of Hinnom. There an image of Moloch was set up for his worshipers. The Hebrew word for "valley" is *gai*. From the expression Gai-Hinnom was derived the word Gehenna, the Jewish hell, a more fiery place than the Greek Hades.

The mild interpretation of Rashi was brilliantly refuted by Nachmanides, the Ramban (1194-1270), who based himself on Abraham ibn Ezra (1098-1146) in identifying Moloch with Milcom, the detestation of the Ammonites. Rashi had described the Moloch ritual as consisting of the father handing over a son to priests. The priests, having lit two large pyres, had the son pass on foot between the two fires, without there being any actual burning of the child. Nachmanides argued that there was a burning with real fire and that the child was completely consumed by the flames. He cited scriptural verses which asserted that the children passed through the fire to be *devoured* by it.

Jeremiah prophesied that punishment would be meted out to

the king and inhabitants of Jerusalem for the abominable practices carried on in Gai-Hinnom: "They have filled this place with the blood of innocents; and have built the high places of Baal, to burn their sons in the fire for burnt-offerings unto Baal. . . . Therefore, behold the days come, saith the Lord, that this place shall no more be called Tophet, nor the Valley of the Sons of Hinnom, but the Valley of Slaughter" (Jeremiah 19:4-6).

That the Baal referred to was Moloch emerges from Jeremiah 32:35, which stated in the name of the Lord: "And they built the high places of Baal, which are in the Valley of the Sons of Hinnom, to set apart their sons and their daughters unto Moloch; which I commanded them not, neither came it into My mind, that they should do this abomination, to cause Judah to sin."

Despite the many biblical references to the worship of Moloch, the biblical texts did not include any detailed descriptions of the features of this devouring idol or of the exact ritual performed by the priests of Moloch. Such details were first supplied by the Midrash on Lamentations, *Ekha Rabbah* 1:9, based on only partly extant earlier sources. According to this fifth-century commentary, a hollow image of the idolatrous god was set up in Gai-Hinnom within the innermost of seven chambers. The image held a copper plate in its hand, and upon the plate a fire-pan was placed. Worshipers who brought an offering of flour were admitted into the first chamber but not beyond, those who brought an offering of doves or pigeons could pass into the second chamber, those who brought a lamb were admitted into the third chamber, those who brought a ram got as far as the fourth chamber, those who brought a calf got to the fifth chamber, those who brought an ox were welcomed in the sixth chamber, but only those who brought a child as a burnt-offering could enter into the seventh, or innermost, chamber in which stood the idol. The priests would place the child on the copper plate, kindle the fire in the furnace, and sing before the image: "May the sacrifice be pleasant and sweet to thee!" The hymn would drown out the crying of the child so that the parents would not be tempted to retract their precious sacrifice at the last moment.

According to the Harvard historian of religion George F.

Moore, the rabbinical authors of the Midrash probably borrowed their notion of Moloch and his worship from Greek sources. Since the Bible repeatedly mentioned the offering of children by fire to Moloch as an abomination of the Canaanites, it was natural that, when the Jewish sages came across accounts of such sacrifices in Carthage, which was founded in 846 B.C.E. as a colony of Tyre, they assumed that the worship of Moloch in Jerusalem was similar if not identical.

The principal Greek sources for the Moloch cult of Carthage were the historian Diodorus of Sicily, who lived in the second half of the first century before the common era, and the biographer Plutarch, who lived a century later.

In describing the war between Carthage and Syracuse in 406 B.C.E., Diodorus Siculus narrated that the Carthaginian commander, Hamilcar, supplicated Cronus (Moloch) by sacrificing a young boy to the god. About a century later, in 310 B.C.E., the Greeks of Sicily and the Carthaginians were again at war. When the latter were besieged and hard pressed, they attributed their misfortune to Moloch's turning against them because, while in former times they had sacrificed to him the noblest of their sons, more recently they had bought and nurtured children of lesser lineage and sent these to the sacrifice. To make amends for their earlier subterfuge, they now selected two hundred of the noblest children and sacrificed them. Three hundred others also volunteered to sacrifice themselves.

Diodorus described the image of Moloch at Carthage as made of bronze, with hands extended palms up and sloping toward the ground, so that each of the children when placed thereon rolled down and fell into a sort of gaping pit filled with fire.

In a treatise on superstitions, Plutarch called attention to Carthaginian fathers who were religiously motivated to offer up their own children or to buy infants from poor people for the sacrifice. Before handing the child over to the priests for burning, such fathers would cut its throat as if it were a lamb or a young bird. Meanwhile the mothers would stand by without a tear or a moan. If a mother uttered a single moan or let fall a single tear, she had to forfeit the money for which the child was bought and her child was sacrificed nevertheless. The entire area before the statue was filled with a loud noise of flutes and drums so that the cries of the wailing children should not reach the onlookers (Plutarch, *Moralia*, Loeb Classics, II, 493).

George Rawlinson suggested, in his book *Phoenicia* (1896, p. 114), that the story of Theseus and the Minotaur of Crete was probably based on the cult of Moloch. "The Cretan monster with human body and bull's head, to whom young men and women were sacrificed, was the Moloch who had come from Phoenicia, and the overcoming of him by Theseus was the destruction of the bloody rite." Rawlinson held that the Baal worshiped in Tyre and its colonies was identical with the Moloch worshiped by the Canaanites. He was the sun-god, the god of consuming fire. His anger could be pacified by burnt-offerings. Children were the dearest possession of their parents, hence these pure and innocent offerings of atonement were most pleasing to him.

John Milton's superb knowledge of biblical lore and classical mythology led him to include Moloch in the pantheon of pre-Christian deities not only in his epic *Paradise Lost* but also far earlier, when he was only twenty-one. His first description of this heathen god was incorporated in his ode "On the Morning of Christ's Nativity," which he composed or began to compose on Christmas Day, 1629. He outlined how, at the birth of the Christian savior, all the heathen gods who had previously been worshiped on earth no longer dared to abide there but had to troop back to their infernal jail. The twenty-third stanza was devoted to Moloch.

> And sullen Moloch, fled,
> Hath left in shadows dread
> His burning idol all of blackest hue;
> In vain with cymbals' ring
> They call the grisly king,
> In dismal dance about the furnace blue.

In the first book of *Paradise Lost*, the poet presented Moloch as the first chief of the vanquished crew of apostate angels to be roused by Satan, the archfiend, from the pit of hell. Moloch is introduced as the future grim idol of the Ammonites, who will reign besmeared with the blood of human sacrifices and with the tears of parents whose children pass through fire.

Milton identified Moloch as the god who, by fraud, will get Solomon to build him a temple opposite the Temple of the Lord, the true God of Israel, on the hill of Tophet. As a result, Moloch's grove in the pleasant valley of Hinnom, or Gehenna, will thereafter be abhorred as a type of hell.

In the council of Satan's crew that is convoked to decide on whether or not to resume war against the Lord of Heaven, Moloch is the fiercest, the most impatient, the first to speak up for war. As the strongest spirit in the original revolt in heaven, he has become even fiercer by defeat and despair. He fears neither God nor hell. He will even accept complete annihilation, complete dissolution into nonbeing, rather than be less than the Lord of Heaven. He, therefore, counsels open warfare, but his counsel is temporarily rejected, while other stratagems are explored. However, in Book VI of Milton's epic, he has his way and is given the opportunity of participating in a renewed struggle against the hosts of heaven. It is the Archangel Gabriel who pierces the deep array of Moloch until this defiant, furious, blasphemous opponent of heaven, "down cloven to the waist, with shattered arms and uncouth pain, fled bellowing" (*Paradise Lost*, bk. VI, ll. 361 f.).

Milton, far more than any other poet, influenced the mystical visions of William Blake, who included Moloch as one of the Seven Eyes of God in his poetic allegory *Jerusalem*. The Seven Eyes represented for Blake the seven stages of man's spiritual development, from Lucifer, dominant in the first stage, to the Christian savior, dominant in the final stage. Moloch, who demands human sacrifices, succeeds Lucifer as the Second Eye. He delights in war. He rejoices when a curtain of blood is let down from heaven to the valley of the Jebusites, the pre-Israelite inhabitants of Jerusalem. He presides over the orgies of the warriors with the daughters of Albion, for the explosion of war always brings in its wake an explosion of sex orgies and saturnalian revels, a love that is mingled with cruelty and makes horrible demands.

> Bring your offerings, your first begotten,
> pampered with milk and blood,
> Your first-born of seven years old,
> be they males or females.
> ... Human blood is the life
> And delightful food of the warrior; the well-fed
> warrior's flesh
> Of him who is slain in the war fills the valley of
> Ephraim with
> Breeding women walking in pride and bringing forth
> under green trees
> With pleasures, without pain, for the food is blood
> of the captive.
> Moloch rejoices through the land from Harilah to Shur.
>
> (*Jerusalem* III, 68)

In Blake's visions of love as allied with cruelty, hatred, war, Moloch, he anticipated August Strindberg's concept of *Liebeshass*, "love-hate," as the force that impels the sexes to each other, and also young Sigmund Freud's concept of a primeval devil religion, about which he wrote in a letter to the physician Wilhelm Fliess on January 24, 1897: "I have an idea shaping in my mind that in the perversions, of which hysteria is the negative, we may have before us a residue of a primeval sexual cult which in the Semitic East (Moloch, Astarte) was once, perhaps still is, a religion" (Sigmund Freud, *Complete Psychological Works*, 1966, I, 243).

Samuel Taylor Coleridge, a contemporary of Blake and allied with him in opposition to Albion-Britain's war against the revolutionary French, was especially irked by his native land's being leagued with petty German princelings, each of whom was nursed in gore. He felt that the most vicious of them was the former prince of Hesse, who received money from Britain for the flesh of his subjects in the American War of Independence. In Coleridge's "Religious Musings," a poem written on Christmas eve of 1794, he lashed out against the warmongers and the Moloch priest who preferred the prayer of hate rather than the prayer of love.

More than a quarter of a century later, Robert Southey, brother-in-law of Coleridge, saw the spirit of Moloch coming to the fore in the "Satanic School" of Lord Byron, the author of *Don Juan*. The younger poet had satirized the romantic triumvirate of Wordsworth, Coleridge, and Southey in his early poetic polemic *English Bards and Scotch Reviewers* (1809). He dubbed Southey a ballad-monger, a poet who plodded his weary way verseward. When Southey became poet-laureate of England in 1813, Byron regarded him as a renegade to the cause of freedom ushered in by the French Revolution. When the laureate was requested to compose an elegy on the death of King George III, he did so, entitling it "A Vision of Judgment" (1821), and prefacing it with an attack upon the more popular Byron as a leading member of the Satanic School that also included Shelley and Leigh Hunt. He called them poets who were inspired by the spirit of Belial in their lascivious verse and by the spirit of Moloch in their loathsome images of atrocities and horrors which they delighted to portray. Byron replied with a vitriolic attack in the preface to his own *Vision of Judgment*, which effectively annihilated Southey's reputation as a major poet.

Less belligerent was the later poet-laureate of Queen Victoria, Alfred Tennyson. In "The Dawn," a poem written at the end of his life and published in 1892, the year of his death, he began with the age of the Moloch worshipers at the dawn of mankind and emphasized the slow pace of progress, while conceding the inevitability of man's ascent. The opening lines were:

>Red of the Dawn!
>Screams of a babe in the red-hot palms
>   of a Moloch of Tyre,
>Man with his brotherless dinner on man
>   in the tropical wood,
>Priests in the name of the Lord passing souls
>   through fire to the fire,
>Head-hunters and boats of Dahomey that float
>   upon human blood.

The reference in the last line was to a report that, on the accession of a king of Dahomey, enough women victims were killed to float a small canoe with their blood. The later stanzas voiced Tennyson's view that if sunlight would still shine upon earth for another twenty million years, as the physicist William Thomson estimated, then there would be sufficient time for the human race, which was far from its noon, to continue growing. The poet wondered how long it would take to rid ourselves of the brute within us and what our descendants would be like, a hundred thousand or a million years away.

The concept and the word Moloch were gaining ever wider currency both in England and on the Continent. The atrocities of Moloch and his worshipers at which the English poets hinted were elaborated with greater vividness in the plays of the German dramatists Christian Dietrich Grabbe and Friedrich Hebbel and in the novels of the French realist Gustave Flaubert and the American master of historical fiction James Michener.

Grabbe's *Hannibal* (1835), portrayed how one of the world's supreme military geniuses was brought low by the greed and pettiness of Carthaginian politicians. In the conflict with the besieging Romans, general fear prevailed that Moloch, the idol of Carthage, might be angry with his city and its people. To ward off defeat, bloody sacrifices were needed to appease him.

The fourth act of the tragedy takes place in the square before the gigantic iron idol of Moloch, whose hands glow and steam. Mothers with infants in their arms kneel in a circle while priests pass up and down between them and the idol, and take the children for the sacrifice. To the plea of a mother that she be taken in lieu of her innocent child, a priest replies that Moloch wants only innocent blood. To win Moloch's favor, the religiously incited crowd also demands grown-up victims of the noblest families. To the request of one of these victims that he be strangled before being delivered to the flames, the answer comes that Moloch does not desire corpses but only living flesh for his fire.

Grabbe's Moloch scene gave the impetus to Friedrich Hebbel's selection of the Moloch cult as the best subject for a drama portraying the introduction of a new religion to a primitive people. However, Hebbel's grandiose dramatic plan never materialized beyond two acts, with the remaining acts surviving mainly in outline form. Richard Wagner and Robert Schumann, whom Hebbel sought to win as composers for his text, were unavailable, and only after Hebbel's death did Max Schillings complete the opera *Moloch*, based upon a modified text.

In the Hebbel play, the high priest of Moloch and the Carthaginian leader Hieram manage to escape during the fall and burning of Carthage. They take with them the image of Moloch and sail to distant Thule, then inhabited by a primitive Germanic tribe. It is Hieram's plan to introduce the worship of Moloch in this new land, inflame the wild inhabitants with religious zeal, and civilize them so that they will be strong enough to march upon Rome and avenge Carthage. He himself became irreligious on the day when the conflagration in Carthage destroyed Moloch's temple and he realized that the god was no more than a lump of iron. However, as a patriot of fallen Carthage, he also realized that he could make use of the idol for his own purposes, by implanting the Moloch cult in Thule.

In the end, when Hieram succeeds in this endeavor, he discovers that he is no longer the master and the idol his tool. A god in whom a people believes, though the most monstrous of idols, is stronger than the mightiest man. Moloch, whom the people have learned to fear, can no longer be destroyed but rather destroys Hieram, the creator of the new religion.

Hebbel died in 1863 before completing and staging his grandly conceived drama on Moloch worship, probably unaware that a year earlier the French novelist Gustave Flaubert had dealt with the Moloch cult in *Salammbô*, a novel about Carthage in the days of Hamilcar Barca, the father of Hannibal. Flaubert's earlier and more famous novel, *Madame Bovary*, had established his reputation as a realist dealing with the contemporary French scene. His reversion to dealing with a remote age and a ruined civilization of North Africa was regarded as a reversion to the romantic fashion, which was on the decline.

The novel takes place in 241 B.C.E., after the conclusion of the First Punic War. Its main theme is the revolt of the mercenaries who were brought back to Carthage. It abounds in violent passions and reaches a climax in the Moloch festival. When the fate of the Carthaginians is in the balance, they seek the help of Moloch by offering their children to this mighty monster, whose body contains seven storied compartments. In each of six compartments, less valuable sacrifices are brought. The seventh is reserved for the children who are hurled in throughout the day from Moloch's horrible hands and arms, on which they are placed. While the devout exclaim: "Lord, eat!", the victims disappear like drops of water on a red-hot plate, and white smoke rises amid the great scarlet color. The people howl in terror and mystic voluptuousness. "Then the faithful came into the passages, dragging their children, who clung to them; and they beat them in order to make them let go, and handed them over to the men in red. The instrument-players sometimes stopped through exhaustion; then the cries of the mothers might be heard, and the frizzling of the fat as it fell upon the coals" (Flaubert, *Salammbô*, Everyman's Library, 1931, p. 234).

Hamilcar Barca, though commander-in-chief of the Carthaginian forces, also has to agree to hand over his ten-year-old son Hannibal to the priests of Moloch. But he manages to save him by substituting the son of a slave, disguised as Hannibal.

While Flaubert, like Grabbe and Hebbel before him, described the cult of Moloch as practiced in Carthage, the American novelist James Michener reverted to ancient Canaan as the scene of this worship. His novel *The Source* (1965), though reaching a climax in contemporary Israel, covered the rise of civilization in this area since prehistoric millennia. It did so by imagining an archaeological dig in a fictitious tell, Makor, that uncovered various layers of rubble and artifacts and then detailing events that might have transpired during the periods of the succeeding levels.

The Moloch cult was pushed back to the prepatriarchal period, when Astarte, goddess of life and fertility, and Moloch or Melak, god of war and death, were worshiped. The archaeologist William F. Albright, in his book *Archaeology and Religion of Israel* (1953), had revealed that in Mari a god named Muluk was worshiped about 1800 B.C.E. Michener, therefore, felt justified in introducing at a somewhat earlier date this new god imported from the north and added to the pantheon of local gods, of Baalim.

The fiery-throated Melak can forestall the threat of war if appeased by receiving firstborn children for burning, especially those of the leading families. The mothers of the chosen victims are required to be present at the ceremony, otherwise it might be rumored that they were offering their sons with a grudging spirit. They, as well as the fathers, have to watch as the infants are lifted up by the priests onto the arms of the stone idol, arms which incline downward so that whatever is placed on them rolls into the huge gaping mouth and plunges into the fire which leaps from the god's mouth. The god accepts each sacrifice with a belch of fire and rancid smoke. The people who witness the ceremony are then certain that Moloch will thereafter protect them. "There was something grave and stately in the picture of a father willing to sacrifice his first-born son as his ultimate gift for the salvation of a community, and in later years, not far from Makor, one of the world's great religions would be founded upon the spiritual idealization of such a sacrifice as the central, culminating act of faith" (p. 113).

For eight hundred years Moloch's ritual of terror is enacted annually in the community described by Michener, his authority being shared only by Astarte, the goddess of passion. The severe religious demands prove the power of this idol. He has not been forced upon the inhabitants, but he answers their need for a powerful god before whom they can stand in awe. It is only eight centuries after his cult was introduced that a desert clan of Hebrews, who worship the invisible El-Shadai, burst out of the desert and overthrow this abominable idol of the Canaanites.

The Yiddish poet Hirsh Osherowitch, a contemporary descendant of the Hebrew people, who experienced the terror of Stalin in a Gulag camp from 1949 to 1956, brooded on the dictatorial Moloch who had drowned in blood Russia's revolutionary fighters for freedom and who was nevertheless worshiped as a god by millions. He saw the tragedy of mankind in its acceptance of cruel idols, to whom the dearest possessions of body and mind were sacrificed. He penned his long poem "Moloch" in 1962 after his return to Vilna, but he could not publish it until 1979, after he had found refuge in Israel, his ancestral home.

In this poem, the copper-headed Moloch, with a bellyful of ashes, relaxes, sated after the bloody red day has yielded to black night. Terrified fathers and mothers are sleepless, their still surviving children awaiting immolation on the morrow. Hearts yearn for life and pray for pity to the pitiless, red monster. But Moloch is blind. Moloch is deaf. Moloch dominates through terror, until one night a desperate father falls upon this devourer of children. His intrepid example is followed by others, and the idol is toppled and fragmented. Then it becomes clear to the long-suffering and believing worshipers that their god was but a lump of iron.

As wars in the twentieth century flared with ever greater ferocity, and aerial bombings of cities failed to discriminate between civilians and combatants, children and grown-ups, Moloch was often used as a synonym for the force that rained down destruction from the skies. When infants were fed into the ovens of extermination camps, along with fathers and mothers, to satisfy racial dogmas embraced with religious fervor, it seemed as if the cult of Moloch had rearisen and was demanding such sacrifices. When Hiroshima went up in flames, was it the God of Abraham and of the Christian savior, or was it not more likely Moloch, who savored this burnt-offering? As arsenals of nuclear armaments increased, an uneasy balance of terror kept nations in leash. Would these armaments ever be unleashed in a holocaust engulfing all things living and permit Moloch, the god of fire and destruction, to reign supreme? All believers in moral creeds pray for the avoidance of such a cataclysm and the retention of sanity by the human species.

27

Belshazzar's Folly

Pride goeth before a fall is the basic moral of the Belshazzar theme in the fifth chapter of the Book of Daniel, and it is reiterated with variations and elaborations in the literary versions based on the biblical narrative.

In English literature, one of the earliest Anglo-Saxon manuscripts contains a poetic rendering of the Book of Daniel which some scholars ascribed to Caedmon, the shepherd-poet of the seventh century. However, the evidence for Caedmon's authorship is not adequate, and the rendering is fairly literal.

Chaucer (1340-1400) treats the Belshazzar theme in "The Monk's Tale." The Monk, who participates in the pilgrimage to Canterbury, is called upon to entertain his fellow-travelers with a tale. Instead of a single long story, he prefers, in accordance with his religious calling, to narrate several short episodes that illustrate a moral. He chooses the moral that all those who attain to great prosperity and become overweeningly proud are ultimately cast down from their high estate into calamity. He begins with Lucifer, the brightest of all angels, who sinned and was hurled down to hell. He continues with Adam, who was not satisfied with everything granted to him for enjoyment in Paradise but he must needs partake also of the forbidden tree, a deed which drove him from the Garden of Eden to toil and misery outside its boundaries. The Monk then narrates the tragedies of the proud heroes Samson and Hercules, who put too much trust in their mightiness, only to learn too late their human limitations. Then follow the tales of the Babylonian kings Nebuchadnezzar and Belshazzar. The former conquered Jerusalem and took to his capital, Babylon, the vessels of God's Temple, as well as the fairest children of Israel, including wise Daniel. Yet, this mighty and haughty king of kings was cast from power after his victories and forced to roam as an animal among the beasts of the forest until he recognized the greater power of God and swore to sin no more.

Belshazzar, the last king of Babylon, took no warning from the fate that had befallen his predecessor, Nebuchadnezzar. He too became all too proud of his high estate and was unheedful of the fact that fortune comes and goes as God wills. He gave a feast at which he put on a great display of the vessels from the Jerusalem Temple. While he, his wife, his lords, and his concubines were drinking out of these vessels in honor of false gods, an armless hand appeared and wrote on the wall symbols that made all of the banqueters quake. Daniel interpreted these symbols as foretelling the king's doom for rebelling against the one true God. That same night Belshazzar was slain and Darius ascended the throne.

The moral repeatedly stressed by Chaucer is that no dominion is secure. Glory, wealth, power are but transitory, and friends acquired in periods of affluence turn to enemies when ill fortune strikes. Had Belshazzar but paid heed to the warning God sent to Nebuchadnezzar, he might have avoided premature, sudden death.

A similar moral pervades the morality play, *La Cena del Rey Balthasar* by the Spanish dramatist Calderón (1600-1680), written about three centuries after Chaucer. The baroque dramatist was a deeply religious churchman, unsurpassed in his generation as a writer of *Autos Sacramentales*, of which his play about Belshazzar is generally acknowledged to be his best.

Calderón believed both in the omnipotence of God and in the free will of man. Hence, he depicted his principal character, Balthasar, as a king who is free to choose between good and evil, and who deserves to pay the penalty of death for making the wrong choice. However, every human being should be offered an opportunity to repent. Only if he still persists in his evil course is his punishment to be carried out. Calderón's morality play was, therefore, structured in such a way that Balthasar, though guilty of arrogance and impiety, is twice reprieved from death by the intervention of Daniel. Only after he twice relapses into overweening pride and defiance of the true God is he finally handed over to Death, the young, dark knight with sword, dagger, and skeleton-braided cloak, who is ever ready to carry out God's bidding.

In Calderón's dramatic allegory, Daniel, who stands for God's wisdom, is contrasted with the king's companion Pensamiento, who stands for Human Thought, in reality Human Folly. Balthasar, married to Vanity, decides to take Idolatry as his second wife. Only Daniel dares to question the king's decision. Daniel feels that the king's marriage to Idolatry is an act of infidelity to the Supreme Creator of the universe. Nevertheless, he asks Death not to slay Balthasar but only to threaten him, to convince him that every mortal is but dust, and to make him give up Idolatry. Balthasar does indeed hesitate for a moment when he receives Death's message, but he soon yields once more to the allurements of both wives. Death then succeeds in putting the king to sleep. However, on drawing his dagger to slay the sleeper, he again meets with interference by Daniel. On awakening, the still unchastened and unrepentant king prepares for the impious feast. At this feast he drinks to the health of the false god Moloch from the consecrated vessels of Jerusalem's Temple. It is then that the fiery inscription appears on the palace wall, and neither Vanity nor Idolatry, the king's two wives, can prevent Death from executing the well-deserved doom, which Daniel no longer cares to arrest. On witnessing Balthasar's end, Idolatry resolves to abandon the many gods for the one true God.

If Calderón's morality play may be regarded as the best literary treatment of the Belshazzar theme in the seventeenth century, then Georg Friedrich Handel's dramatic oratorio *Belshazzar*, which he completed in 1744 and which experienced its first performance during the following year, is undoubtedly the finest artistic treatment of the eighteenth century. It is true that its popularity was exceeded by his *Messiah*, his *Samson*, and his *Judas Maccabaeus*. However, the text by Charles Jennens is of a quality comparable to the other libretti. The libretto and music of *Belshazzar* stress the death-throes of the Babylonian Empire as symbolic of a civilization in the final stages of decay and as a warning to all aspiring empires that their dominance will be but temporary and that their decline is bound to follow sooner or later.

The opening monologue, or aria, by Nitocris, the mother of Belshazzar, sounds the moral of the drama, the mutability of human empires. At a time when British imperialism was in the ascendancy and British might was reaching out to all continents, Babylon's fate was presented in this oratorio as a warning to British audiences that all empires were doomed. Imperial rule was vain and fluctuating. Empires begin as small and weak powers in need of the protection of mightier neighbor-states. They are nursed along until they attain to wealth and formidable strength. Arrived at full maturity, they become rapacious. They rob, ravage, and oppress their terrified neighbors. They grow fat with conquest. Pride, luxury, corruption, perfidy begin to eat away at their vitals. When such an aging imperial power becomes flabby, advantage is taken of its infirmities by some other, newly arisen power, which brings about its downfall. The victorious young state then runs the same shadowy round of fancied greatness and meets the same tragic end as its predecessor.

The opening aria sets the keynote to the unfolding drama. Aging Babylon is nearing the end of the imperial cycle. Persia is the young, aspiring power. Belshazzar, nevertheless, retains his haughty, imperious demeanor. Despite the raging conflict with Cyrus, he proclaims a festival, during which promiscuity is to reign. Paying no attention to the unhappiness of the Jewish captives, he vows to drink from the sacred vessels of their destroyed Temple. At the royal banquet, surrounded by his wives, concubines, and lords, he does indeed drink out of the Jerusalem vessels and sings the praises of the Babylonian gods. It is then that a hand appears and writes mysterious symbols on the wall. Trembling overtakes Belshazzar, his knees knock against each other, and the bowl of wine drops from his grasp. Daniel alone can interpret the handwriting, which foretells the doom of Belshazzar and his empire.

The dramatic oratorio ends with Belshazzar slain and with the triumphant Cyrus promising to release the Jews from captivity and to rebuild their sanctuary in Jerusalem.

A generation after the Jennens-Handel oratorio, young Goethe planned a Belshazzar drama, as well as a second biblical drama on Jezebel, but he never wrote either. There does, however, survive an outline of the former play in *Wilhelm Meisters Theatralische Sendung* (bk. II, chap. 4; bk. III, chap. 9).

Goethe's Belshazzar was conceived as a young, good-natured, frivolous king. At his court, a plot is forged to overthrow him. Its leaders are Princess Kandace, whose father was dethroned by Nebuchadnezzar, and the courtier Eron, who resents the waning of his earlier influence upon the royal establishment. Darius, king of the Medes, offers to help the conspirators. Disguised as his own envoy, he appears at Belshazzar's court. His true identity is unknown even to the conspirators when he joins in their deliberations. They plan the murder of Belshazzar during the feast being arranged for his birthday. The conspirators would then elevate the princess to the throne of Babylon and marry her off to the king of the Medes. The disguised Medean envoy promises to bring the proposal to Darius but makes no firm commitments.

As the action develops, the princess falls in love with the envoy and would prefer him as her consort. The disguised Darius, however, has fallen in love with Nitocris, the wife of Belshazzar, but fears that she would never agree to become the mate of her husband's murderer. He, therefore, persuades the conspirators to delay the execution of their plans. Eron becomes suspicious of the envoy. Can it be that Darius intends to bypass the princess and seize the throne for himself? When Eron learns about the handwriting on the wall and Daniel's interpretation, he feels that immediate success is assured for the overthrow of Belshazzar. But the envoy of Darius still counsels a delay.

The final act shows the intoxicated Belshazzar terrified by the mysterious words that seem to foretell his doom. As he leaves the banquet hall, he is killed by the conspirators. The princess claims the throne for herself. But then suddenly Darius, no longer in disguise, appears at the head of his troops, who have forced their way into the city. He is accepted by all as the new ruler of Babylon. He rewards the princess magnanimously but does not marry her. As the final curtain descends, he is comforting Belshazzar's widow with words that leave the impression that a union between them is likely soon.

Though Goethe never got beyond a single monologue before abandoning the Belshazzar theme, the English dramatist Hannah More, who was born in 1745, four years before Goethe, and who died in 1833, a year after him, did complete and publish, in 1782, a *Belshazzar* as one of her so-called *Sacred Dramas*. This play, however, did not rise above mediocrity.

Nor are the two poems on this theme which Lord Byron (1788-1824) composed a generation later of a superior quality. Indeed, only one of them, "The Vision of Belshazzar," did he deem sufficiently significant to include in his *Hebrew Melodies* (1815). The other "To Belshazzar," was written in the same year but was not published until 1831, seven years after his death. Its three stanzas are addressed to the arrogant king whose soul expired ere youth decayed. The monarch is admonished to turn from banqueting and from sensuality. He is not a mighty despot but rather a weakling who was weighed in the balance and found worthless, unfit to govern, live, or die.

"The Vision of Belshazzar" consists of six stanzas that retell the biblical episode of the festival in greater detail: the king and his satraps drinking the godless wine from the sacred vessels, the handwriting on the wall which the Chaldean seers cannot read but which the captive Hebrew youth deciphers and whose prophetic message proves to be true on the following morning when Belshazzar's grave is made and his kingdom taken over by the Medes and the Persians.

Byron's poem probably stimulated the far more magnificent ballad of Heinrich Heine (1797-1856). Although the German poet claimed in 1849 that he composed his "Belsatzar" before his sixteenth year, hence before Byron's *Hebrew Melodies* appeared, his memory must have been at fault. The original impulse to compose a poem on this theme may have come so early. He recalled intoning in his boyhood the Hebrew hymn intoned by Jews annually at the Passover Seder, "Va'i bekhatzi halayla"—"And it was at midnight." This opening line of the Hebrew hymn is echoed both rhythmically and in meaning in Heine's opening verse, "Die Mitternacht zog näher schon." By 1820, Byron's poem was available to German readers in translation and probably stimulated Heine to attempt a new poetic version of the biblical scene. The German poet may also have read it in the original English, since he was an avid reader of Byron and was soon to be dubbed the German Byron because of the Byronic, or *Weltschmerz*, tone in his early lyrics.

The entire action of Heine's ballad takes place during a single night, the night of the banquet. Heine omits all mention of Daniel and of the Persian army at the gates of Babylon. While midnight silence envelops the entire city, the imperial palace is astir with loud carousing. The king, under the influence of wine, blasphemes the Lord, God of the conquered Jews, and calls for the vessels robbed from the shrine in Jerusalem. As the ruler of a mighty empire, he feels himself superior to the vanquished captives and their deity. However, hardly has he voiced his scorn of God when horror overcomes him and the loud laughter of his courtiers yields to corpselike silence, a foreboding of doom for the blasphemer. In the midst of this absolute silence, a hand becomes visible inscribing letters of fire on a white wall. Horror is intensified, as no one knows the meaning of the flaming signs. But that very night spells the end of the haughty ruler, who is slain by his own underlings.

Heine's poem was set to music by Robert Schumann. It has been sung and recited to German and international audiences ever since its publication and is thus far better known than all the Belshazzar versions that preceded or followed it.

Subsequent Belshazzar versions in the nineteenth century include "Belshazzar's Feast" by the poetess Felicia Hemans; "Impious Feast," a poem by Robert Landor, the brother of the more famous Walter Savage Landor; *Belshazzar*, a drama by Henry Hart Milman; "Belshazzar's Feast" and "Belshazzar," two poems by Bryan Waller Procter, who wrote under the pseudonym of Barry Cornwall; and *The Feast of Belshazzar*, a narrative poem by Edwin Arnold.

Of these poetic versions, Edwin Arnold's long tale of 1853 is the most elaborate and the most moving. It depicts King Belshazzar in his arrogance decreeing a high festival. Though the foe is at the gate of Babylon and a battle is to be fought on the morrow, the king wants to feast with royal extravagance. He gives orders that the bowls and goblets carried off from Judah's Temple when Jerusalem was conquered be filled with wine for Jerusalem's conquerors. But the handwriting on the wall casts a pall of fear over the revelers. Daniel the Hebrew, who reads visions, is summoned to decipher the mysterious symbols. Fearlessly he faces the mighty monarch and his satraps. He reminds them of Nebuchadnezzar's arrogance, which was humbled when God drove him out into the desert, to roam among the wild asses, far from kingly majesty and from the brotherhood of fellow-men. Had Belshazzar bowed to the Lord's will, as did his repentant predecessor, then he might have continued to retain his scepter. However, he had mocked the majesty of heaven, hence the message whose spectral letters proclaim his coming end. Before the night was over, Belshazzar lay crownless and scepterless, a robe of purple round a form of clay.

The symbolic words written on the wall of Babylon's palace while its lords feasted were often referred to as ominous warnings to more recent rulers and arrogant dictators. On the eve of the Revolution of 1848, the words "Mene, Mene, Tekel, Upharsin" formed the title of lyrics by Emanuel Geibel in 1846 and by Hermann Semmig in 1847. Later, the warning spelled out by the handwriting on the wall recurred as a leitmotif in William Walton's splendid oratorio of 1931, *Belshazzar's Feast*, which was based on a text by Osbert Sitwell, and throughout the novel of resistance to Nazi arrogance, *Sansibar*, by Alfred Andersch in 1956.

In the poem by Geibel, the leader of the Munich Group of

poets, high society carouses, candles sparkle, music resounds, and scantily dressed maidens serve foaming wine. Outside the palace walls, thousands of hungry faces gather in the darkness of night. Led by an Amazon with a red flag, they surround the banquet-hall. Still the carousers dance on, though hollow-eyed death is all about them, ready to overwhelm them.

In the novel by Andersch, one of Germany's most popular writers of the post-Nazi decade, the hero, Pastor Helander, waits throughout the arrogant Nazi years for a handwriting to appear on the church wall with the message that the realm of evil will soon come to an end. Since the victory of the Nazis in 1933, his community, his church, and his house have become empty, echoless space. God seems so remote, far too remote to write in invisible ink even a few letters on the church wall with the slightest message of hope which could comfort him in his isolation. The Nazis continue to stride from victory to victory and seem to be invincible. Finally, the long awaited message of God does come to him in his last hour, after he has completed his courageous deed of defiance of the Nazi establishment, and as the bullets of the Gestapo riddle him. His dying thought is that now the message for which he waited throughout the long years of silent and heroic resistance must appear. God must bring retribution upon the Nazis. "He turned and glanced at the wall and, as he read the writing, he hardly felt the fire that entered into him. His only thought was 'I am alive,' as the small, hot fires burned in him. These fires hit him everywhere."

Down the many centuries, the fiery symbols of the Book of Daniel—Mene, Mene, Tekel, Upharsin—have been hurled by literary spokesmen at tyrants and tyrannical systems, and have brought hope and comfort to oppressed groups and national entities, including Jewish communities under the heels of brutal conquerors from Belshazzar to Hitler. These symbolic words remain an eternal affirmation of divine justice that humbles the proud and uplifts the lowly.

28

The Biblical Tradition of Democracy

Throughout the long march on the road of history, there were many centuries when Jews existed without a land of their own and had to content themselves with only an unquenchable longing for the land of their origin and with a messianic hope of their ultimate return to it. There were also many centuries when Jews had no common spoken tongue and had to modify the languages of their neighbors to suit their own linguistic needs. Thus there came into being diverse Jewish languages ranging from Judeo-Greek, spoken in the Balkans, Judeo-Persian, spoken by the Jews of Iran, Tat, spoken by the Mountain Jews of the Caucasus, to Ladino, spoken by Sephardim, Yiddish spoken by Ashkenazim, and other tongues that arose, flourished, and declined. However, Jews did have a common written language, the sacred Hebrew of the Bible, which they cherished so ardently that they could revive it as their common spoken tongue when they returned to Israel from the lands of the Diaspora, a miracle of linguistic rebirth that no other people has been able to duplicate.

Jews survived for millennia, scattered over many territories far from their ancestral soil, amidst alien peoples and alien tongues, and without a government of their own capable of guiding their destinies and protecting their common interests, because they did have a quasi-territory, a portable fatherland, the Torah, which they carried with them on their wanderings in many exiles; they did have a common legal code expounded in the Talmud; they did have a common core of linguistic expressions and idioms gleaned from their prayers, folkways, festivals, and historical memories; they did have, in addition to the alien governments that lorded over them, a quasi-government based on the Mosaic legal code which they respected, obeyed, and reinterpreted to meet their changing needs. Above all, they were able to maintain themselves as a united, disciplined historic group because, since their national birth, they had been trained to exercise popular sovereignty and to practice popular democracy—not representative democracy, such as prevails in Central and Western Europe and in America, and not the so-called people's democracy of Eastern Europe, which is neither the expression of a people's will nor really democratic. Theirs was a genuine participation of all the Hebraic individuals, men and women, in decision-making. Theirs was an adherence by consensus to laws, written and oral, that guided their group behavior.

From their beginnings, when they stood at the foot of Mount Sinai and freely accepted their first code of laws after their liberation from slavery, until their most recent historical experiences when, as denizens of Eastern European townlets and North African mellahs, they retained autonomous behavior-patterns which guaranteed survival under stress; and when, as citizens of contemporary states ranging from North America to South Africa and Australia, they reacted with almost complete unanimity in defense of imperiled Israel, Jews have shown themselves to be a disciplined people, a people that acts with a common will and a common purpose in periods of adversity and danger, even though at other times, in periods of prosperity and relative stability, they indeed argue vehemently, rage against restraints, and often rebel against their traditional uniqueness.

There is a legend that the Torah was originally offered to other peoples but was rejected. It was then offered to the liberated Hebraic slaves. These included adherents of Moses and Aaron, dissidents like the horde of Korah, and wavering groups. Ultimately, all the men, women, and children assembled at Sinai accepted the Torah by acclamation. It has been the constitution under which their descendants have lived until this day, descendants who freely chose to do so, freely and not under compulsion, since whosoever wished to secede from Judaism could generally do so.

Popular democracy prevailed during the forty years of wandering in the desert of Sinai, and Moses needed ever anew his marvelous gifts of persuasion to win approval of his proposals and ordinances. He could not assume automatic obedience. He had to strive for a consensus, and he was not always successful, for his people was from its very beginning a stiff-necked people.

Popular democracy was retained under Joshua, the successor of Moses. After the crossing of the Jordan and the conquest of Canaan, this military leader assembled the entire people at Shechem. And there, at a great conclave, he spoke to them about their past since the days of Abraham. He then presented them with the basic issue that now faced them as they settled down to a more stable existence. They could choose to serve the gods of the Amorite population in whose midst they were now to live or the God of their patriarchal ancestors and of Moses. The people answered that they would accept their historic God. Joshua warned them that it was not an easy fate they were about to accept. A second time they gave their assent to serve the God who had liberated them from Egypt. A third time Joshua reminded them that they were still free to choose. A third time they replied that they would obey the voice of the Lord. After these three presentations—a tradition of three readings is still practiced by Israel's Knesset today whenever a new law is proposed—the basic law or covenant of the Jewish people, which had earlier been accepted at Sinai, was considered as having been again ratified by the voluntary acclamation of all those who were assembled, and it was then written down by Joshua as a permanent record before the assembly dispersed, each family to its own home.

For generations thereafter the people ruled themselves within the framework of the accepted covenant and under tribal judges of their own choosing, judges who interpreted the laws for them in times of peace and who led them into battle in times of war. Whenever danger threatened, the Hebraic tribes united for common action, but otherwise each tribe did what was pleasing in its eyes.

During the era of Samuel, however, the need to ward off the incursions of the Philistines led to a call for a strong central authority, a king who would be able to bring about greater unity among the divided tribes. Samuel warned the people not to give up their sovereign power to a monarch who might become a dictator and a tyrannical oppressor, who would expropriate their fields, vineyards, olive groves to give to his retinue, who would take the best of their sons and daughters to be his servants. The people, however, were prepared to take the risk, since disunity imperiled their survival. They outvoted Samuel, and he, in true democratic fashion, had to accept their decision. They did, however, reserve final legislative authority for themselves, turning over to their chosen rulers primarily executive and judicial power.

Amidst the changes of fortune throughout the First Monarchy, basic sovereignty continued to be vested in the people and found expression in the assemblies convoked when critical issues came up. Kings had to be confirmed by the people. Thus, when Solomon died and his son Rehoboam was to be confirmed as his heir, the people were ready to do so only under certain specified conditions, chiefly a lessening of the tax burden that had been imposed earlier. When Rehoboam refused to accept these conditions, the sovereign people decided not to confirm him. Ten of the twelve tribes chose Jeroboam as their executive officer, and only two tribes, Judah and Benjamin, voted for Rehoboam and the Davidic dynasty.

Popular democracy prevailed during the centuries of the First Temple and found eloquent spokesmen in the prophets from Elijah to Jeremiah. These gifted orators stood on guard against the infringement of the popular will by the monarchs both in Judea and in the Northern Kingdom. The most spectacular assertion of the popular will came to the fore during the reign of the

Judean King Josiah. This young monarch was able to carry out his basic reformation of state and cult because he had the backing of public opinion and because he received a mandate to put his reforms into practice in an assembly of all the inhabitants of his kingdom. At this assembly the king read out the words of the legal code that was found in the house of God, and all the men of Judah and all the inhabitants of Jerusalem reached an agreement, which they ratified by a covenant, to keep the Lord's commandments and His statutes with all their heart and all their soul. "And all the people stood to the covenant."

After the ascension of King Jehoiakim to the throne of Judea, the consensus that had been reached during the reign of his father, Josiah, and had been embodied in a covenant, no longer prevailed. Pressured by rival superpowers, Babylonia and Egypt, the new administration faced critical problems involving its very survival as an independent state, and its decisions were not always wise. But the tradition of popular democracy was retained, and prophets, true and false, spoke up at assemblies convoked in Jerusalem and tried to win over the masses, each to his own viewpoint.

The twenty-sixth chapter of Jeremiah depicts vividly this prophet's presentation to the entire people of his minority view about the political crisis that was brewing. All the people listened to him, princes, priests, and commoners, as he foretold a coming catastrophe, but they were not convinced. Hotheads shouted him down and even demanded that he be put to death for his treasonable utterances that undermined public morale at a dangerous time. Nevertheless, the prophet continued his efforts to convince the majority of his listeners to change their political position on the burning issues. At the same time he accepted their democratic right to outvote him. His defense and final summation are reminiscent of the speech of Socrates before the Athenians two centuries later. Jeremiah tells his listeners that they are wrong in their appraisal of current realities, even if they are in the majority. "As for me, behold, I am in your hand. Do with me as seems good and proper in your eyes. But know for certain, that if you put me to death, you shall surely put innocent blood upon yourselves, and upon this city, and upon its inhabitants, for of a truth the Lord has sent me to you to speak all these words in your ears." And like Socrates, he makes no promise that he will desist from agitating for his minority view.

Jeremiah was no less a "gadfly" than was Socrates, but he was not forced to drink the hemlock because of his voiced subversive opinions. In true democratic fashion, his opponents against whom he railed protected him in his right to speak out and to attack the establishment and its policies.

Popular democracy survived the fall of Judea and the destruction of the Temple, the symbol of Jewish unity. It survived the Babylonian exile and was fully restored upon the return to Zion of the pioneers under Zerubbabel and of the contingents that followed under Ezra and Nehemiah.

Nehemiah, in chapter 8 of his narrative, describes the democratic procedure of his generation, when the men and women came up to Jerusalem from their various settlements in the month of Tishri. On the first of the month Ezra brought up for their consideration a reaffirmation of the earlier Hebraic constitution, the laws that had governed them since the original adoption at Sinai. Standing on an elevated platform and flanked by thirteen prominent settlers, he read out the relevant passages of the Torah, a reading which took up the entire morning. All the people listened attentively. And when Ezra finished his presentation, the thirteen distinguished persons and the Levites explained section by section the sense of the laws the people were asked to reconfirm. The implications of the laws were clarified not only for the assembled men but also for the women and all those who could hear with understanding, meaning children above a certain age. Then the people dispersed for the day, to eat, drink, and discuss.

On the following morning, the second day of Tishri, the chiefs of the households, together with the priests and the Levites, met for further consideration of the practical application of the proposed ordinances. They arrived at a consensus that immediate priority be given to the ordinances for the celebration of Succoth two weeks later. To prepare properly for this celebration, it was necessary for the *chalutzim* who had come back out of captivity to go out to the mountain and fetch the prescribed materials, branches of thick trees, as well as olive, myrtle, and palm branches, needed for the making of succahs in which to dwell during the coming holiday.

For seven days, amidst great gladness at their return to Jerusalem, the people celebrated Succoth as they had not done to that extent since the days of Joshua ben Nun. On each day they read and discussed the Torah. This constituted the second reading. On the eighth day, Shemini Atzereth, they again were called into assembly to hear the report of the central committee headed by Ezra, which had during the preceding weeks made a thorough study as to what changes in communal life-style would be necessary and how the ordinances of the Torah could be applied to the contemporary situation in which the returnees from Babylon found themselves.

Before a vote was taken at this assembly, the relevant passages of the Torah were again read out, a reading which consumed one-fourth of the day and which constituted the third, or final, reading. Then the leaders harangued the assembly. They recalled the glorious days of the past since the generation of Abraham, and the less glorious days of the people's backsliding, which had resulted in catastrophes and the recent exile. They reminded their audience of the special relationship of the Hebraic community to God. The recommendation was made that final approval and ratification be formalized by a written covenant.

Nehemiah, the high commissioner, was the first to attach his signature. He was followed by the outstanding priests, then Levites, gatekeepers, singers, Temple servants, and all who had separated themselves from the non-Jewish inhabitants by this covenant, men and women, their sons and daughters, everyone who was old enough to understand the significance of his vote. Before the assembly dispersed, all took an oath to observe the commandments, ordinances, and statutes agreed upon. This was an oath of allegiance not to an individual but to the ratified constitution, the code of laws embodied in the Torah.

The most onerous of the endorsed laws bound them to refrain

from mixed marriages and to dissolve those they had already entered into with foreign wives. The covenant also obligated them to be more scrupulous in observing the Sabbath ordinances, not to engage in buying or selling or engaging in any business enterprise on the Sabbath and on Holy Days, to be meticulous during a Sabbatical year in forgoing the exaction of debts and in letting the land lie fallow, and finally to pay the various taxes of the religious cult.

During the ensuing two to three centuries, the Jewish people lived under its autonomous democratic traditions in its homeland and in the growing diasporas from Babylon to Alexandria, after the latter city was founded by Alexander the Great. Successive overlords of Judea, from the Persian satraps to the Ptolemaic successors of Alexander, did not interfere too much with Jewish communal and religious institutions and did not attempt to splinter the unity of the Jewish people. Synagogues arose as Houses of Learning and as centers of discussion on religious and civic matters. Though no new prophets came to the fore after Haggai and Zechariah as spokesmen for the common man, popular democracy continued to flourish. Scholars tried to win the approval of the masses for their interpretations of the Torah, the constitution which ruled the internal organization of the Jewish people. This people endured passively foreign political domination as long as it did not interfere with the cherished basic precepts of the Torah. However, when the Seleucid ruler Antiochus IV tried to force Hellenization and the worship of Zeus upon the Jews, they rose up in revolt under the leadership of the Hasmoneans. They fought desperately to maintain their traditional way of life, as they had covenanted again and again, and they won out. Individual Jews, generation after generation, especially those of the upper social rank, might succumb to the lure of Hellenism and might freely choose assimilation to alien ways, but the masses were always ready to fight to the death for their God and their freely accepted constitution, the Torah.

This constitution vested ultimate sovereignty in the entire people as trustees of God's will, and the people exercised this sovereignty through their democratic institutions down the centuries. Pharisees and Sadducees argued, debated, quarreled, approved, and disapproved Hasmonean leadership. The various factions of the Hasmonean dynasty tried to manipulate the popular will, but they recognized its paramount importance.

When Rome seized control of Judea as decay overtook the Hasmoneans, Roman rulers too had to respect Jewish democratic institutions. The Jews paid taxes and gave lip service to the Romans, but they sought and followed the guidance of their own rabbis and scholars who expounded the Torah ordinances to them. When a Roman emperor, who was able to impose his godhood upon other provinces of his farflung empire, tried to have his statue as god-emperor installed also in Jerusalem's Temple, he had to recognize the limits of his authority over the Jewish masses, for they lined the highway to Jerusalem, prepared to die to prevent this desecration of their faith. Their action was not dictated from above but was a spontaneous upsurge of the Jewish population in defense of its freely chosen way of life. Nor was the revolt that led to the destruction of the Second Commonwealth and the exile of the Jewish people from its homeland in 70 C.E. dictated by any one Führer. It too was an upsurge of Hebraic democratic forces and an expression of the popular will. Whether this revolt or the desperate Bar Kochba revolt two generations later was politically wise may be argued, but there is no doubt that both revolts were expressions of a democratic people that took great risks in order to preserve its national uniqueness.

Biblical democratic traditions continued to rule Jewish life. Jewish neighborhoods, ghettos, townlets were Jewish national enclaves in non-Jewish states. Without compulsion, Jews listened to the directions of great scholars and voluntarily followed the leadership of charismatic personalities with gifts of persuasion who arose in the various diasporas. The centuries of exile dragged on and on, but Jews did not give up their democratic processes and self-governing institutions. They retained the laws of the Torah and pored over the Talmud's interpretations of the Torah as their guides to individual and communal behavior, not only in the dark days of the Middle Ages but also in modern times. Communities freely chose martyrdom to apostasy and dissociation from the Jewish national entity. Yet, even when communities felt that apparent conversion to avoid extermination was the wiser decision, they temporarily became Marranos and later reverted to the faith of their fathers as soon as mortal danger abated.

In every townlet and in every synagogue, popular democracy prevailed. Though aberrations occurred, and communal leaders now and then proved faithless to their trust, the voice of the scholar and of a man of the masses arose to chastise and to demand a reckoning in the name of the Torah, the enduring constitution. Any ten Jews could form a minyan and conduct public religious services, and they did not need a rabbi or religious officer to call them together or to lead them. Any individual man or woman who felt aggrieved by a fellow-Jew and who failed to get justice in any other way could stop holy services by mounting the rostrum before the ark of the Torah scrolls and insist on being heard before permitting the Torah to be read.

When pogroms threatened and catastrophes loomed, the Jewish people united in defense of its unique way of life and rushed to save the imperiled sectors or organs of the Jewish national organism. In the early decades of the present century, Jewish unity was displayed in the worldwide relief activities for the victims of tsarist pogroms and of the revolutionary and counter-revolutionary Russian hordes. In the Nazi decades, Jewish efforts on a worldwide scale were directed to lessen the impact of the decrees promulgated for the annihilation of Jews and to rescue survivors of concentration camps and ruined ghettos. Since the mid-century decades Israel has been at the center of Jewish concern everywhere. Jews felt new fire in their veins as they sensed the opportunity to renew and to consolidate Jewish sovereignty in their historic land. With unbroken unity, the Jewish masses throughout the Diaspora have been unwavering in the defense of Israel's right to its national resurrection. Though governments of hostile and at times even friendly states sought to splinter this unity because of their own national interests, such efforts have met with little success and will undoubtedly continue to fail. Individual Jewish intellectuals, alienated from the traditions rooted in the Bible, might decry the unswerving unity which often sets the little, heroic biblical people in opposition to non-Jewish world opinion. But this unity has been an historic fact ever since the Jews were constituted as a people, one people, with democratic ideals and individual responsibility for the preservation of these ideals as embodied in their freely accepted covenants since Sinai and last renewed on Israel's sovereign soil in Israel's covenant of 1948.

For the preservation and security of the Jewish national entity, the Jewish masses are closing ranks today, as in all earlier generations when this entity was imperiled, and are again reaffirming by their sacrifices in war and peace their adherence to their millennial covenant by which they have lived since their national birth in the days of Moses.

Afterword

By Elie Wiesel

Before giving the Law to the Jews, God offered it to all the other peoples on earth. They all refused it. It contained too many prohibitions. Even the children of Israel accepted it only under constraint. Under God's threat of death, they declared themselves ready to receive the divine commandments even before knowing what they were. The Talmud tells us about this.

As a child I thought that the Bible interested only talmudic commentators and their readers. I told myself that it only concerned the Jews. Later on I realized my error. The history of our people is linked to the history of humanity.

An inspired work, the Bible is also a source of inspiration. Its impact has no equal, whether on the social and ethical plane or on that of literary creation. We forget too often that the Bible pertains equally to the artistic domain. Its characters are dramatic, their dramas timeless, their triumphs and defeats overwhelming. Each cry touches us, each call penetrates us. Texts of another age, the biblical poems are themselves ageless. They call out to us collectively and individually, across and beyond the centuries.

It is not surprising that so many writers and poets, both Jewish and non-Jewish, felt the need to take themes from the Bible for their works. This is the subject of the book which I am now enthusiastically recommending to the reader.

Thanks to his erudition, both Jewish and secular, Sol Liptzin shows us, with a remarkable talent as a storyteller and literary commentator, the Bible's influence on the great figures of world literature.

Cain's fascination for Coleridge and Schiller, Joseph's for Thomas Mann, Moses as interpreted by Alfred de Vigny and Freud, the relationship between Ruth and Medea, Voltaire's pity for King Saul, D. H. Lawrence's dramatization of David—you must read and reread these analyses and studies in the chapters of this admirable and enriching book.

Perhaps even more stimulating are the sections which the author devotes to minor characters of the Bible; for example, Hagar, Sarah's servant, and Asenath, Joseph's wife. Why are they neglected in the Scriptures and even in postbiblical commentaries? And why such fierce hostility to Lilith? And what explains Jephthah's cruelty to his daughter?

For generations writers and poets, dramatists and painters, composers and historians have been drawn to these men and women of the biblical realm, who, although mortal and profoundly human, have achieved some measure of immortality. Thanks to Sol Liptzin, you will know them better, and perhaps yourself as well.

Translated from the French
by Martha Liptzin Hauptman

Bibliography

1. Rehabilitation of Lilith

Anski, S. *Ashmedai*. St. Petersburg, 1905.
Browning, Robert. "Adam, Lilith, and Eve." In *Poems and Plays*, p. 1098. New York, 1934.
Eisenmenger, J. A. *Entdecktes Judentum*, I, 165; II, 413-421. Frankfurt a. M., 1700.
France, Anatole. "La Fille de Lilith." In *Oeuvres Complètes*, IV, 175-193. Paris, 1925.
Ginzberg, Louis. *Legends of the Jews*, I, 65 f. Philadelphia, 1938.
Gourmont, Remy de. *Lilith*. Boston, 1946.
Hadas, P. W. *In Light of Genesis*. Philadelphia, 1980.
Hoffman, Rainer. "Liliths Erlösung." *Neue Züricher Zeitung*, May 6, 1978.
Kurz, Isolde. *Die Kinder der Lilith*. Stuttgart, 1908.
Lilith, The Jewish Women's Magazine. New York, 1976–.
Macdonald, George. *Lilith*. London, 1895; Stuttgart, 1977.
Manger, Itzik. "Lilith un Monish." In *Shtern in Shtoib*, pp. 103 f. New York, 1967.
Peretz, Y. L. "Monish." In *Ale Verk*, X, 223-247; XIII, 41-55. Buenos Aires, 1944.
Rigney, B. H. *Lilith's Daughters*. Madison, Wis., 1982.
Rossetti, D. G. "Lilith." In *Poems and Translations*, p. 146. London, 1913.
———. "Eden Bower." In *Poems and Translations*, pp. 18-23. London, 1913.
Shaw, G. B. *Back to Methuselah*. London, 1921.
Widmann, J. V. *Der Heilige und die Tiere*. 1905.
Wolfskehl, Karl. "Sanctus. Ein Mysterium." In *Gesammelte Werke*, I, 344-358. Hamburg, 1960.

2. Defiant Cain

Baudelaire, Charles. "Abel et Cain." In *Oeuvres Complètes*, pp. 115 f. Paris, 1961.
Birnbaum, Uriel. "Biblische Sonette." In *Gedichte*, pp. 557-578. Amsterdam, 1957.
Brieger, Auguste. *Kain und Abel in der deutschen Dichtung*. Berlin, 1934.
Byron, Lord. "Cain." In *Complete Works*, pp. 626-654. Boston, 1905.
Coleridge, S. T. "The Wanderings of Cain." In *Complete Poetical Works*, I, 285-292. Oxford, 1912.
Fairlies, Alison. *Leconte de Lisle's Poems on the Barbarian Races*, pp. 244-279. Cambridge, 1947.

Gertner, Meir. "Else Lasker Schüler's Biblical Poems." *Jewish Quarterly* 17, nos. 3-4 (1969).
Gessner, Salomon. *Der Tod Abels.* Leipzig, 1760.
———. *The Death of Abel.* London, 1761.
Hugo, Victor. *La Legende des Siècles.* Paris, 1962.
Illies, Joachim. *Der Brudermord. Zum Mythos von Kain und Abel.* Munich, 1975.
Lasker-Schüler, Else. "Abel." In *Gesammelte Werke,* I, 293. Munich, 1959.
Leconte des Lisle, C. M. R. "Qain." In *Oeuvres,* II, 2-18. Paris, 1976.
Manger, Itzik. "Cain." In *Shtern in Shtoib,* p. 56. New York, 1967.
Mellinkoff, Ruth. *The Mark of Cain.* Berkeley, Cal., 1981.
Nerval, Gèrard de. *Voyage en Orient.* Paris, 1867.
Reed, Bertha. *Influence of Salomon Gessner upon English Literature.* Philadelphia, 1905.
Rothschild, Jacob. *Kain und Abel in der deutschen Literatur.* Würzburg, 1933.
Schiller, Friedrich. *Die Sendung Moses und Etwas über die erste Menschengesellschaft.* Hamburg, 1960.
Shaw, G. B. *Back to Methuselah.* London, 1921.
Wildgans, Anton. *Kain.* Leipzig, 1920.
Yehoash. "Cain." In *Poems,* p. 61. London, Ont., 1952.

3. The Tower of Babel

Borst, Arno. *Der Turmbau von Babel,* 6 vols. Stuttgart, 1957-63.
Defoe, Daniel. *Works,* Vol. III: *Political History of the Devil.* London, 1912.
Donne, John. *Poems.* London, 1929.
Dürrenmatt, Friedrich. *An Angel Comes to Babylon.* New York, 1964.
Friedlander, Gerald, ed. *Pirke de Rabbi Eliezer,* pp. 174-178. New York, 1965.
Gaster, M., ed. *The Chronicle of Jerahmeel.* London, 1899.
Goethe-Handbuch, I, 518-523. Stuttgart, 1961.
Gressmann, Hugo. *Tower of Babel.* New York, 1928.
Hart, Heinrich. *Gesammelte Werke,* I, 221-388. Berlin, 1907.
Herder, J. G. *Vom Geist der Ebräischen Poesie,* I, 231-235. Leipzig, 1825.
Herodotus. *History,* bk. I, chap. 181.
Jenny, Uwe. *Dürrenmatt: A Study of His Plays.* London, 1978.
Josephus Flavius. *Jewish Antiquities,* bk. I. Loeb Classics, ed. London, 1934.
Judson, A. C. *Life of Edmund Spenser.* Baltimore, 1945.
Kurfess, Alfons, ed. *Sibyllinische Weissagungen,* pp. 76-80. Münster, 1951.
Locke, John. *Two Treatises of Civil Government.* London, 1924.
Milton, John. *Paradise Lost.* Cambridge, 1934.
Minkowski, Helmut. *Aus dem Nebel der Vergangenheit Steigt der Turm zu Babel.* Berlin, 1960.
Osherowitch, Hirsh. *Tanakh-Poemes.* Tel Aviv, 1979.
Philo Judaeus. *The Confusion of Tongues.* Loeb Classics ed., IV, 1-119. London, 1932.
Ponten, Josef. *Der Babylonische Turm.* Stuttgart, 1918.

Rubinstein, Anton. *Der Turm zu Babel.* Leipzig, 1872.
Strabo. *Geography.* Loeb Classics ed., VII, 197-201. London, 1966.
Tseno Ureno, I, 43-45. New York, 1910.
Wordsworth, William. *Poetical Works.* London, 1928. *The Excursion,* Book IV.
Wünsche, August, ed. *Bereshith Rabba,* pp. 163-172. Leipzig, 1881.
Zweig, Stefan. *Der Turm zu Babel.* Vienna, 1964.
———. *Europäisches Erbe.* Frankfurt, 1960.

4. Princess Hagar

Adams, F. L. "Hagar." In *Oxford Book of Scottish Verse,* pp. 457 f. London, 1966.
Arnold, Edwin. "Hagar in the Wilderness." In *Poems, Narrative and Lyrical,* pp. 58-67. Oxford, 1953.
Auerbach, Ephraim. "Ishmael." In M. Bassin, *Amerikaner Yidishe Poezie,* pp. 459 f. New York, 1940.
Coleridge, Hartley. "Hagar." In *New Poems,* p. 44. London, 1942.
Costa, Isaac de. *Hagar.* Zutphen, 1941.
Eybers, Elisabeth. "Hagar." In *Penguin Book of South African Verse,* p. 221. Harmondsworth, 1968.
Forbes-Mosse, Irene. "Hagars Klage." In H. Hakel, *Die Bibel im deutschen Gedicht des 20.Jahrhunderts,* pp. 18-20. Basel, 1958.
Grünbaum, Max. *Neue Beiträge zur semitischen Sagenkunde.* Leiden, 1893.
Hale, E. E. "Hager Departed." In G. A. Kohut, *Hebrew Anthology,* I, 58. Cincinnati, 1913.
Hardy, W. G. *Father Abraham.* London, 1935.
Inghelran, Daan. *Sarai und die Ägypterin.* Cologne, 1956.
Lasker-Schüler, Else. "Hagar und Israel." In *Gesammelte Werke,* I, 295. Munich, 1959.
Lindheimer, Franz. *Hagars Liebe.* Heidelberg, 1896.
Manger, Itzik. *Lid un Balade,* pp. 224-229. New York, 1952.
———. "Hagar's Last Night in Abraham's House." In I. Howe and E. Greenberg, *A Treasury of Yiddish Poetry,* pp. 277 f. New York, 1969.
O'Neal, Cothburn. *Hagar.* New York, 1958.
Philo Judaeus. Loeb Classics ed., IV, 465-551. London, 1932.
Pirkê de Rabbi Eliezer. New York, 1965.
Potash, Rikudah. "Hagar." In *Lider,* pp. 167 f. Tel Aviv, 1917.
Sowden, Lewis. "Ishmael." In *Poems on Themes Drawn from the Bible,* pp. 11-14. London, 1960.
Tighe, Mary. "Hagar in the Desert." In *Psyche,* pp. 299-302. London, 1812.
Tseno Ureno, I, 84-86. New York, 1910.
Willis, N. P. "Hagar in the Wilderness." In *Poetical Works,* pp. 64-70. London, 1888.
Wolfskehl, Karl. "Hagar die Verstossene vor der Tür." In *Gesammelte Werke,* I, 362-364. Hamburg, 1960.
Wolfson, H. A. *Philo.* Cambridge, Mass., 1947.

5. Rebekah's Beguilement of Isaac

Beer-Hofmann, Richard. *Jaakobs Traum*. Berlin, 1918.
Birnbaum, Uriel. "Rebekka." In *Gedichte*, p. 582. Amsterdam, 1957.
Cabries, Jean. *Saint Jacob*. Paris, 1954; New York, 1958.
Ehrenstein, Theodor. *Das Alte Testament im Bilde*. Wien, 1923.
Fineman, Irving. *Jacob*. New York, 1941.
Housman, Laurence, *Palestine Plays*. London, 1942.
Manger, Itzik. *Lid un Balade*. New York, 1969.
Mann, Thomas. *Die Geschichten Jaakobs*. Berlin, 1933.
Van Doren, Mark. *Collected New Poems*. New York, 1964.

6. Lady Asenath

Archiv far der Geshikhte fun Yidishn Teater un Drame. Vilna: YIVO, 1930.
Burchard, Christoph. *Untersuchungen zu Joseph und Asenath*. Tübingen, 1965.
Favir, Eliezer. *Gdolas Yosef*. Zholkov, 1801.
Grimmelshausen, H. J. C. *Des vortrefflich keuschen Josephs in Egypten Lebensbeschreibung*. Tübingen, 1968.
Mann, Thomas. *Joseph und seine Brüder*, vol. III. Berlin, 1936.
Pirkê de Rabbi Eliezer. New York, 1965.
Vincent de Beauvais. *Speculum Historiale*. Copenhagen, 1971.
Zesen, Philip von. *Assenat*. Amsterdam, 1670.
Zunser, Eliakum. *Mekhiras Yosef*. Vilna, 1874.

7. Schiller's Moses

Freud, Sigmund. *Der Mann Moses*. Amsterdam, 1939.
———. *Moses and Monotheism*. New York, 1939.
Schiller, Friedrich. *Die Sendung Moses und Etwas über die erste Menschengesellschaft*. Hamburg, 1960.

8. The Death of Moses

Ahad Haam. "Moses." In *Selected Essays*, pp. 306-329. Philadelphia, 1944.
Asch, Sholem. *Moses*. New York, 1951.
Birnbaum, Uriel. *Gedichte*, pp. 585 f. Amsterdam, 1957.
Bonhoeffer, Dietrich. "Der Tod des Mose." In *Auf dem Wege zur Freiheit. Gedichte und Briefe aus der Haft*, pp. 24-29. Berlin, 1952.
Bryant, W. C. "No Man Knoweth His Sepulchre." In *Poetical Works*, pp. 36 f. New York, 1919.
Eidlitz, Walter. *Kampf im Zwielicht*. Berlin, 1928.
Eliot, George. "The Death of Moses." In *The Spanish Gypsy and Other Poems*, pp. 450-454. Edinburgh, 1901.
Fichman, Jacob. "Nebo." In *Kitve*, p. 28. Tel Aviv, 1959.
Fleg, Edmond. *Moise*. Paris, 1956.
———. *Life of Moses*. London, 1928.
Freiligrath, Ferdinand. "Nebo." In *Werke (Bong Klassiker)*, I, 95-97. Berlin, 1909.

Freud, Sigmund. *Moses and Monotheism*. New York, 1939.
Goddard, Donald. *Last Days of Dietrich Bonhoeffer*. New York, 1976.
Hauptmann, Carl. *Moses*. Munich, 1906.
Herder, J. G. *The Spirit of Hebrew Poetry*. Burlington, 1833.
Montgomery, James. "The Death of Moses." In G. A. Kohut, *Hebrew Anthology*, I, 120. Cincinnati, 1913.
Moore, Thomas. "Weep, Children of Israel." In *Poetical Works*, pp. 261 f. London, 1910.
Sellin, Ernst. *Mose und seine Bedeutung für die israelitisch-jüdische Religionsgeschichte*. Leipzig, 1922.
Shapiro, Karl. "The Murder of Moses." In *Selected Poems*, pp. 183 f. New York, 1973.
Stoddard, R. H. "The Death of Moses." In G. A. Kohut, *Hebrew Anthology*, I, 125 f. Cincinnati, 1913.
Vigny, Alfred de. "Moses." In *Poèmes, Antiques et Modernes*, pp. 3-15. Paris, 1857.
Wolfskehl, Karl. "Vom Nebo." In *Gesammelte Werke*, I, 58 f. Hamburg, 1960.

9. Rahab of Jericho
Gottschall, Rudolf. *Rahab*. Leipzig, 1898.
Izban, Shmuel. *Jericho*. Buenos Aires, 1966.
Josephus Flavius. *Jewish Antiquities*. Loeb Classics ed., bk. 5. London, 1934.
Kartun-Blum, Ruth. *From Tyre to Jerusalem: The Literary World of Matityahu Shoham*. Berkeley, 1969.
Shoham, Matityahu. *Jericho*. Tel Aviv, 1974.
Slaughter, F. A. *The Scarlet Cord*. New York, 1956.

10. Jephthah's Literary Vogue
Asch, Sholem. *Yiftakh's Tokhter*. Vilna, 1913.
Buchanan, George. *Jephtha; or, the Vow*. In *Sacred Dramas*, pp. 1-85. Edinburgh, 1906.
Byron, Lord. "Jephtha's Daughter." In *Hebrew Melodies*, pp. 13 f. London, 1815. in *Complete Poems*, p. 218. Boston, 1905.
Coleridge, Hartley. "On a Picture of Jephthah and His Daughter." In *Poems*, II, 350 f. London, 1851.
Dean, Winton. *Handel's Dramatic Oratorios and Masques*, pp. 589-624. London, 1959.
Feuchtwanger, Lion. *Jefta und seine Tochter*. Hamburg, 1957.
Fichman, Jacob. "Bat Yiftakh." In *Kitve*, p. 28. Tel Aviv, 1959.
Freytag, Ludwig. *Jephthah*. Berlin, 1871.
Frug, S. S. "Bat Yiftakh." In *Shirim*, pp. 221-230. Warsaw, 1914. English translation in B. Beinkenstadt, *Anthology of Hebrew Poetry*, pp. 152-160. Capetown, 1930.
Gershon, Karen. "Jephtha's Daughter." In *Coming Back From Babylon*, pp. 15 f. London, 1979.

Händel, G. F. *Jephta, Oratorio.* Leipzig, 1965.
Herrick, Robert. "Dirge of Jephthah's Daughter, Sung by the Virgins." In *Poetical Works*, pp. 349-351. London, 1951.
Johannessen, K. L. *Zwischen Himmel und Erde. Eine Studie über Joost van den Vondels biblische Tragödie*, pp. 165-187. Oslo, 1963.
Lissauer, Ernst. *Das Weib des Jephta.* Berlin, 1928.
Manger, Itzik. "Yiftakh's Tokhter." In *Shtern in Shtoib*, p. 15. New York, 1967.
Porwig, Johanna. *Der Jephtastoff in der deutschen Dichtung.* Breslau, 1932.
Robert, Ludwig. *Die Tochter Jephthas.* Stuttgart, 1820.
Saphire, Saul. *Yiftakh un sein Tokhter.* New York, 1937.
Schwartz, I. I. "Yiftakhs Tokhter." In *Literatur*, II, 93-99. New York, 1910.
Sypherd, W. O. *Jephthah and His Daughter.* Newark, Del., 1948.
Tennyson, Alfred. *A Dream of Fair Women.* London, 1833.
Van Doren, Mark. "Jephthah's Daughter." In *Collected and New Poems*, pp. 428 f. New York, 1963.
Vigny, Alfred de. "La Fille de Jephté." In *Poèmes Antiques et Modernes*, pp. 127-156. Paris, 1857.
Vondel, Joost van den. *Jephta of Offerbelofte.* Groningen, 1959.
Willis, N. P. "Jephthah's Daughter." In *Poetical Works*, pp. 44-48. London, 1888.
Yehoash. "Yiftakhs Tokhter." In *Gezamelte Lider*, pp. 26 f. New York, 1910.

11. Samson in the Twentieth Century
Bab, Julius. "Der Jude." In *Ausgewählte Gedichte*, pp. 16 f. Berlin, 1930.
Bernstein, Henry. *Samson.* Paris, 1908.
Birnbaum, Uriel. "Simson und Delila." In *Gedichte*, pp. 609-620. Amsterdam, 1957.
Burte, Hermann. *Simson.* Leipzig, 1917.
Dean, Winton. *Handel's Dramatic Oratorios and Masques*, pp. 326-364. London, 1959.
Eulenberg, Herbert. *Simson.* Leipzig, 1910.
Fichman, Jacob. "Shimshon." In *Kitve*, pp. 133-146. Tel Aviv, 1959.
Frug, S. S. "Mot Shimshon." In *Shirim*, pp. 351-358. Warsaw, 1914.
Gerlach, Kurt. *Der Simsonstoff im deutschen Drama.* Berlin, 1929.
Gershon, Karen. "Samson in Gaza." In *Coming Back From Babylon*, pp. 17 f. London, 1979.
Händel, G. F. *Samson. Oratorio.* Leipzig, 1904.
Jabotinsky, Vladimir. *Samson the Nazarite.* London, 1930.
Johannessen, K. L. *Zwischen Himmel und Erde. Eine Studie über Joost van den Vondels biblische Tragödie*, pp. 188-207. Oslo, 1963.
Milton, John. *Samson Agonistes.* In *Poetical Works*, pp. 503-551. London, 1950.
Saint-Saëns, Camille. *Samson et Delilah.* Paris, 1892.
Salten, Felix. *Simson, das Schicksal eines Erwählten.* Berlin, 1928.
Saphire, Saul. *Shimshon Hagibor.* New York, 1935.

Wedekind, Frank. *Simson oder Scham und Eifersucht.* In *Gesammelte Werke*, VI, 219-312. Munich, 1920.
Yehoash. "Delila." In *Neie Shriftn*, pp. 165-167. New York, 1910.

12. Ruth and Medea

Beer-Hofmann, Richard. *Der junge David.* Berlin, 1933.
Euripides. *Medea.* Harmondsworth: Penguin Books, 1963.
Fichman, Jacob. "Ruth." In *Kitve*, pp. 113-122. Tel Aviv, 1959.
Grillparzer, Franz. *Das goldene Vliess.* In *Sämtliche Werke*, vol. IV. Leipzig, 1903.
Saphire, Saul. *Ruth.* New York, 1936.
Sheirich, R. M. "Ruth und Boas, Ein unbekanntes Drama von Richard Beer-Hofmann." In *Neue Züricher Zeitung*, October 26, 1979, pp. 37 f.

13. Saul's Tragedy

Alfieri, Vittorio. *Saul.* Florence, 1949.
Beck, Karl. *Saul.* Leipzig, 1840.
Beer-Hofmann, Richard. *Der junge David.* Berlin, 1933.
Browning, Robert. "Saul." In *Poems*, pp. 26-33. London, 1910.
Byron, Lord. "Song of Saul Before His Last Battle." In *Complete Works*, p. 219. Boston, 1905.
Dean, Winton. *Handel's Dramatic Oratorios and Masques*, pp. 274-310. London, 1959.
Du Ryer, Pierre. *Saul.* Paris, 1918.
Fischer, J. G. *Saul.* Stuttgart, 1862.
Fontain, R. J. and Wojcik, Jan, eds. *The David Myth in Western Literature.* Purdue, 1980.
Gutzkow, Karl. *König Saul.* Hamburg, 1839.
Händel, G. F. *Saul.* Leipzig, 1965.
Knappert, L. *Saul, Koning in Israel.* Utrecht, 1920.
Lamartine, Alphonse de. "Saul." In *Oeuvres*, I, iv, 152.
Lancaster, H. C. *Pierre Du Ryer, Dramatist.* Washington, 1912.
Pinski, David. "Shaul." In *Di Goldene Keyt*, no. 23 (1955), pp. 16-78.
Rilke, R. M. "David Singt vor Saul." In *Neue Gedichte*, pp. 12-14. Leipzig, , 1907.
Rückert, Friedrich. *Saul und David.* Erlangen, 1843.
Sorge, R. J. "König David. Ein Schauspiel." In *Werke*, III, 69-163. Nuremberg, 1967.
Thiel, M. A. *La Figure de Saul et sa representation dans la littérature dramatique française.* Amsterdam, 1926.
Voltaire. "Saul." In *Oeuvres*, vol. VII. Paris, 1831.
Wolfskehl, Karl. "Saul." In *Gesammelte Werke*, I, 323-343. Hamburg, 1960.
Yehoash. "Saul." In *Neie Shriftn*, I, 17-30. New York, 1910.
Zweig, Max. *Saul.* Vienna, 1964.

14. The Love of David and Michal
Cohen, M. R. *King Saul's Daughter*. Glencoe, Ill., 1952.
Gordon, J. L. *Kol Shire*, III, 1-91. Tel Aviv, 1930.
Heym, Stefan. *Der König David Bericht*. Munich, 1972.
———. *The King David Report*. New York, 1972.
Kaufmann, Walter. *Cain and Other Poems*. New York, 1962.
Lawrence, D. H. *David*. London, 1926.
Malvern, Gladys. *Saul's Daughter*. New York, 1956.
Pinski, David. "King David and His Wives." In J. C. Landis, ed. *Great Jewish Plays*, pp. 161-215. New York, 1966.
Schmitt, Gladys. *David the King*. New York, 1946.
Tramer, Hans. *Michal, Liebe und Leid einer Königin*. Tel Aviv, 1940.
Wohl, Louis de. *David of Jerusalem*. Garden City, N.Y., 1965.

15. Nabal and Abigail
Austin, G. J. *Abigail*. Bloomington, 1924.
Manger, Itzik. "Abigail." In *Lid un Balade*, pp. 252 f. New York, 1952.
Pinski, David. "Abigail." In *Dramen*, V, 29-54. New York, 1920.
Shamir, Moshe. *David's Stranger*. London, 1964.
Van Doren, Mark. "Abigail." In *Collected and New Poems*, p. 432. New York, 1963.
Zweig, Arnold. *Abigail und Nabal*. Leipzig, 1913.

16. Noble Jonathan
Beer-Hofmann, Richard. *Der junge David*. Berlin, 1933.
Liptzin, Sol. *Richard Beer-Hofmann*. New York, 1936.
Neumann, H. G. *Richard Beer-Hofmann*. Munich, 1971.

17. Abishag the Shunammite
Birnbaum, Uriel. "Abisag." In *Gedichte*, p. 590. Amsterdam, 1957.
Fichman, Jacob. "Abishag." In *Kitve*, p. 29. Tel Aviv, 1959.
Gershon, Karen. "David and Abishag." In *Coming Back from Babylon*, pp. 25 f. London, 1979.
Hardt, Ernst. *König Salomo*. Leipzig, 1915.
Johannessen, K. L. *Zwischen Himmel und Erde. Eine Studie über Joost van den Vondels Biblische Tragödie*, pp. 227-245. Oslo, 1963.
Manger, Itzik. "Abishag." In *Lid un Balade*, pp. 254-261. New York, 1962.
Mayer, Jochen. *Briefe an Ernst Hardt*, p. 94. Marbach, 1975.
Mayer, T. H. *David Findet Abisag*. Leipzig, 1925.
Michener, James. *The Source*. New York, 1965.
Miegel, Agnes. "Abisag von Sunem." In *Gedichte*, pp. 104 f. Berlin, 1901.
Pinski, David. "Abishag." In *Dramen*, V, 88-106. New York, 1920.
———. "Adoniyahu." In *Dramen*, V, 107-128. New York, 1920.
Rilke, R. M. "Abisag." In *Neue Gedichte*, pp. 10 f. Leipzig, 1907.
Schmitt, Gladys. *David the King*. New York, 1946.

Spire, André. "Abishag." In N. Ausubel and M. Ausubel, *Treasury of Jewish Poetry*, pp. 32 f. New York, 1957.
Zahn, Ernst. *Tochter Dodais*. Stuttgart, 1929.

18. The Judgment of Solomon
Brecht, Bertold. *Der kaukasische Kreidekreis*. Frankfurt a.M., 1969.
Forke, Alfred. *Die indischen Märchen*. Berlin, 1911.
Gressmann, Hugo. *Die älteste Geschichtsschreibung und Prophetie Israels*. Göttingen, 1921.
Guenther, Johannes von. *Der Kreidekreis*. Stuttgart, 1953.
Gunkel, Hermann. *Das Märchen im Alten Testament*. Tübingen, 1917.
Hubler, R. G. *Love and Wisdom: A Novel About Solomon*. New York, 1968.
Klabund. *Der chinesische Kreidekreis*. Berlin, 1925.
Li Hsing-tau. *Der Kreidekreis*. Leipzig, 1958.
Noth, Martin. *Könige*. Neukirchen, 1968.
Poser, Therese. *Interpretation zu Berthold Brecht, Der kaukasische Kreidekreis*. Munich, 1972.
Talmud. *Makkot* 23b.
Tschong Dao Kim. *Berthold Brecht und die Geisteswelt des Fernen Ostens*. Heidelberg, 1919.
Yaari, Yehuda. "The Judgment of Solomon." In *A Whole Loaf: Stories from Israel*, ed. by S. J. Kahn, pp. 65-85. Tel Aviv, 1957.

19. Solomon and the Queen of Sheba
Abercrombie, Lascelles. *Poems*. London, 1930.
Browning, Robert. "Solomon and Balkis." In *Poems and Plays*, pp. 1095 f. New York, 1934.
Budge, E. A. W. *History of Ethiopia*, I, 194-204. London, 1928.
―――. *The Queen of Sheba and Her Only Son Menyelek I*, pp. 16-84. London, 1932.
Chastel, André. "L'Episode de la Reine de Saba dans la Tentation de St. Antoine." *Romanic Review*, 40 (1949): 261-267.
Dean, Winton. *Handel's Dramatic Oratorios and Masques*, pp. 511-534. London, 1959.
Don Passos, John. *Three Soldiers*. New York, 1921.
Eisenmenger, J. A. *Entdecktes Judentum*, II, 440-444. Frankfurt a.M., 1700.
Flaubert, Gustave. *La Tentation de St. Antoine*. Paris, 1971.
Freeman, John. *Solomon and Balkis*. London, 1926.
Frishman, David. "Ophir." In *Yidishe Folksbibliotek*, ed. Shalom Aleichem, pp. 211-223. Kiev, 1888.
Goldmark, Karl. *Die Königin von Saba*. Vienna, 1926.
Gounod, C. F. *La Reine de Saba*. Paris, 1862.
Hammer-Purgstall, Joseph. *Rosenöl*, I, 154-166; I, 174 f. Stuttgart, 1813.
Händel, G. F. *Solomon*. Leipzig, 1965.
Josephus Flavius. *Jewish Antiquities*, bk. VIII. Loeb Classics ed., London, 1934.

Kipling, Rudyard. *Just-So Stories*. London, 1952.
Koran. Sura 27.
Kuprin, Alexander. *Sulamith*. New York, 1926.
Lord, Edith. *Queen of Sheba's Heirs*, pp. 25-27. Washington, 1970.
Nerval, Gèrard de. *Voyage en Orient*. Paris, 1867.
Payne, E. R. *Sapientia Solomonis*. Yale Studies in English, no. 89. New Haven, 1938.
Peretz, Y. L. *Ale Verk*, I, 214-272. Buenos Aires, 1944.
Pritchard, J. B. *Solomon and Sheba*. London, 1974.
Rhodes, S. A. *Gèrard de Nerval*. New York, 1951.
Russell, Bertrand. *Nightmares of Eminent Persons*. London, 1954.
Silberman, L. H. "The Queen of Sheba in Judaic Tradition." In J. B. Pritchard, *Solomon and Sheba*. London, 1974.
Symons, Arthur. "The Love of the Queen of Sheba." In *Poems*, II, 93-102. London, 1911.
Tseno Ureno, II, 735 f. New York, 1910.
Ullendorff, Edward. "The Queen of Sheba in Ethiopian Tradition." In J. B. Pritchard, *Solomon and Sheba*. London, 1974.
Voragine, Jacobus de. *The Golden Legend*, pp. 269-276. New York, 1969.
Whittier, J. G. "King Solomon and the Ants." In *Poetical Works*, I, 369-371. Boston, 1892.
Yeats, W. B. "Solomon to Sheba." In *Collected Poems*, pp. 332 f. New York, 1957.
Yehoash. "Queen of Sheba." In *Neie Shriftn*, I, 46-58. New York, 1910.

20. Sulamith Unallegorized

Brod, Max. *Heidentum, Christentum, Judentum*. Munich, 1921.
Broderzon, Moshe. "Shulamis." *Lodzer Folksblat*, March 30, 1923.
Fichman, Jacob. "Shulamith." In *Kitve*, p. 37. Tel Aviv, 1959.
Frug, S. S. "Shulamis." In *Ale Shriftn*, II, 21-23. New York, 1910.
Goldfaden, Abraham. *Shulamis*. Odessa, 1883.
Heine, Heinrich. "Salomo." In *Werke*, II, 107 f. Leipzig, 1924.
Herder, J. G. *Vom Geist der ebräischen Poesie*. Dessau, 1782; Gotha, 1890.
Heyse, Paul. *Die Weisheit Salomons*. Berlin, 1886.
Kuprin, Alexander. *Sulamith: A Tale of Antiquity*. New York, 1926.
Lasker-Schüler, Else. "Sulamith." In *Hebräische Balladen*, p. 14. Berlin, 1913. Also in *Gesammelte Werke*, I, 37, 310. Munich, 1959.
Lebensohn, M. J. *Shire Bat Zion*. Vilna, 1859.
Molodowsky, Kadia. *Lider*, pp. 130, 135. Buenos Aires, 1935.
Peretz, Y. L. "Venus un Shulamis." In *Ale Verk*, IV, 188-194. Buenos Aires, 1944.
Rosenfeld, Morris. "Shulamis." In *Shriftn*, I, 144-151. New York, 1904.
Shalom Aleichem. "Shir Hashirim." In *Ale Verk*, VI, iv, 7-74. New York, 1944.

21. Solomon's Humiliation

Chaucer, Geoffrey. "Nabugodonosor." In *Canterbury Tales*, pp. 249 f. Oxford, 1900.

Eisenmenger, J. A. *Entdecktes Judentum*, I, 351-361. Frankfurt a. M., 1700.
———. *Traditions of the Jews*, pp. 75-81. London, 1732.
Fuks, L. *Das altjüdische Epos Melokhim-Bukh*. Assen, 1965. Publications of the Bibliotheka Rosenthaliana.
Gaster, Moses. *Exempla of the Rabbis*, pp. 80 f. London, 1924.
Gordin, Abba. *Shlomo Hamelekh*. Tel Aviv, 1960.
Gronemann, Sammy. *Der Weise und der Narr, König Salomo und der Schuster*. Tel Aviv, 1942.
Hammer-Purgstall, Joseph. *Rosenöl*, I, 170-174. Stuttgart, 1813.
Langbein, F. E. "Märchen von König Luthbert." In *Sämtliche Schriften*, IV, 155-163. Stuttgart, 1841.
Longfellow, H. W. "King Robert of Sicily." In *Poems*, pp. 403-407. London, 1909.
Maase-Book. Translated by M. Gaster. Philadelphia, 1934.
Morris, William. *The Earthly Paradise*. London, 1890.
Pesikta de Rav Kahane, pp. 395 f. Philadelphia, 1975.
Saphire, Saul. *Shlomo Hamelekh*. New York, 1931.
Tal, Josef. *Ashmedai*. Tel Aviv, 1971.
Tseno Ureno, II, 807 f. New York, 1910.
Varnhagen, Hermann. *Ein Indisches Märchen auf seiner Wanderung durch die Asiatischen und Europäischen Literaturen*. Berlin, 1882.
Wedekind, Frank. *König Nicolo, oder So Ist das Leben*. In *Gesammelte Werke*, IV, 99-181. Munich, 1920.
———. *Such Is Life*. Philadelphia, 1912.

22. Elijah in Yiddish Literature
Bialostotsky, Benjamin. *Lid Tsu Lid*, pp. 276-278. New York, 1958.
Ginzberg, Louis. *Legends of the Jews*, IV, 195-235. Philadelphia, 1947.
Glanz-Leyeles, Aaron. *Baym Fuss Fun Barg*, pp. 273-282. New York, 1957.
Grade, Chaim. *Der Mames Tzevoe*, pp. 137-171. New York, 1949.
Gross, Naftoli. *Lider*, p. 300. New York, 1958.
Hirshbein, Peretz. *Einaktike Dramen*, pp. 125-145. New York, 1951.
Katz, Alef. *Gut Morgen, Alef*, pp. 23 f. New York, 1950.
Leivick, H. *Geula Komedie*. Chicago, 1934.
———. *Der Golem*. New York, 1921. English translation in J. C. Landis, *Great Jewish Plays*, pp. 217-356. New York, 1972.
———. *Die Kehtn fun Moshiakh*. In *Ale Verk*, II, 393-418. New York, 1940.
Liessin, Abraham. *Lider un Poemen*, pp. 176-187. New York, 1938.
Liptzin, Sol. *Stories from Peretz*, pp. 15-93. New York, 1947.
Maase-Book. Translated by Moses Gaster. Philadelphia, 1934.
Manger, Itzik. *Lid un Balade*, pp. 373 f., 403 f. New York, 1952.
Mani-Leib. *Lider un Baladen*, pp. 250-255. Tel Aviv, 1963.
Meitlis, Jacob. *Das Maasebuch, seine Entstehung und Quellengeschichte*. Berlin, 1933.
Menes, Abraham. *Eliyahu Hanavi*. New York, 1955.
Molodowsky, Kadia. *Der Melekh Dovid Aleen Is Geblibn*, pp. 6-8. New York, 1945.

Peretz, Y. L. *Ale Verk*, I, 57-61; I, 99-103; I, 159-213; XIII, 124 f. Buenos Aires, 1944.
Rosenblatt, H. *Herodes*, pp. 38-40. Los Angeles, 1930.
Shalom Aleichem. *Ale Verk*, I, iv, 117-124. New York, 1944.
Yehoash. *Fabeln*, pp. 101-103. New York, 1912.

23. The Literary Impact of Jonah

Andres, Stefan. *Der Mensch im Fisch*. Munich, 1963.
Ben-Chorin, Schalom. *Die Antwort des Jona*. Hamburg, 1966.
Blackburn, R. A. *Biblical Drama under the Tudors*. The Hague, 1971.
Bonhoeffer, Dietrich. "Jona." In *Auf dem Wege zur Freiheit. Gedichte und Briefe aus der Haft*, p. 30. Berlin, 1952.
Fichman, Jacob. "Jonah." In *Kitve*, p. 38. Tel Aviv, 1959.
Goddard, Donald. *The Last Days of Dietrich Bonhoeffer*. New York, 1976.
Goodman, Paul. "Jonah." In *Three Plays*, pp. 203-261. New York, 1965.
Grade, Chaim. "Yona Oifn Yam." In *Der Mames Tzevoe*, p. 179. New York, 1949.
Housman, Laurence. *Palestine Plays*. London, 1942.
Jarrell, Randall. "Jonah." In *Complete Poems*, pp. 103 f. New York, 1969.
Leivick, H. "Yona Hanavi." In *Lider Tsum Eybikn*, pp. 146-152. New York, 1959.
Melville, Herman. *Moby Dick*. New York, 1957.
Molodowsky, Kadia. "Yona." In *Likht fun Dornbush*, p. 165. Buenos Aires, 1965.
Nathan, Robert. *The Son of Amittai*. London, 1925.
———. *Jonah*. New York, 1925.
Quarles, Francis. "A Feast for Wormes." In *Complete Works*, II, 1-25. Hildesheim, 1971.
Rutenborn, Guenther. *The Sign of Jonah*. New York, 1960.
Sowden, Lewis. "Jonah." In *The Jaffe Road*, pp. 29-38. Tel Aviv, 1974.
Steffen, Uwe. *Das Mysterium von Tod und Auferstehung: Formen und Wandlungen des Jona-Motivs*. Göttingen, 1963.

26. The Cult of Moloch

Albright, W. F. *Archaeology and Religion in Israel*. Baltimore, 1953.
Blake, William. *Poetry and Prose*. London, 1927.
Blaustein, Leopold. *Das Gotteserlebnis in Hebbels Dramen*. Berlin, 1929.
Buber, Martin. *Kingdom of God*, pp. 177-184. New York, 1967.
Coleridge, S. T. *Poetical Works*, pp. 53-60. London, 1903.
Curry, Kenneth. *Southey*. London, 1975.
Diodorus Siculus. *History*. Loeb Classics ed., V, 365; X, 179. London, 1962.
Eissfeldt, Otto. *Molk als Opferbegriff im Punischen und Hebräischen und das Ende des Gottes Moloch*. Halle, 1935.
Flaubert, Gustave. *Salammbô*. London: Everyman's Library, 1931.
Freud, Sigmund. *Complete Psychological Works*, I, 243. London, 1966.
Grabbe, C. D. "Hannibal." In *Werke*, II, 317-396. Meyers Klassiker.
Hebbel, Friedrich. "Moloch." In *Werke*, V, 5-60. Meyers Klassiker.

Michener, James. *The Source*. New York, 1965.
Midrash Rabbah, Lamentations. London, 1939.
Milton, John. *Paradise Lost*, New York, 1951.
Moore, G. F. "The Image of Moloch." *Journal of Biblical Literature* 16 (1897): 161-165.
Osherowitch, Hirsh. *Tanakh-Poemes*. Tel Aviv, 1979.
Plutarch. *Moralia*. Loeb Classics ed., II, 493. London, 1962.
Ramban (Nachmanides). *Commentary on the Torah*. New York, 1974.
Rawlinson, George. *Phoenicia*. London, 1896.
Tennyson, Alfred. "The Dawn." In *Poems*, p. 1453. London, 1969.

27. Belshazzar's Folly

Andersch, Alfred. *Sansibar*. Olten, 1956.
Arnold, Edwin. "Feast of Belshazzar." In *Poems, Narrative and Lyrical*, pp. 34-46. Oxford, 1853.
Byron, Lord. *Hebrew Melodies*. London, 1815.
———. "The Vision of Belshazzar." In *Complete Works*, p. 220. Boston, 1905.
———. "To Belshazzar." In *Complete Works*, p. 185. Boston, 1905.
Calderón de la Barca, Pedro. *La Cena del Rey Balthasar*. In *Obras Completas*, III, 153-177. Madrid, 1952.
Chaucer, Geoffrey. "Balthasar." In *Canterbury Tales*, pp. 250-252. Oxford, 1900.
Dean, Winton. *Handel's Dramatic Oratorios and Masques*, pp. 434-459. London, 1966.
Fichman, Jacob. "Daniel." In *Kitve*, p. 38. Tel Aviv, 1959.
Geibel, Emanuel. "Mene, Mene, Tekel, Upharsin." In *Werke*, II, 91. Stuttgart, 1893.
Goethe, J. W. *Wilhelm Meisters Theatralische Sendung*, bk. II, chap. 4; bk. III, chap. 9. In *Gedenkausgabe der Werke, Briefe und Gespräche*, vol. VIII. Zurich, 1961.
Händel, G. F. *Belshazzar*. Leipzig, 1965.
Heine, Heinrich. "Belsatzar." In *Werke*, I, 53 f. Leipzig, 1924.
Hemans, Felicia. "Belshazzar's Feast." In G. A. Kohut, *Hebrew Anthology*, I, 436 f. Cincinnati, 1913.
Landor, Robert. *Impious Feast*. London, 1828.
Milman, H. H. *Belshazzar*. London, 1822
More, Hannah. *Belshazzar*. In *Sacred Dramas*, pp. 125-189. London, 1782.
Procter, B. W. (Barry Cornwall). "Belshazzar." In G. A. Kohut, *Hebrew Anthology*, I, 436 f. Cincinnati, 1913.
Semmig, Hermann. "Mene, Mene, Tekel, Upharsin." In Sol Liptzin, *Lyric Pioneers of Modern Germany*, pp. 177 f. New York, 1928.
Walton, William. *Belshazzar's Feast, Oratorio*. London, 1931.
Weir, L. E. *The Ideas Embodied in the Religious Drama of Calderón*, pp. 21-25. University of Nebraska Studies, Lincoln, 1940.

Index

Aaron, 283
Abel, 13-24, 254
Abercrombie, Lascelles, 189
Abiathar, 172, 180
Abigail, 95, 145, 151, 155-163, 177, 212
Abimelech, King, 52
Abimelech, Priest of Nob, 130
Abishag, 95, 116, 151, 172-179
Abner, 129, 133, 136, 141, 146, 151, 159
Abraham, 1, 26, 33, 39-60, 66, 79, 98, 100, 107, 112, 193, 251, 255-258, 284, 288
Absalom, 173, 177
Achan, 100f
Achinoam, Wife of David, 145, 151
Achinoam, Wife of Saul, 167
Achish of Gath, King, 126, 133, 146, 165
Adah, 18f
Adam, 1-11, 13, 18, 22f, 25, 28-30, 190, 195, 205, 273
Adams, F. L., 48
Adoniram, 21, 196f
Adoniya, 170-173, 175, 178, 180
Adriel, 145, 148
Aeneas, 211
Agag, King, 135, 139f, 142, 151, 164f
Agamemnon, 104f, 112
Ahab, King, 98, 228, 241
Ahad Haam, 83, 116
Ahasverus, King, 191
Ahaz, King, 259
Akhnaton (Ikhnaton), 78, 90
Akiva, Rabbi, 43, 204

Albright, W. F., 270
Alexander the Great, 289
Alfieri, Vittorio, 128f, 131
Alphabet of Ben Sira, 4
Amalek, 88, 134f, 139f, 142, 151
Ammonite, 102-105, 111, 132, 220f, 259, 261, 265
Amon, King, 259
Amorite, 97f, 284
Amos of Tekoa, 241, 246
Anamelech, 14
Anchises, 211
Andersch, Alfred, 281
Andres, Stefan, 242, 245-247
Andreyev, Leonid, 254
Anski, S., 10
Antigone, 61
Antiochus IV, 289
Aphrodite, 9, 122
Apis, 71
Apollo, 216
Arabian Nights, 225
Argov, Alexander, 225
Arion, 237f
Aristotle, 104
Arnold, Edwin, 47, 189, 280
Aronson, Naum, 103
Artemis, 96
Asasel, 8
Asch, Sholem, 88f, 108f
Asenath, 63-73
Ashmedai, 10, 190, 220-222, 276f
Astarte, 96, 99, 107, 241, 266, 270f
Auden, W. H., 7

Augustine, St., 113
Augustus, Emperor, 27
Austin, G. J., 161

Baal, 31, 33, 51, 228, 261f, 264
Bab, Julius, 115f
Bacchus, 217
Bacharach, Naphtali, 221
Balaam, 100
Barbier, Jules, 197
Bar Kochba, 290
Bathsheba, 95, 151, 162, 164, 170, 176f
Baudelaire, Charles, 21
Beardsley, Aubrey, 200
Beck, Karl, 133-135
Bede, the Venerable, 195
Beelzebub, 202
Beer-Hofmann, Paula, 125
Beer-Hoffmann, Richard, 55, 125-128, 138f, 149, 166-169
Beethoven, Ludwig van, 74
Begin, Menahem, 117, 120
Belial, 267
Belshazzar, King, 131, 273-281
Belus, 31f
Benaiah, 222
Ben-Chorin, Schalom, 247
Ben-Gurion, David, 141
Benjamin, 66, 138, 144, 168
Bereshith Rabba (*Genesis Rabba*), 28
Bergner, Elizabeth, 183
Bernstein, Henri, 114
Betar, 117
Bialostotsky, Benjamin, 232
Bilderdijk, Willem, 46
Bileam, 100
Birnbaum, Nathan, 85, 176
Birnbaum, Uriel, 23, 85f, 176f
Bismarck, Otto von, 34
Blake, William, 103, 265f
Boaz, 94, 123, 125
Bodmer, J. J., 71
Boleyn, Anne, 189
Bonhoeffer, Dietrich, 85-88, 242-244
Borst, Aron, 28
Bostansky, Shlome, 228
Brecht, Bertold, 68, 182-184
Breughel, Pieter, 198

Brieger, Auguste, 21
Brod, Max, 206
Broderzon, Moshe, 214
Browning, Robert, 5, 136f, 189, 196, 198f
Bryan, W. J., 241
Buchanan, George, 103
Buddha, 181
Budge, E. A. W., 190
Bunyan, John, 15
Burchard, Christoph, 64
Burte, Hermann, 114
Byron, Lord, 14f, 17-22, 105f, 114, 130-133, 195, 267, 278f

Cabbala, 1, 190, 228
Cabries, Jean, 55, 59f
Caedmon, 273
Cahen, J. L., 228
Cain, 13-24, 31, 114, 139, 254
Calderon de la Barca, 189, 274f
Caleb, 99, 156
Carré, Michel, 197
Chagall, Marc, 55, 60, 189
Charles V. Emperor, 217f
Chateaubriand, F. R., 195
Chaucer, Geoffrey, 216, 273f
Christopherson, John, 104
Chronicles II, 187
Cleopatra, 106, 202
Clytemnestra, 105
Cohen, M. R., 149-151
Coleridge, Hartley, 47
Coleridge, S. T., 15f, 47, 266f
Constantine, Emperor, 195
Contarini, Cardinal, 29
Cornwall, Barry, 280
Costa, Isaac da, 46f
Costa, Uriel da, 46, 133
Crammer, Archbishop, 189
Creon, King, 61
Cronus, 27
Cybele, 9
Cyrus, King, 276f

Dagon, 241
Dan, 66, 116-119, 122, 168
Daniel, 216, 273-275, 279f

D'Annunzio, Gabrielle, 122
Dante, 15
Darius, King, 277f
Darrow, Clarence, 241
Darwin, Charles, 240
David, King, 94, 109, 116, 121, 123, 125-142, 144-180, 187, 193, 203, 205
Deborah, 95, 205
Defoe, Daniel, 15, 31
Degas, Edgar, 103
Delilah, 10, 95, 114-116, 119, 212
Deuteronomy, 260
Diana, 100
Dinah, 67, 72
Diodorus, 27, 263
Doeg, 142
Donne, John, 29
Dos Passos, John, 189
Dürrenmatt, Friedrich, 36f
Dowson, Ernest, 200

Ebers, Georg, 96
Eblis, 22
Edom, 56f
Eisenmenger, J. A., 4
Ekha Rabbah, 262
Electra, 104
Eliezer, 54, 59f
Elijah, 100, 228-235
Eliot, George, 85
Eliphas, 57
Eliraz, Israel, 226
Elizabeth I, Queen, 189
Enoch, 20
Enos, 15f
Ephraim, 62f, 103, 105, 118
Erasmus, Desiderius, 104
Esau, 54-61
Esther, Queen, 10, 71, 95, 109, 212
Euripides, 9, 104, 122, 124
Eve, 1-11, 13, 18f, 22f, 31, 190, 205
Ezra, 287f

Fairlie, Alison, 21
Falasha, 81
Faust, 4, 18, 84, 250-253
Favir, Eliezer, 71
Feuchtwanger, Lion, 110-112

Fichman, Jacob, 176
Fineman, Irving, 55, 58f
Fischer, J. G., 135
Flaubert, Gustave, 189, 198, 268-270
Fleg, Edmund, 83
Fliess, Wilhelm, 266
Fonesca, Wollheim da, 183
Forbes-Mosse, Irene, 48
France, Anatole, 6f
Freeman, John, 189, 200f
Freiligrath, Ferdinand, 84
Freud, Sigmund, 75, 78, 80, 89-91, 137, 266
Freytag, Ludwig, 107
Fritz, W. H., 23f
Frug, S. S., 107f, 213

Gabriel, Archangel, 10, 85, 244f, 265
Gad, 66
Gaster, Moses, 229
Gautier, Théophile, 195
Geibel, Emanuel, 280f
Gemara, 2
Genesis, 2f, 25f, 39f, 42, 54, 62f, 67, 69
Genesis Rabbah, 28, 43
George III, King, 267
Gessner, Salomon, 14f
Gesta Romanorum, 216, 218f
Ghiberti, Lorenzo, 188
Gibeonites, 150
Gide, Andre, 128, 137f
Ginzberg, Louis, 228
Giorgione, 181
Glanz-Leyeles, Aaron, 232
Glicenstein, Enrico, 103
Goethe, J. W., 4, 18, 32, 84, 96, 100, 250, 252, 277f
Goldfaden, Abraham, 72, 210f
Goldmark, Karl, 189, 197
Goliath, 129, 132-135, 144f, 147, 156, 160
Gordin, Abba, 216, 220
Gordon, S. L., 207
Gorky, Maxim, 208
Gottschall, Rudolf von, 95-97, 100
Gounod, Charles, 189, 197f
Gourmont, Remy de, 5
Grabbe, C. D., 268, 270

Grade, Chaim, 234
Gressmann, Hugo, 182
Grillparzer, Franz, 114, 124f
Grimmelshausen, H. J. C., 68-70, 128
Gronemann, Sammy, 216, 225f
Gross, Naftoli, 232f
Grünbaum, Max, 44
Gunkel, Hermann, 182
Gutzkow, Karl, 133, 135f, 164

Habiru, 50-52, 98
Hagar, 39-53, 67
Haggai, 289
Haile Selassie I, Emperor, 193
Hale, E. E., 48
Ham, 26, 29
Hamilcar Barca, 263, 269f
Hamilton, Newburgh, 114
Hammer-Purgstall, Joseph von, 196, 223f
Hammurabi, 51
Handel, G. F., 103, 114, 123, 189, 275-277
Hannibal, 268-270
Hardt, Ernst, 172-174
Hardy, W. G., 51f
Hart, Heinrich, 33f
Hasmonean, 289f
Hauptmann, Carl, 83f
Hauptmann, Gerhart, 225
Hayim Abraham ben Arye Leib Hacohen, 71
Hebbel, Friedrich, 268-270
Heine, Heinrich, 6, 92, 206, 278f
Hekate, 9
Helen of Troy, 9, 106
Helena, Empress, 195
Hemans, Felicia, 279
Hercules, 122, 237, 274
Herder, J. G., 31f, 82, 205f
Hermes, Uwe, 7
Herodotus, 26f, 32
Herrick, Robert, 105
Herzl, Theodor, 116
Heym, Stefan, 151-154
Heyse, Paul, 207f
Hezekiah, King, 261
Hippolytus, 122

Hiram, King, 133, 241
Hirshbein, Peretz, 230
Hitler, Adolf, 86, 88, 142, 152, 166, 227, 243, 255, 281
Hoffmann, Rainer, 7
Holbein, Hans, 188
Holberg, Ludwig, 225
Honneger, Arthur, 128
Horodetsky, S. A., 229
Housman, Laurence, 55, 57f, 248
Hugo, Victor, 5, 21, 195
Hulda, 94
Hunt, Leigh, 267
Hyksos, 98

Ibn Ezra, Abraham, 261
Ibsen, Henrik, 8
Ikhnaton, 78, 90
Illies, Joachim, 23
Iphigenia, 96, 100, 103f, 106, 112
Isaac, 40f, 44, 46, 51f, 54-61, 66, 79, 107, 112, 193, 205, 254-257
Isaiah, 2
Ishmael, 39-42, 44-49, 52, 60, 67
Isidore, Archbishop, 195
Isis, 5
Israels, Joseph, 128
Izban, Shmuel, 95, 98f

Jabotinsky, Vladimir, 114-120
Jacob, 54-61, 66-68, 72, 79, 116, 122, 138, 166, 193, 205
James, Apostle, 94
James I, King, 2
James II, King, 30
Japhet, 27
Jason, 173f
Jebb, Bishop, 240
Jebusites, 133, 152, 265
Jehoiakim, King, 286
Jelusich, Mirko, 172
Jennens, Charles, 276f
Jephthah, 95, 102-112, 198
Jerahmeel, Chronicles of, 28
Jeremiah, 259, 261f, 285-287
Jeroboam, King, 246, 285
Jerome, St., 4
Jesse, 125, 140, 147, 156, 178

Jezebel, Queen, 98, 100, 228, 277
Joab, 133, 162-172, 177, 180
Job, 71, 139, 250-258
Jonah, 236-249
Jonathan, 129, 131f, 134, 138f, 147, 149-151, 153f, 159, 164-169, 172
Joseph, 57, 59, 62-73, 88, 91, 109, 122
Joseph Della Reina, 229
Josephus Flavius, 26-28, 40, 42, 63, 69, 94, 111, 190
Joshua, 82f, 93, 95, 97-101, 109, 118, 284, 288
Josiah, King, 259, 286
Jovinian, Emperor, 216, 218f
Judah, 118, 121, 144, 146, 150, 152, 154, 168, 188, 262
Judges, 102f
Julian, Emperor, 216, 219
Julien, Stanislas, 183
Jupiter, 4

Kalonymus, 86
Katz, Alef, 234
Keats, John, 9
Kebra Nagast, 190, 193f
Ketura, 46
Kienecker, Friedrich, 23
Kings I, 170, 180f, 187, 221
Kings II, 261
Kipling, Rudyard, 189
Kish, 144
Klabund, 182f
Klopstock, F. G., 71
Knappert, L., 136
Koheleth, 207, 216f, 222, 227
Korah, 284
Koran, 69, 188, 192, 196, 222
Kori, Torahiko, 128
Kuprin, Alexander, 201, 208-210
Kurz, Hermann, 8
Kurz, Isolde, 8-10

Laban, 54, 59f
Laish, 145
Lamartine, Alphonse de, 131-133, 195
Lamia, 2, 4
Landor, Robert, 279
Landor, W. S., 280

Langbein, A. F. E., 224
Lasker-Schüler, Else, 22f, 49
Lawrence, D. H., 147
Leah, 61, 66f
Lebensohn, M. J., 206f
Lehman, Shmuel, 228
Leivick, H., 231, 254-258
Lemaire, Fernand, 114
Levi, 66
Leviticus, 260
Liessin, Abraham, 231
Li Hsing-tao, 182f
Lilith, 1-12, 139, 190
Lindheimer, Franz, 52
Lisle, Leconte de, 21
Lissauer, Ernst, 109f
Locke, John, 30f
Longfellow, H. W., 216, 218
Lorelei, 6
Lorraine, Claude, 188
Louis XIV, King, 31
Lucifer, 3, 10, 14, 19, 265, 273
Luke, Gospel, 194, 237
Luther, Martin, 2, 113

Maacha, 151
Maase-Book, 216, 229
Macdonald, George, 6f
Macleish, Archibald, 254
Manasseh, King, 259, 261
Manasseh, Son of Joseph, 62, 118
Manger, Itzik, 48f, 60f, 161f, 175f, 234
Mani-Leib, 233f
Mann, Thomas, 56f, 72f
Marduk, 26f
Mars, 211
Marx, Karl, 153
Matthew, Gospel, 94, 194, 236f
Mayer, T. H., 177
Medea, 121-127
Meitlis, Jacob, 229
Melanchton, Philipp, 104
Melville, Herman, 239f
Mendele Mocher Sforim, 229
Menelik, King, 190, 193f
Menes, Abraham, 228
Mephibosheth, 167, 172
Mephistopheles, 4, 250-253

Merab, 144-148
Mercury, 211
Meribaal, 167
Methuselah, 11f, 22
Michael, Archangel, 29, 65, 67, 85, 195, 244f
Michal, 95, 129, 144-154, 160, 177
Michener, J. A., 179, 270f
Miegel, Agnes, 171
Milcom, 261
Milman, H. H., 280
Milton, John, 29f, 113f, 264f
Miriam, 212
Mohammed, 46, 49
Moloch, 107-109, 259-272, 275
Molodowsky, Kadia, 214, 233f, 248f
Montgomery, James, 84
Moore, G. F., 263
Moore, Thomas, 84, 195
More, Hannah, 71, 278
Morell, Thomas, 103
Morris, William, 216, 219
Mosenthal, S. H., 197
Moses, 74-93, 99, 109, 139, 142, 205, 283f
Münchhausen, Börries von, 101
Murillo, Bartolomé, 55

Naamah, Princess, 220f
Nabal, 145, 155-163
Nabopolassar, King, 26
Nachmanides, 42, 44f, 261
Nachor, 66
Naomi, 123, 125
Naphtali, 118
Napoleon, 224
Nathan, Prophet, 132, 162
Nathan, Robert, 106, 241
Nebuchadnezzar, King, 26, 37, 190, 216, 274, 277
Nehemiah, 287f
Neith, 62
Nerval, Gerard de, 21, 189, 196f
Nietzsche, Friedrich, 114
Nimrod, 25-29, 31, 33f, 37f
Noah, 25-27, 29, 32f
Noth, Martin, 182

Obed, 125
Oedipus, King, 61
Og, King, 97
O'Neal, Cothburn, 51
Orestes, 96, 104
Osherowitch, Hirsh, 37f, 271f
Othniel, 100

Paltiel, 145f, 149-152, 159
Parsifal, 9
Patterson, J. H., 119
Paul, Apostle, 40-42, 94
Peretz, Y. L., 1, 192, 211f, 229f
Perseus, 237
Pesikta de Rav Kahane, 217
Phaedra, 122
Philcol, 52
Philistine, 59, 116-119, 122, 125f, 129, 131, 133, 138f, 142, 145-149, 160, 165-168, 285
Philo, 40-42
Pinchas, 99
Pinski, David, 141f, 147, 155, 159f, 174f
Pirke de Rabbi Eliezer, 28f, 43f, 67
Plutarch, 263f
Poe, E. A., 7
Ponten, Josef, 34
Porwig, Johanna, 104
Potash, Rikudah, 49
Potiphar, 62f, 67-70, 72f, 122
Poti-phera, 62, 65, 67
Poussin, Nicolas, 55, 181
Prichard, J. B., 189
Proctor, B. W., 280
Prometheus, 17, 32
Pylades, 96

Quarles, Francis, 238f

Rachel, 61, 63f, 67, 116, 205, 212
Racine, Jean, 122
Rahab, 93-101
Ramban, 42, 44f, 261
Rameau, J. P., 114
Raphael, Archangel, 244
Raphael, Santi, 181

Rashi, 44-46, 261
Rav, 217, 220
Rawlinson, George, 264
Rebecca, 54-61, 63, 67, 205
Rebekah, 54-61, 63, 66, 205
Reed, Bertha, 15
Rehoboam, King, 194, 221, 285
Reinhardt, Max, 183
Reinig, Christa, 23f
Rembrandt, 60, 143
Reni, Guido, 55
Rilke, R. M., 85, 171f
Robert, King, 216, 218
Robin Hood, 163
Rodenberg, Julius, 33
Rolland, Romain, 35
Rosa, Salvator, 198
Rosenblatt, H., 233
Rosenfeld, Morris, 213f
Rossetti, Christina, 227
Rossetti, D. G., 1, 5f
Rothschild, Jacob, 21
Rubashov, Zalman, 229
Rubens, P. P., 181, 188
Rubinstein, Anton, 33
Rückert, Friedrich, 131f
Russell, Bertrand, 201
Rutenborn, Guenther, 242, 244f
Ruth, 66, 109, 121-127
Ryer, Pierre de, 128

Sachs, Hans, 103, 113, 216, 219
Sahle Selassie, King, 193
Saint-Saëns, Camille, 114
Sakhr, 222
Salten, Felix, 114-116
Samael (Zamael), 85
Samson, 109, 113-120, 122, 139, 197, 274
Samuel, 125, 128, 130-136, 139-142, 144, 148, 151, 157, 164f
Samuel of Nahardea, 217, 285
Saphire, Saul, 109, 114, 216
Sarah, 39-53, 61, 63, 67, 95
Satan, 5, 31, 250, 255-257, 265
Saul, King, 125, 128-160, 164-169, 172
Schiller, Friedrich, 16f, 74-80

Schillings, Max, 269
Schmitt, Gladys, 151f, 177-179
Schumann, Robert, 269, 279
Schwartz, I. I., 108
Scopes, J. T., 240f
Scylla, 4
Sefira, 63, 67, 70
Segal, J. I., 234
Segal, S. M., 228
Selicha, 63, 69f, 79f
Sellin, Ernst, 89
Semadar, 118f
Semmig, Hermann, 280
Seneca, 122
Sepher Hayashar, 69
Sephira, 63, 67, 70
Septuaginta, 2
Seth, 195
Shakespeare, William, 15, 105, 189, 225
Shalom Aleichem, 212f, 229
Shamir, Moshe, 162
Shapiro, Karl, 85, 89-91
Shatzky, Jacob, 72
Shaw, G. B., 11f, 22
Shazar, Zalman, 229
Sheba, Queen of, 10, 21, 95, 187-203
Shechem, 17
Shelley, P. B., 195, 267
Shem, 196
Shoham, Matityahu, 95, 100f
Sihon, King, 97f
Simeon, 66, 168
Simeon Bar Yohai, Rabbi, 43
Slaughter, F. G., 95, 97f
Socrates, 286f
Solomon, King, 21, 109, 153f, 170-173, 175-178, 180-227, 259, 285
Song of Songs, 204-214
Southey, Robert, 267
Sowden, Lewis, 50, 248
Spenser, Edmund, 29
Spiro, André, 176
Stalin, J. V., 37f, 112, 255
Steffen, Uwe, 237
Stoddard, R. H., 82
Strabo, 27

Strauss, Johann, 135
Strindberg, August, 266
Sulamith, 10, 95, 170, 197f, 201, 204-214
Suleika, 63, 69f, 72f
Swinburne, A. C., 9
Sybil, Jewish, 27
Symons, Arthur, 189, 199f
Sypherd, W. O., 104

Taille, Jean de la, 128
Tal, Josef, 226
Talmud, 3f, 63, 181, 190, 196, 204, 221, 255
Tamar, 10
Tandrup, Harald, 242f
Tannhäuser, 6, 9
Targum Jonathan, 67
Targum Sheni, 190-192
Teniers, David, 198
Tennyson, Alfred, 106, 267f
Terach, 51, 66
Testament of Joseph, 63
Testament of the Twelve Patriarchs, 70
Theocritus, 15
Theseus, King, 122, 264
Thoas, King, 96
Thorvaldsen, A. B., 55
Thousand and One Nights, 223
Tiepolo, G. B., 181
Tighe, Mary, 47
Tintoretto, Jacopo, 188
Titan, 27
Tseno Ureno, 28f, 44-46, 216
Tubal-Cain, 21, 196
Twain, Mark, 224

Ullendorff, Edward, 193
Uriah, 162, 164

Van Beek, G. W., 189
Van Doren, Mark, 60, 151, 155, 161
Vashti, Queen, 10
Venus, 6, 9, 211, 216

Verdi, Giuseppi, 96
Verhaeren, Émile, 35
Veronese, Paolo, 188
Victoria, Queen, 267
Vigny, Alfred de, 5, 84, 105f
Vincenz of Beauvais, 65
Voltaire, 114, 128, 133, 136, 164
Vondel, Joost van den, 104f, 113, 171
Voragine, Jacobus de, 195
Vulcan, 211
Vulgate, 2

Wagner, Richard, 6, 9, 197f, 269
Walton, William, 280
Wedekind, Frank, 114, 216
Weinreich, B. S., 228
Whittier, J. G., 189
Widmann, J. V., 7f
Wilde, Oscar, 137, 200
Wildgans, Anton, 22
Willis, N. P., 47f
Wolfskehl, Karl, 52, 85f, 139f
Wooley, C. L., 51
Wordsworth, William, 15, 32, 267

Yaari, Yehuda, 182-185
Yeats, W. B., 189
Yehoash, 108, 202, 234

Zahn, Ernst, 177f
Zechariah, 289
Zephaniah, 28
Zerubbabel, 287
Zesen, Philip von, 68-71
Zeus, 17, 289
Zillah, 18
Zipporah, 82, 99
Zohar, 4
Zoller, Anton, 55
Zuleika, 63, 69
Zunser, Eliakum, 72
Zweig, Arnold, 155-159
Zweig, Max, 140f
Zweig, Stefan, 35f, 173f